THE MAGIC IN
St Andrews

BY THE POSITIVE GOLFER

Finding Inspiration at Golf's Spiritual Home

Kevin Davidson

GOOD BOUNCE
PUBLISHING

Copyright © 2025 Kevin Davidson

Paperback ISBN: 978-1-9192503-0-4

eBook: 978-1-9192503-1-1

All rights reserved.

No part of this publication may be reproduced, stored in a retrieval system, or transmitted, in any form, or by any means (electronic, mechanical, photocopying, recording or otherwise) without the prior written permission of the publisher.

The author has asserted his right under the Copyright, Designs and Patents Act 1988 to be identified as the author of this work.

Design: Spiffing Publishing

Mum: Thanks for a lifetime of positive words which continue to inspire me every day.

CONTENTS

The Magic in St Andrews: Part I: 1
    Chapter 1:   My First Time 3
    Chapter 2:   To Augusta and Beyond! 13
    Chapter 3:   The Wilderness Years 35
    Chapter 4:   I Will Not Be Signing Your Masters Flag, Sir! 37

The Positive Golfer: Part I 61
    Chapter 5:   Moving to St. Andrews 63
    Chapter 6:   10 to 1.5 in 10 Months! 69
    Chapter 7:   My Eight Pillars for Positive Golf 73
    Chapter 8:   Chipping Woes and Winning Ways 105

The Magic in St Andrews: Part II 113
    Chapter 9:   St Andrews Beach to Pebble Beach 115
    Chapter 10: The 150th Open Comes To Town 137
    Chapter 11: Finding Love On The Links 175

The Positive Golfer: Part II 205
    Chapter 12: Lost My Job, Found My Chipping 207
    Chapter 13: Introducing The Golfing Gods 217
    Chapter 14: In Pursuit of Rory 231

The Magic In St Andrews: Part III. 239
    Chapter 15: Playing The Old Course 241
    Chapter 16: My Take On The Town 263
    Chapter 17: Other People's Stories 272
    Chapter 18: Where The Magic Never Ends 284
    Acknowledgements 291
    Appendix: My Favourite Golf Courses ... so far! 292

What happens when Magic meets Positivity?

Your handicap can tumble from 10 to 1.5 in 10 months
You can win trophies and a scratch club championship
You can shoot a gross 67 around The Old Course
You can get to hang out with amazing people
You can build fantastic lifelong friendships
You can party with Major Champions
You can spend 7 days at The Masters
You can get to play Pebble Beach
And …
You can find love!

THE MAGIC IN ST ANDREWS
Part I

CHAPTER 1: MY FIRST TIME

TOUCHED BY ST ANDREWS

The first encounter I had with St Andrews and The Old Course was with my father, Wallace, at a Wednesday Practice Day at the Open, when I was a gawky, acne-ridden fifteen-year-old. The date was 18th July 1984; the year Seve Ballesteros fist pumped majestically after sinking his putt on the 18th green to claim the second of his three Claret Jugs.

My forty-three-year-old Dad had thought that this was a great opportunity for a father and son trip to go to The Open when it was almost on our doorstep, just under one hundred miles away. We had previously only marvelled at the world's greatest golfers on TV and had stayed up late together to watch the BBC's coverage of the last nine holes of The Masters from Augusta when Seve had won it the year before. The Masters was my first love.

Magic may well have been in the air that Wednesday, but all that the fifteen-year-old version of me could think about was the long walk back to the car park and the three-hour car journey back home to the Northeast of Scotland in Dad's Ford Sierra 2.0; I was known to suffer from the occasional bout of car sickness and wasn't looking forward to it.

For me, then, it wasn't love at first sight with St Andrews, but in time the most famous golf town in the world would eventually transform my life.

FATHERLY LOVE

My dad had a habit of taking my younger brother Rory and me to big sporting events over the years. Looking back, we were very fortunate and just didn't really appreciate the efforts he made to take us there.

One time, he'd queued for hours to get tickets for an Alex Ferguson-managed Aberdeen Football Club's European Cup match against former European champions Liverpool at Pittodrie Stadium. Willie Miller was Ferguson's captain, 'the best penalty box defender in the world' was how Ferguson described him, and he was our favourite player. That twenty-five-year-old Willie Miller and the eleven-year-old me would go on to become great friends, business partners and golfing buddies some twenty-five years later.

Anyway, tickets for the Liverpool game were like gold dust and had quickly sold out, with some fans buying ten at a time. Knowing how disappointed his two young sons would be if he returned home empty handed, and going against his strong morals, he paid well over the odds for tickets from one lucky punter and that's how we got to see the biggest match, at that time, in Aberdeen's history.

Dad was a strict man. For example, he wouldn't allow us to wear jeans, making us stand out amongst our friends at a time you just wanted to blend in. No white socks were to be worn either, even when that was the teenage fashion at the time.

The measure of the man, though, was in June 1979 when there was a TV strike and a resulting blackout which included the Scotland football match against the newly crowned world champions, Argentina, with an eighteen-year-old Diego Maradona due to play. Dad surprised Rory and me by getting us up early that Saturday morning and onto the train. We were headed down to Hampden Park in Glasgow to take in the match live.

Rory and I were beyond excited, but much less so when we were walking back along the Mount Florida streets around the stadium after Scotland had lost 3-1 to a Maradona-inspired side. Rivers of urine were flowing everywhere you walked - supporters relieved themselves where they stood…it was all too much for our Dad as he tried to manoeuvre his two young boys through the throngs, vowing never to take us to a Scotland match ever again. London's streets may be paved with gold, but Glasgow's streets were paved with a different golden liquid that day!

However, watching the enigma that was Diego Maradona had eased the disappointment of the result and my disgust at the walk back. It was like catching my first glimpse of Rory McIlroy playing the Open for the first time as an amateur at Carnoustie back in 2007; you knew you were in the presence of a generational talent.

A TRAGIC TEATIME TALK

My Dad is no longer hacking up the fairways, as he sadly passed away less than ten years after our jaunt to The Open, having come off the rugby field early in the second half of a match; he was still playing the game he loved, at age fifty-three. They found him lying beside the boot of his car in the car park. He had suffered an ischemic heart attack, meaning he was alive one second and dead before he'd even hit the ground.

I was on the phone to my Mum on our usual early evening Saturday night call just after 5pm, when I heard the doorbell ring at her end of the phone, and she asked me to hold on as the police were at the door. She put the phone down and went to answer the door. I could hear every word over the phone as the police told Mum that that they were sorry, but he had collapsed and died in Elgin.

I couldn't believe what I was listening to, but Mum quickly came back to the phone to confirm the news to me herself that my 'North Star' was indeed gone. Dad had died on Sat 26th March 1994 at 16:15, the time set on the three carriage clocks that my Mum bought soon after for herself, Rory and me. All the clocks are still set to that time in each of our houses, and every year on that date, Mum, Rory and I fall silent for two minutes wherever we are, remembering him, and then we text each other just afterwards. One year, I'll remember to change out of my jeans for it!

THANKS DAD

It was my Dad who introduced me to the wonderfully evil and addictive game of golf at the age of eight. Because rugby was his first love, golf was just a pastime, but I'll be forever grateful to him for the introduction to a game that would change my life.

The Clubhouse at our local McDonald Golf Club in Ellon, which was best known for producing the 1984 Scottish Amateur Champion Angus Moir, was a wonderful social hub where drinks and dinners could be shared with others on a Friday and Saturday evening. The golf course itself was just an unwelcome distraction for him and my long-suffering mum, Maureen. My Mum recalls having to religiously endure mixed foursomes golf on a Friday evening on the promise of a lovely mixed grill and a nice bottle of wine thrown in at the end of it.

For me, there were no parental dreams of their eldest son becoming a professional golfer and no one-to-one lessons with a professional to acquire all the good habits at an early age. All my terrible habits were self-taught and self-inflicted from whatever felt comfortable, and my resting handicap of sixteen during my teenage years reflected this.

IT ALL COMES DOWN TO THIS

Aged seventeen, I was thrilled to be appointed Junior Captain by the Golf Club, and I led a team of much better, much lower handicap players to a 'major victory' when we become the local Junior Pennant winners in the 1986 final against a Cruden Bay Golf Club team which was sprinkled with players who would eventually join the professional ranks. It was a great achievement for our small club, and the photo of that team still adorns the walls of the Club nearly forty years later.

My everlasting memory from that time, though, was during the semi-final when all the other matches were finished and we were tied. The result now depended on my fourball match.

All the other players and dads, including mine, were following our game as we played the seventeenth and eighteenth holes at Ellon. These were amongst the most challenging closing holes in the Northeast of Scotland, maybe even the world, for all I knew, with my golfing travels yet to extend beyond those boundaries.

I knew by the gathering numbers and the excited whispers that the result had come down to us. We were tied all square standing on the 18th tee, tucked far back in the trees. My partner rattled his ball into the trees down the right as did one of our opponents.

Some players don't want to know and feel pressure, but this was thrust upon me, and I remember feeling calm and even happy that it all seemed to depend on me now. This was the first time in my short golfing life that I'd been called upon to step up, and I marvelled at this new feeling of nerves and the excitement of being watched by others and being relied on to get the result. However, regardless of how much I enjoyed being the centre of attention, I needed to deliver.

FRIEND OR FOE?

Having cracked a lovely drive two hundred and thirty yards to the left-hand side of the 18th fairway, I still had to negotiate the thirty-yard space between the trees. I reached for my three iron and a hush descended over the crowd. What could this sixteen handicapper do? The ball launched as straight as an arrow through the gap, but then it started fading towards the bunker on the right-hand side of the green.

I've learned in golf to keep my mouth shut and never make a call out loud until the ball has come to a complete standstill. You just never know what the Golfing Gods are going to deliver to you by way of a good or a bad bounce.

I could hear the collective sharp intake of breath from all around. Their doubting minds could see the ball fall into the back of the bunker and, with it, our chances of winning the match and progressing to the Final. I kept my silence and walked up the fairway, as unsure as they were about where the ball had come to rest. Was it friend or foe? What did the Golfing Gods have in store for me that day?

As we walked over the slight brow, I spotted my ball nestling at the back of the green, having obligingly missed the bunker, as it too also wanted to see what I was made of. Could I handle the 30-foot putt that was left?

Down in two putts would win us the match and get us into our first Junior Pennant Final for many years; a three putt would not!

CHOKER OR CLUTCH?

I could see my dad out of the corner of my eye, standing behind the green with everyone else. Goodness knows what was going through his mind ...

'Do I have a son who's a choker or one who can step up and clutch when required?'

Would Dad be able to show his face for those weekend drinks

and dinners again in the clubhouse anytime soon or would the old school golf club banter of "How's Kev the Choker?" haunt him for however long?

Thankfully, I wasn't privy to whatever unwelcome thoughts were going on in his head, as the added weight of my mum and dad having to forego their weekly mixed grills for a few weeks might have been too much for me to deal with.

I stepped up to my thirty-footer and devoured the hole with my eyes. It looked like a straight putt with a slight turn right over the last three feet. I still remember those damned nerves, searching out places in my body that had never felt tingling sensations like that before, not even as a teenage boy.

Nervously, I took the putter back, and forward it went through the ball, rolling towards the hole, snaking one way and then the other, finishing three and a half feet short of the hole. I hadn't seen if it did turn slightly right just before the hole, because I'd left it short of the hole-one of golf's cardinal sins.

Hold on though, three and a half feet-wasn't that a gimme? Not this time it wasn't. Now I had to face this knee-knocker to get us into to the Final.

I'm glad I didn't stop to analyse the consequences of what might happen if I missed that putt. I would probably have seen a lifetime of therapy ahead of me, trying to recover from the ignominy and social shunning from those who'd witnessed my golfing capitulation. Thankfully, though, my brain was slumbering and not salivating at an impending disaster.

As I looked at the hole and back at the ball and took the putter back, I watched as my ball decided that its favoured home was not above ground anymore, but after taking a slight turn to the right, it was nestling comfortably at the bottom of the cup.

I had done it. We were in the Final!

A PROUD MOMENT

Pandemonium broke out amongst the home support of twenty or so, and as I raised my arms and then respectfully shook hands with my opponents, I remember turning towards my Dad and seeing the immense pleasure and pride on his face. He strode over and gave me a handshake that said it all and probably also said, "Thanks for not buggering up my weekends at the Club"

Dad wasn't one for showing much emotion, and hugging was off the agenda, but I knew that what I'd just done had made him incredibly proud and I've got golf to thank for that unforgettable moment in time.

NATURE, NURTURE OR MAGIC?

Not once during those closing holes had any negative thoughts entered my mind. The Positive Golfer had stepped forward that day.

Maybe I'd been born positive or just nurtured that way.

Maybe I'd got my positivity from my visit to St Andrews two years before, when I'd breathed in the air surrounding that magical place.

In St Andrews, I'd walked in the footsteps of legends around the Old Course on that practice day as Dad and I stood in awe of Masters Champions, Seve Ballesteros (1980, 1983), Jack Nicklaus (1963, 1965, 1966, 1972, 1975), Gary Player (1961, 1974, 1978) and Tom Watson (1977, 1981).

Less than two years after breathing in that same magical air, Jack Nicklaus won his final and eighteenth major at Augusta in 1986 at the age of forty-six, having not won a major since 1980!

Arnold Palmer (1958, 1960, 1962, 1964) was there too and I would have the privilege of seeing him play in his last Masters twenty years later during a week-long visit to Augusta, through a turn of events which were also linked to St Andrews.

We also followed Masters Champions-to-be, Bernard Langer (1985,1993), Fred Couples (1992), Nick Faldo (1989,1990,1996) Sandy Lyle (1988), Jose-Maria Olazabal (1994, 1999), Ian Woosnam (1991) and Larry Mize (1987).

I would meet them all in person in the years to come.

Whatever was in the air in St Andrews that day, it changed my life and those of a few others there as well forever. I had been touched by the Magic in St Andrews for the very first time.

There was much more to come!

CHAPTER 2: TO AUGUSTA AND BEYOND!

BUMPING INTO BYRON

After Seve's Open in 1984, my next visit to St Andrews came eighteen years later. A long time had passed, especially when the famous town was only eighty-five miles from where I lived now in the 'big city' of Aberdeen, just sixteen miles south of where I grew up in Ellon. I hadn't flown far from the nest.

St Andrews had just never come across my radar again, despite it hosting three more Opens in 1990 (Nick Faldo), 1995 (John Daly), and 2000 (Tiger Woods).

During my twenties I played football, or soccer for my American friends, and had also discovered alcohol and women, and I loved the nightlife Aberdeen had to offer at that time. Hard working during the week, hard living at the weekends, meant that golf occupied a place much further down the pecking order, and life was far too exciting after the teenage acne had cleared off and women had turned up!

I had just started my own legal and sports agency firm called K.W.A.D and had a core following of clients, but I needed to spread the word about my new business far and wide. So, I joined a networking group called BNI, Business Network International, which held their weekly early morning meetings from 7-8.30 so as not to interfere with the traditional 9-5 working day.

At around this time, I'd developed and was marketing a scheme called Proshare™, which allowed anyone to buy a share in a professional golfer and then receive a percentage back from their on-course earnings over the next five years. Three Scottish professional golfers had already signed up to the scheme and this was one of the concepts I was discussing on a weekly basis with my fellow members at our BNI Delta Chapter in the city.

In the autumn of 2002, with plenty of Proshare™ promotional material with me, I headed to a BNI 'Masters of Networking' event at the St Andrews Bay Hotel (now The Fairmont), which is spectacularly located about a seven-minute drive outside of the town on a clifftop looking back towards St Andrews. The event was organised by the late Ron Hain with Ivan Misner, the founder of BNI, also in attendance, as was one Byron Casper, a golf professional and son of Billy, three-time Major champion, including the Masters in 1970.

Byron, was a great friend of Ron's, having moved to Scotland from the States after meeting, falling in love with and marrying a Scottish girl and was now teaching golf in and around St Andrews.

From the first time we were introduced by Ron, Byron and I hit it off. He loved the Proshare™ concept and was convinced that his father would love it too. He gave me his card, and a copy of the book called *'Billy Casper's Golf Tips'* which he'd co-written with his Dad, and we said our goodbyes.

As I drove back to Aberdeen that evening after a productive day full of meetings and talks, the entrepreneur and opportunist in me couldn't help wondering how I could take that chance meeting with Byron and make it work for me and Proshare™.

That opportunity was to raise itself less than a year later.

FROM ZERO TO HERO

Aberdeen golfer Paul Lawrie won the Open at Carnoustie in 1999, coming from ten shots behind on the final day to get into a play-off. His opponents in the play-off were American Justin Leonard, who'd won The Open two years earlier at Royal Troon, and the unfortunate Frenchman Jean Van De Velde.

Van De Velde made a real mess of the 18th hole, having gone into it with a three-shot lead and come out of it - having taken on the infamous Barry Burn in front of the green, with millions watching around the world on tv - with a triple bogey seven, prompting BBC TV commentator Peter Alliss to surmise that "his golfing brain had stopped about ten minutes ago." He wasn't wrong.

However, Paul Lawrie had grasped the nettle superbly after some great psychology from his coach, Adam Hunter, who told Paul to look into the eyes of Leonard and Van de Velde on the fifteenth tee, the first of the four play-off holes, and that he would see nerves. Paul did just that. Seeing that they were as nervous, if not more so, than he was, he went on to win the four-hole play-off by three shots over possibly the hardest closing four holes in golf at the fifteenth, sixteenth, seventeenth, and eighteenth, finishing with two magnificent birdies at the seventeen and eighteen to become The Champion Golfer of the Year.

I was, and still am, good friends with Paul's brother Stephen or 'Zero' to his friends. Zero is a taxi driver and, unlike Paul, Zero is one of life's louder characters, but his banter was always top notch, telling you how good he was and how bad you were. The

Muhammed Ali of golf! In fact, I'm sure every golf club has a loveable motormouth like Zero.

Anyway, in October 2003 I had taken a table at Aberdeen Football Club's Centenary Gala Dinner. Zero was driving me and some of my guests across the city to the Exhibition Centre where the 1,000-person black tie event was being held. When he found out our destination, he excitedly shared with us that his brother Paul was donating two of his Masters guest tickets to the Auction and that these included access to the Clubhouse. (As a result of Paul's Open win in 1999, he got with it a five-year exemption to play in The Masters!)

Wow!!

An idea started to form at the back of my head in the back of his taxi, and it had managed to work its way to the front of my head by the time we'd arrived at the venue. When we got into the auditorium, I headed for our table and quickly skimmed the Programme for the evening. There in big bold writing was indeed ...

- 2 tickets for the 2004 Masters - donated by Paul Lawrie.

The rest of the evening was a blur, filled with fun and laughter and memories of the first one hundred years of my beloved football team ... and then came the Auction.

The compère read through and auctioned off four or five prizes including:

- Dining at Old Trafford and access to the manager's private after match area, donated by Sir Alex Ferguson.
- Corporate hospitality for 10 people at an upcoming Elton John concert at Pittodrie Stadium.

And then came the big one ...

- 2 tickets for The 2004 Masters courtesy of Paul Lawrie, giving access to the grounds on all 8 days from the Sunday to the Sunday including practice days, the par three tournament and the tournament days.

The Masters was the first golf tournament I remember watching on TV live from Augusta at the start of April each year, albeit with very limited coverage in those days, on the BBC with Peter Alliss commentating. The greenness and lushness of the fairways and the putting surfaces, the colourful Azaleas in bloom all over the golf course and the seemingly constant sunshine and blue skies seemed a far cry from the grey skies and patchy fairways we'd be enduring at that time of year in the North of Scotland.

Augusta was a mythical place.

Memories came flooding back of Jack Nicklaus's charge up the leaderboard in 1986, Larry Mize's chip in at the 11th hole in 1987 to snatch the Green Jacket from a shell-shocked Greg Norman, and Sandy Lyle's majestic bunker shot in 1988 leading to his first Green Jacket and his second major.

Here was a chance, maybe my only chance to make it there and spend not just one day, but seven days at that hallowed place. However, Business Kev kicked in, banishing such emotional thoughts.

"What was this package worth. Who could I take to make this a worthwhile business trip? What else needed to be added in cost-wise?" Business Kev asked.

So, here's how my mind worked based on ticket costs. (These are 2025 reseller prices per ticket[1])

- Sunday (Drive, Chip, and Putt) – $450
- Monday (Practice Round) – $1600
- Tuesday (Practice Round) – $1900
- Wednesday (Practice Round + Par 3 Tournament) – $2800
- Thursday (Tournament Round) – $2850

[1] https://www.mybucketlistevents.com/product/masters-ticket-packages/

- Friday (Tournament Round) – $2450
- Saturday (Tournament Round) – $2450
- Sunday (Tournament Round – Championship Sunday) – $2450

The total came to $14,100 which, at the 2024 exchange rate, equalled £10,575. Adjusting for inflation, this would have amounted to £6,000 per ticket in 2003.

So, the value of seven-day ticket per person was £6,000.

Tickets for 2 people equalled £12,000, but access to the Clubhouse was priceless.

My mind then started turning as to whom I could invite as my guest. I could promote Proshare™. Could I invite Sam Torrance, the 2002 European winning Ryder Cup captain as a paid ambassador? I didn't know Sam or have any contacts connecting me with him, but he was Scottish, well known in golfing circles and I'd worry about that later.

Other stuff for me and Sam?
- Flights = £1,000
- Accommodation = £700
- Food etc = £1,000
- Hire Car = £300
- Total = £3,000
- Total for Trip = £15,000
- Ambassador Fee for Sam = Unknown

I'd made my mind up. I'd worked out a value for the tickets, so I could at least gauge what to go up to when the bidding for this auction prize commenced, although I'd no idea what anyone else in the room might bid or how much they might want those tickets. Did they have a business idea which would benefit from this or was this just the trip of a lifetime for an oil rich businessperson based in the oil capital of Europe, of whom there were plenty in the room that night? I was a mere property professional, albeit one with a little bit of capital after leaving my previous business a couple of years earlier to set up KWAD.

Me v. the Oil Barons; what chance did I have?!

The compères at these events always start high and then rein it back in, only to get things moving again quickly. I wasn't surprised then when I heard them ask for an opening bid of £6,000.

No response from the audience.

I was biding my time, and it looked as if others were playing that game too; I had recognised some of the faces in the vast room as veterans from around the Aberdeen fund raising dinner circuit.

"Do I have £5,000?" bellowed the compère.

Nothing!

"£4,000?"

Still nothing!

Maybe no one fancied going to The Masters in April, swapping the cold grey skies and five degrees in the Northeast of Scotland for the brilliant blue skies and 80 degrees of heat in Augusta.

Aye, right!

Suddenly the compère announced he had a bidder at £4,000, and it wasn't me.

I strained to see who it was but struggled to achieve this in the vast hall of a thousand people organised into a hundred tables. I also hadn't heard any counter bid, and I could see the compère looking nervously at the organiser to see if he should wind this up and take the money and move on.

This was my chance.

My table guests appeared shocked and concerned as my hand shot up when the compère asked if there was £5,000 anywhere in the room.

"I have £5,000 from Table 10," shouted the compère. My table, that was me!

There was no time to bask in the glory, as the compère asked for £6,000.

The invisible bidder went to £6,000.

Bugger!

"Do I have £7,000?"

All eyes, from my mix of friends and business associates, on my table turned back to me, joined by others seated at tables around our Table 10.

My hand went up, as did the audible gasps from the guests at my table.

"What was I doing? Had I had too much to drink?" … I felt their thoughts poking into me.

"I have £8,000," boomed out the compère.

That invisible bidder was extremely keen to swap Aberdeen for Augusta in April next year.

"Do I have £9,000?"

Like the tennis final at Wimbledon, heads swivelled back to me. 'Future Kev' urged me to put my hand up and grab the opportunity. My friends were looking at me in amazement, urging me not to be so daft. I'd had my fun and grabbed the attention, but now I needed to sit on my hands. My right hand, though, was listening to Future Kev.

"I have £9,000 from sports agent Kevin Davidson," shouted the compère who I knew and who'd decided to unmask me to the room.

"Do we have £9,500?"

Of course he would get that. However, it was now £1,500 more than the invisible oil baron had bid a minute earlier. Maybe the oil baron had a budget to work to?

"I have £9,500," said the compère.

No budget for the baron! Double bugger!

"Do we have £10,000?"

I hesitated, as reality and friend's stares kicked in. I could see it in their eyes. £10,000?! This was an eye-watering sum, a large part of my very small fortune!

What was Kevin doing, what was Kevin thinking? Kevin had had his fun competing against the oil baron, but it was time for Kevin to stop now, you frigging imbecile! Those were the unsaid, but not unheard thoughts.

Future Kev's voice was louder though. Future Kev would still be around in fifteen to twenty years' time, unlike those transient 'going out' friends. He knew what moments and memories would be in store, if only I would take that £10,000 leap of faith and be Future Kev's Hero.

My hand responded to Future Kev's invisible prompts. Up it went to the utter amazement of my table guests. I could hear their gasps, and I could see their nudges under the table. The gasps around the hall were audible too, as the five-figure limit was breached for the first time in Aberdeen in a very long while.

All heads turned back towards the oil baron.

Hesitation from the baron. Maybe their table and their 'future oil baron' had prevailed?

Was £10,000 their limit?

Surely not. This was the Oil Capital of Europe!

But a second booming "£10,000 going twice" left the compère's mouth.

Surely the oil baron was teasing and waiting until the last second to jump in with a dream busting sized 11 or £12,000 bid.

"Sold! At £10,000 to Kevin Davidson at Table 10," the compère's words boomed around the room.

10 was indeed the magic number that the oil baron wasn't going

to go beyond.

Oh bollocks! I wasn't sure whether to celebrate or not and neither was the rest of my table.

Future Kev was celebrating, though, and back slapping me, as he knew that Current Kev's boldness was going to be rewarded with a lifetime of priceless moments and memories, which would far outweigh the number paid that night.

Meetings in Augusta and St Andrews with Major Champions would come to pass many times over the following years and that night of bidding boldness was the catalyst.

Thanks, Future Kev. Thanks, Zero. And, of course, thanks, Paul Lawrie, for winning The Open in the first place!

DONALD, WHERE'S YOUR TROOSERS?

Accommodation was going to be the next issue, so I reached out to Paul Lawrie's Manager and asked if he could help. He said that he could, but only after I'd paid the third and last chunk of money due at the end of December. The week after the auction, I'd negotiated payment by instalments. Once an Aberdonian, always an Aberdonian!

After the last of the £10,000 had left my bank account, he confirmed that he could get me a deal at a hotel on the outskirts of Augusta. It was used by IMG, the International Management Group, which looked after Paul now, for the players it represented and its staff, but it wasn't cheap.

I enquired about a twin room and was delighted to learn that one was still available but at a very unreasonable rate! In for a penny, in for Ten Thousand Pounds (plus) on this trip of a lifetime.

Sam Torrance and I were going to be roomies!

However, Sam never made it to that twin room in Augusta.

I'd spoken to a contact at Glenmuir Clothing, who I was in early talks with about getting involved as a sponsor of Proshare™ and for whom Sam was an ambassador. They indicated they could speak to him but that the price was likely to be prohibitive and he was also likely to be doing media duties around it too. Whether any of that was true or it was just that they didn't want to make a fool of themselves by asking Sam Torrance, recent winning Ryder Cup Captain, such an impertinent question, I'll never know. I hadn't even mentioned the sharing a room with me thing at that stage either!

Instead, I settled for organising a competition amongst the mortgage brokers I knew. Whoever passed my firm the most business in the next eight weeks would be the winner and get an all expenses paid trip to The Masters. (This was well before the Bribery Act came into force in 2010!).

I announced it at a reception evening at our office in front of ten brokers and you could hear the excitement in the room afterwards.

We probably covered the costs of the entire trip with the work that was passed during that time and by the end of it, Donald was the winner and would be coming to Augusta. He was no Sam Torrance, but he was a decent golfer and a top guy to boot. We were off to Augusta, and we were sharing a room!

When we arrived, I was so glad I'd taken the bold step to book the IMG hotel at that unreasonable rate. On the first morning, as we ventured down to breakfast, past Masters Champions Mike Weir and Vijay Singh stepped into the elevator with us. Donald, grabbing his moment, wished them both good luck for the week ahead.

Mike Weir, the first left hander to win The Masters the year before, acknowledged him, but I'm not sure that Vijay understood what the gruff Scotsman Donald had barked at him. Vijay stayed silent and just looked ahead for the remainder of the journey to the ground floor, although his eyes seemed to be searching for a 'Skean Dhu'[2] hidden about Donald's kilted person.

[2] A Skean Dhu is a small dagger worn by Scottish Highlanders in full dress

Our evenings were spent in the bar with golfers' mind coach, the gruff and straight-talking Jos Vanstiphout. He was in town working with the 'Big Easy' Ernie Els, the current European Order of Merit winner, amongst others.

When Els was in contention going into the final day, Jos told us that we could join him as his guests at the after party at Els's house if Ernie won. Suddenly, we had a favourite we were rooting for other than Paul Lawrie.

Ian Baker-Finch, the 1991 Open Champion came over to say hi to Jos on the Tuesday evening and Donald and I ended up having a putting competition with Jos and Ian for an hour or so in the bar. Other than Paul Lawrie, this was my first brush with a major champion.

My next and most memorable one was to come the following day.

INSIDE THE CHOCOLATE FACTORY

In April 2004, the town of Augusta was quite a non-descript place, where nothing much else seemed to happen for fifty-one weeks of the year. There was a nightclub where the locals hung out at the weekend which resembled a school disco, a few eating places, including 'Hooters', and the car park which John Daly and his own merchandising truck took over during Masters week.

It wasn't as if you could make a pilgrimage to the town any other time of the year, drive up Magnolia Lane and play the fabled course. The Augusta National Golf Club was, and still is, a very exclusive, private course with only around three hundred invited members.

Waiting to get through the gates that first morning just before 8am was like waiting at the gates of Willy Wonka's Chocolate Factory as a kid with a golden ticket. Like them, we were going to get to venture inside and see around. Donald had come dressed in his kilt for the occasion. I was leaving mine until the final day.

Mornings were chilly in Augusta at that time of year, like five degrees chilly. It was the same as Aberdeen. Had we been hoodwinked by TV pictures of brilliant blue skies? Was Donald going to regret wearing his kilt? Thankfully, the heat built up during the morning as we walked the course, padding along the pine strewn pathways, marvelling at the holes and how different they looked and edging closer to the par 4 11th, par 3 12th and the par 5 13th, known worldwide as Amen Corner.

Five shots (the 2nd at 11, the par three 12th and the drive at 13) that could ruin your round or set you up for a pop at glory, a green jacket and a place setting at the Champions Dinner every Tuesday evening of Masters week forever more.

Now I realised why Mike Weir hadn't been so chatty in the elevator that morning. As current Masters Champion he got to choose the menu for the Champions Dinner that year and was finalising his menu of elk, wild boar and arctic char washed down with a Canadian beer or two for his room of exclusive guests, the past champions, including Scotland's own Sandy Lyle and Mr Billy Casper.

CASPER THE GREAT

Six months before, just after the auction evening, I'd wracked my brains about how I could use this upcoming trip to Augusta as a business one and I kept coming back to Proshare™. There just had to be something around that.

I was hunting for something on a shelf in my office when a book fell off it. I was never the tidiest of people, so it was not an unusual thing to pull at one thing and have another one or two topple down with them.

'Billy Casper's Golf Tips Edited By Byron Casper'... with weatherproof pages ... Ingenious!

Of course, that was it. I should reach out to Byron Casper and see if he could help. I mean, I had once met him in St Andrews, and I hadn't spoken to him since. He was bound to help me!

I found Byron's contact details and emailed him there and then, not really expecting an answer back. But Byron wasn't that person. Within twenty-four hours he'd responded excitedly, reciting details of Proshare™ back to me from our brief meeting and helping me plan the trip to Augusta, a place he'd been on many occasions with his Dad ... and yes, of course, his Dad would be able to meet me there but only for an hour, as it was always a busy week for him as a past champion.

Byron would organise all of that and email me the details. I just had to be there at a certain time and place. Byron told me that no phones were allowed on the course and had to be left in lockers outside the grounds to be collected on the way out. This seemed a long shot. Planning months ahead to meet a Masters Champion at a pre-arranged time on a small picnic bench within the grounds of Augusta golf course the day after the Champions Dinner!

Mmmmm!

****

BACK TO THE CHOCOLATE FACTORY

On the Wednesday morning at 11 o clock, the imposing figure of William Earl Casper ambled along the path towards my picnic bench to the right of one of the holes close to the Clubhouse. Bang on time, just as Byron said he would be.

I was getting a one-to-one hour long meeting with a Masters Champion, two-time US Open winner, a winning Ryder Cup Captain and World Hall of Golf Famer. One legendary golf figure. Wow, this really was a dream come true.

"Well, hello, Kevin. Great to meet you," the words flowed from

Mr Casper's mouth as if he were chatting to a close friend.

"Great to meet you too, sir, and thanks for agreeing to meet me. I'm sure that you must be very busy this week?" I replied nervously.

"Never a problem for a friend of Byron's. What have you been up to since you arrived here?"

I tried to keep it brief about settling into the hotel and walking the course and that I was looking forward to seeing the Par 3 contest that afternoon.

"Yeah, it's a ball," Mr Casper said. "Well worth getting a place on the hill for."

"And you, have you been busy this week?" I asked Mr Casper

"Last night was the Champions Dinner. I love going to that and seeing old friends," he said.

"Oh yes, Mike Weir was hosting the dinner, wasn't he?" I said, sounding as if Mike and I were old pals and not just elevator buddies.

"Yup, he served up a tasty meal of elk, wild boar and arctic char."

Sounded ok, I thought to myself, but as quite a fussy eater, I was glad now that my parents hadn't invested in golf lessons for me after all and that I wasn't a past Masters Champion! The elk and the wild boar would have been safe from me, and I would have struggled to know what an arctic char was without a mobile phone and a search engine. But Mr Casper had enjoyed it, and he'd enjoyed the company of legends the night before. Donald and I, on the other hand, had been to Hooters restaurant the night before. There were some legends there too, but I didn't share that with Mr Casper!

"Byron tells me you're working on something called Proshare™ just now?"

"Yes, sir," I replied, and went on to explain how it worked and what my vision was for it.

After much toing and froing on it with me, Mr Casper leant back and put his arms behind his head, and then he leaned forward.

"I love the idea, Kevin, and if there's anything I can do to help you with it, just let Byron know."

"Thank you, sir, I will do and thanks for your feedback on it," I managed to get out, excited at the thoughts already beginning to queue up in my brain.

We spent that last part of our time chatting about golf generally and about family and the importance of them supporting you throughout life. He said he was sorry when he learned my Dad had passed away ten years before and that he hoped I was looking after my Mum.

As we teetered towards 12 noon and the end of our chat, Mr Casper leaned down into the bag he'd arrived with and pulled out the three Masters flags, laying them all on the on the wooden picnic table. Signing each one of them smack bang in the centre of the shape of the United States in the middle of the flags, he handed them all to me.

"Don't ever let anyone else other than Masters Champions sign these flags," he demanded.

"I won't, Mr Casper," I promised.

With that, he got up, shook my hand firmly but warmly, tapped my left shoulder and then walked off, bang on 12 noon.

Mr Casper had left the picnic bench. What a golfing legend and an all-round truly nice gentleman.

I sat there for a few minutes trying to take in what had just happened, looking down at the three signed Masters flags. All I needed to start me off was to bump into Mike and Vijay in the elevator again back at the hotel and I would be off and running. My second signature, though, wouldn't come for another ten years and the Ryder Cup at Gleneagles. I wouldn't bump into Vijay for another fourteen years and that would be back in St Andrews. Mike and I have never met again. Maybe I should try elk!

PHIL VS. THE PARTY

Phil Mickelson ... the best player never to have won a major ... until Donald and I, two boys from the Northeast of Scotland turned up to watch him play! You're welcome, Phil!

We knew every blade of grass having been to the course seven days out of seven. We watched Arnie play in his final Masters, saw Tiger and followed Paul Lawrie who made the cut to play the final two days. Paul acknowledged the only two kilted boys standing beside the practice green on the Sunday morning and all because he'd put the two tickets into the auction.

"Nice skirts, boys," Paul said with a smile.

Could Paul come back from ten shots behind again today, as he'd done in 1999 at Carnoustie, and claim his second major? It was a long shot, but we wished him all the best.

"Play well, Paul," we said as we headed off for our own lap of honour around the course before returning to our green Masters chairs which we'd bought and placed at the side of the 18th green at 8 o' clock that morning. Incredibly, you really can leave your chair in the same place all day and no one sits there because your name is on the back of it. Anyone who does, and doesn't move when you return, is thrown out of the grounds.

We followed the leaders off the first tee at 2pm and scurried over to the ninth hole and worked backwards, landing at the iconic 16th as Sandy Lyle and Eduardo Romero played through.

Ernie Els had a share of the lead going into the Back 9 at Augusta and we came across Ernie an hour or so later and watched on as he safely negotiated Amen Corner. We were both rooting for him so that we could join his party that evening with Jos.

Phil went through next. Even from a distance, something about his demeanour was different from normal.

We headed against the crowds up the side of the 11th hole and walked across and up beside the 18th green to take our seats, two full hours ahead of when the leaders would come in, wanting to make sure we got second-row seats to watch golfing history being made. These were the days before multiple tv screens had been spread around a golf course, allowing you to follow play. The only way to know what was going on back then was to watch the Masters leaderboards being changed by volunteers and the oohs and aahs as it happened. This was all in between the world's best golfers walking up and finishing their 2004 Masters right in front of us.

Phil was faltering as he entered the back nine. We were going to get our party! What an ending to the week this was going to be, us partying with the Masters Champion Ernie Els the night before flying home.

Phil had other ideas, though. He reeled off four birdies in six holes to be tied with Ernie who had just completed his round to finish on eight under par.

From the leaderboard, we could see Phil had parred seventeen. We waited and watched until we could see the tops of Phil and Chris Di Marco's heads pop over the hill on 18. They surveyed the scene at the 18th green and played their second shots, with Phil's ball ending just ten feet from the flag.

****

At 8 am we had power walked our way to the eighteenth green. Running at Augusta was banned, of course. We put our chairs down and sat on them like a couple of monarchs surveying the land around us.

Disappointingly, the flag was at the back of the green, so we didn't have a prime view, but we were within thirty yards of it in the second row. Not bad at all.

We sat for twenty minutes or so with everyone else, a full ten and a half hours before the final drama that was to unfold. A couple of greenkeepers and tournament officials sauntered onto the green with a hole cutting tool.

"Wait, maybe this isn't the final day flag position. Maybe this is still Saturday's pin?" I exclaimed to Donald.

The greenkeepers started to use their stimpmeter to roll a golf ball down it ten yards in front of us. Donald and I turned to each other, hoping that what was going on meant what we thought it meant. Not a word was said as we looked hopefully at each other.

They cut the hole there, right in front of us. Of course they did. It was the Sunday pin position. This hole position was in a similar place to where I'd watched on TV as Sandy Lyle holed his birdie putt in 1988. This was after his mercurial shot from the bunker on the left-hand side of the fairway. Landing at the top of the hill near where we were sitting now, Sandy's ball had stopped and then started to roll down the hill to within six feet of the hole. Sandy sank that putt to become only the second man at that time to make a birdie on the closing hole to win The Masters and the Green Jacket.

****

If Phil two putted, it was a play-off with Ernie Els, and our party dreams were still alive. As Phil walked onto the green and paced around the putt, thoughts of our party with Ernie disappeared. We wanted Phil to hole that putt right there in front of us to dramatically win The Masters and his first major. This was what playing and watching golf was all about. Rather than watching it at 11.30 at night on TV from the comfort of our homes in Scotland, we were sat ten yards away on the right of the tv screen as you looked at it, in the second row, level with the hole and the flag that had been placed there ten and a half hours before by some kindly gentlemen, keen to ensure a great end to our dream trip.

Phil's putt looked double the length of Sandy's one and had stopped at the top of the hill, rather than rolling down as Sandy's had.

Sandy Lyle had made the cut that week at age forty-six and had played the 18th hole three hours earlier. Sandy Lyle absolutely knew the break on that putt, but did Phil Mickelson? The Masters was on the line, this was a putt for his first ever Major and the whole golfing world knew that Phil was the best player never to have won a major. You could hear those whispers echo around the 18th green as soon as Phil had hit his second shot and started to walk up the 18th fairway.

We all knew what this twelve-foot putt meant to Phil, but I'm not sure that the other patrons, or Phil for that matter, realised what it meant for Donald and me.

One putt = No Party!

The silence was deafening as Phil settled over his putt. He took the putter back and the ball rolled end over end and didn't stop as it found its way to the bottom of the cup. Phil jumped six feet in the air and so did we. This was golfing history we were part of, and seeing the release of joy for Phil after making his putt was as exhilarating as if I'd made it myself. It was magical and all thoughts of parties disappeared instantly as we shared in Phil's moment.

Partying with a major winner would have to wait until St Andrews eighteen years later, the same time as Phil and I would meet again, but this time a little closer than here in Augusta.

What a finish to a fantastic week! I couldn't help wondering where Mr Casper was watching from.

Photos, flags, memories and major champions, with many more

to come for my £10,000. Well worth it.

Thanks, Past Kev. Thanks, Zero, even though my tickets didn't come with Clubhouse Access! Thanks, Paul Lawrie. Thanks, Byron. Thanks, Mr Casper. And thanks, St Andrews. You really delivered again.

More was to follow!

CHAPTER 3: THE WILDERNESS YEARS

I would not return to St Andrews until 2018, and that absence strangely coincided with my own 'Down Decade' from 2008. During those ten years, I only just survived 'The Credit Crunch', got married, got divorced, built a business, sold a business, got into a relationship, got out of a relationship and had quite a few other bumps and scrapes through those years.

The only real bright spot during this time was meeting Kenny Maciver, who brokered the deal to sell my property-leasing business in 2012. He took me out for a few celebratory drinks in Aberdeen where our conversation that evening was to change the course of my life… but not for another eight years.

He casually mentioned that he had a property in St Andrews and that applications for the St Andrews Links Trust Waiting List had just been opened, having been closed for the last few years. He urged me to apply and pay a deposit of £150. It would still likely take five or so years for my name to come to the top and I could decide then whether to pay the full annual fee of nearly £700.

I couldn't imagine ever making use of this. I loved Aberdeen too much and I could never see myself leaving, but what the heck, it was only £150 out of a decent business sale price and the very next day I submitted my application. I think Future Kev had played his part again!

Five years did pass before I heard from the Links Trust that I'd reached the top of the Waiting List. I turned it down, but only for a year. As per their edict, if I turned it down again, then I would go back to the bottom of the Waiting List, which by now numbered one thousand people! I didn't turn it down again.

In March 2018, I paid my fee, and my Links Ticket was sent to me by post. I shared the joyous news with Kenny. He was a member of The New Golf Club in St Andrews, and I submitted my application for approval to the Club and was thankfully accepted as a member that Spring.

I did still wonder how I was ever going to make use of this Golden Ticket, but it turns out that Fate and Future Kev had prepared the way for me.

I had reestablished contact with St Andrews and suddenly life got better! That time in my life was a hard lesson, but it did teach me not to dwell on negativity and to concentrate on the positives that life had to offer. My 'Down Decade' was about to end.

Behind the scenes, St Andrews was starting to work its magic for me!

CHAPTER 4: I WILL NOT BE SIGNING YOUR MASTERS FLAG, SIR!

Billy Casper died on 7th September 2015. The world was a darker place.

I remembered the promise I'd made to Mr Casper more than ten years before at Augusta and was sorry that I'd not added more signatures to the flags he'd gifted me. I vowed to honour my promise to Mr Casper and add more signatures to my Masters flag, but how was I going to do it?

In the years following, up stepped an unlikely ally in Aberdeen and Scotland: football legend Willie Miller.

WILLIE MILLER'S MATE

I strode into Café Continental in Aberdeen in 2002. It was owned by Willie Miller. It was twenty-two years after Aberdeen Football Club's European Cup match against Liverpool and nineteen years after the Club's greatest ever year.

In 1983 and captained still by Willie, they beat two of the greatest European names in quick succession. First Bayern Munich were seen off 3-2 in the quarter final at a packed Pittodrie Stadium, then the mighty Real Madrid were put to the sword 2-1 in a rain-soaked European Cup Winners Cup Final in Gothenburg. The game was only won in extra time by a never-to-be-forgotten and often reenacted John Hewitt header. They then beat another top German side Hamburg, the then European Cup holders, to claim the Super Cup in December at fortress Pittodrie. It was like sending your wee cousin to wrestle The Rock, and somehow he comes back holding the championship belt and saying, "It wasn't that bad, really."

Willie Miller wasn't flashy. No stepovers, no Ronaldo haircuts, no TikTok dances. He was old school. His idea of skill was booting the ball into Row Z and glaring at the striker so hard they considered a career change. He inspired others around him and together he and Alex Ferguson dragged my football club to glory beyond my wildest dreams.

A serial winner, which is the point of including this in a book about golf, Willie would iconically hold thirteen trophies one handedly above his head, play for Aberdeen 797 times, be given two testimonials for his more than two decades service to the Club he loved, and won sixty-five international caps for Scotland. He was, and still is, an Aberdeen Legend and is simply known by most Aberdeen fans as 'God'.

****

Two of Willie's teammates from Aberdeen's winning team, on that magnificent night in Gothenburg in 1983, John Hewitt and Neil Simpson, had heard that I'd started my sports agency company. They thought that the Club was taking advantage of the locally based players by asking them to attend functions and shake hands with little recompense, other than a thank you. They got in touch to ask if I would represent them and I jumped at the chance to meet my heroes in person. They spoke to Willie, and the late afternoon meeting was arranged.

"Who is this cocky prick?" Willie thought to himself, as I strode confidently into Café Continental, the restaurant he owned down at the beachfront in the city. The front of the building overlooked the North Sea, which was as cold as Willie's stare, and the back of it was within a long par five of Pittodrie Stadium. As a lawyer, I was always suited and booted in those days and probably wearing a tie as well.

All the local players were sitting waiting at the end of the room at the rear of the restaurant. Scotland's most capped goalkeeper, Jim Leighton, fearsome Doug Rougvie, Neil Simpson, the redoubtable Neale Cooper (who would become a great friend and at whose memorial service I would speak in 2018), John Hewitt … and then there was Willie!

Trying not to show my nerves, I put on my big boy pants and walked the long walk to the table, where I shook hands with everyone. Willie's handshake seemed particularly firm.

We talked problems and solutions, and I agreed to act for the players. I would make sure they were properly paid for appearances going forward, especially with the Club's Centenary and the 20th Anniversary of Gothenburg the following year. I undertook to write to the other players who made up the 1983 squad to get their agreement to my acting for them. Until then, the squad had always been known as 'The Gothenburg Legends' in the press, but I felt we needed something catchier and 'The Gothenburg Greats' name was born.

I must have done something right during the meeting because Willie's handshake at the end of it seemed somehow less strong and maybe even warmer too. Willie and I would go on to become drinking buddies, business partners, property developers, client and agent, travellers, roomies and pals. My golfing nickname at an annual golf outing to Kinross even involves him ...

'WMM' standing for 'Willie Miller's Mate'. Somehow, I don't think Willie's would be KDM if he ever made that trip!

A SIGNING SPREE

It was thanks to Willie that I ended up attending The Senior Open at St Andrews in 2018 and adding seven more signatures to my Masters flag.

Less than two months earlier, we'd both had to deal with the sudden death of our close friend Neale Cooper who'd collapsed after a night out watching the Champions League Final, only two weeks after we had done a 'Music and Memories from 1983' event at Pittodrie, as a celebration of the 35th Anniversary of Gothenburg. Neale, or 'Tattie' as he was known, had stolen the show with his stories and mimicking of his old boss, Sir Alex Ferguson.

Willie and I were together at Gleneagles with our partners for a couple of days' break when we received a text on the Gothenburg Greats WhatsApp chat ... "Say it's not true," came in from one of the boys.

It was true, though, and there followed a tremendous outpouring of grief, fan and peer tributes and media interest in the two weeks ahead of his private funeral and then his memorial service on the 8th of June at Pittodrie Stadium, in front of five thousand fans.

Willie, as Captain and media personality, was asked to comment the most and it took a lot out of him. He'd lost a close friend and teammate and the first and youngest of the Gothenburg Greats had gone. He, along with some other very hard men of Scottish football, were all visibly upset that day.

In the week following, Willie suggested that he and I tried to get away for a few days' golf soon, to help recover from the stress of the previous couple of weeks. Willie's sister had a place in Crail and was happy to let us use it if we wanted it. I suggested we tried to do it around The Senior Open in St Andrews and take in some of the golf as well as chill out in wonderful Crail.

When we got there, we decided to ditch the cars and take the Number 95 bus into the Home of Golf. I remembered from previous hospitality visits to The Old Course Hotel that the top players usually stayed there during tournaments. I had my Masters flag with me and suggested to Willie that we had a drink in the surroundings of the Old Course Hotel first, before we ventured down to The New Golf Club for some lunch. Then we could head out to the course and see how golf should really be played.

I told Willie the story of the Masters flag and Mr Casper, and he seemed genuinely impressed when I showed it to him, and was happy to humour me, for a short while at least, as he always enjoyed the surroundings of the Old Course Hotel. I wasn't sure we would even get into the hotel without any security badges, but we tried. As we walked confidently through the front doors, the doorman, recognising an icon of Scottish football, said, "Hi, Willie," and ushered us through.

Result!

We sat down in the Reception area where someone came over and asked us if they could take an order for coffees. It seemed a good idea, if only just to buy a little time as I looked around for any faces I would recognise from the small list of previous Masters winners playing that week. Getting the flag out of the rucksack each time was a bit of a rigmarole, taking it out of its protective sheath and grabbing the thick black sharpie marker to get everything ready for a past champion to sign it, assuming they would even sign it. I'd only gone through this once before and I was out of practice. Like a gun slinger trying to perfect his draw, I was trying to do the same with my flag.

The coffees came and, after five minutes of watching me

nervously fumbling about with the flag for the sixth or seventh time, Willie asked me if I thought that there would be any players staying and playing here this week. He hadn't reckoned on my research. There were nine past Masters champions in the field that week and one of them had just walked into the Reception with a beautiful blonde lady accompanying him.

Quickly breaking off my conversation with Willie, I headed towards the player I'd only ever seen before on television. He had always struck me as a friendly looking guy and I hoped that would hold true for this forty-nine-year-old guy approaching him, flag in hand, about to interrupt his morning.

"Mr Couples," I said, thinking that Masters Champions deserved that respect, "would you mind signing this for me, please? Billy Casper gave it to me back in 2004 and signed it and told me not to let anyone other than Masters Champions sign it."

Fred Couples looked at me with a big grin and smiling eyes.

"Sure," he said, signing along the side of the flag, and added, "Mr Casper, that's kinda cool, isn't it? He was a great guy."

"Yes, it means a lot to me. Thanks for signing it and good luck this week," I said.

With that Fred and his lady exited stage left and I returned to my seat where Willie had watched all this unfold, wondering if I was going to come back with egg on my face or a happy camper.

"She was nice," said Willie.

"So was he," I said, still buzzing from my friendly encounter with Fred Couples, the 1992 Masters Champion.

I could sense that Willie wanted a change of scenery, so I suggested that we head upstairs to the Road Hole Bar where the views across the courses are incredible. It would be a great place to have our first red wine of the day. As we got up, I put my flag back into its sheath, slipping the sharpie in beside it, and pushing the flag back into my rucksack. I spied a familiar walk out of the corner of my eye over Willie's right shoulder, and it was heading towards the Reception. He was asking for something to be sent to his room in English, but with a hint of a German accent. The two-time Masters Champion, from 1985 and 1993, Bernhard Langer was in the building.

At the risk of hacking Willie off, I pulled out my flag again and waited until Bernhard had finished with the Reception team. I could sense Willie was wondering what I was doing. Why hadn't I moved with him towards the elevators up to the fourth floor?

As Bernhard Langer turned round from the Reception desk, I said sheepishly,

"Mr Langer, would you mind signing my Masters flag, please?"

Bernhard looked up at us, giving me not quite a smile, but more of a thin-lipped look. I'm not sure if he knew that Willie was once the best penalty box defender in the world; if he did, then he didn't let on that he did.

"Sure," he said, and I told him the story of Mr Casper giving me the flag and all that went with it.

As he was signing it, he said, "That's pretty cool," smiling this time as he signed it, and off he went towards the elevators with that familiar walk of his.

I wasn't sure how Willie would be with this Teutonic interruption to our day. This was the same Willie Miller who had helped tame and slay top German teams Eintracht Frankfurt, Bayern Munich and Hamburg during his career. The same Willie Miller whose cold steely stare could melt teammates, opponents and referees alike. But it was also the same Willie Miller who, on a trip we'd made together to the World Cup in Germany in 2006, was left alone for two minutes by me in Hamburg while I went to the bar to get some drinks for us. When I turned back, this same Willie Miller had been apprehended by two young German fans and was singing with them, to the tune of 'Football's Coming Home', with his face now painted with two small German flags on each cheek!

"Bernard Langer!" exclaimed Willie. "That was pretty fab eh?!"

It was. I was on a roll. Two signatures within five minutes of arriving in St Andrews!

Forgetting the Road Hole Bar, we walked along to The New Club for lunch. As a new member that year, this was my first trip to the Club. We ordered lunch and a bottle of red wine and sat in the bay window, overlooking the 1st and 18th fairways of the Old Course, watching some of the world's most famous golfers walk past us. Looking right, we watched as they drove off the first tee in front of the R and A Clubhouse, taking aim at the small gorse bush to the right of the Swilcan Bridge. In front of us, we watched drives from the 18th tee bounce over Grannie Clark's Wynd and come to rest just short of the Valley of Sin.

Looking left allowed us to follow players as they teed off at the 18th, with the Old Course Hotel and Jigger Inn behind them and then traverse the most photographed golf bridge in the world, pausing only as a courtesy to watch first hole players negotiate their second shots over the Swilcan Burn which is sadistically located immediately in front of the first green.

For those who play the course, whether it's for the first time or the hundredth time, the Swilcan Burn is always there in your peripheral vision or in the back or the front of your mind. Everyone at some point in their playing careers ends up in it!

The backdrop to this golfing canvas was the Himalayas putting green, eighteen holes of putting joy for adults and kids alike, which sits immediately alongside the first green. Behind that was the West Sands Beach, where the opening running scenes from the film 'Chariots of Fire' were filmed. It was filled with excited holidaymakers, oblivious to the famous golfers on the Links just a pitching wedge from where they were enjoying the unusually hot summer's day. Some brave souls were even swimming in the North Sea. What a way and what a place for us to spend an afternoon!

After a good few hours sitting there, marvelling at the view and the players and enjoying a couple more glasses of red wine, we headed along the cobbled streets to 'The Dolls House' restaurant in Church Square for a bite to eat. As we walked in, in the queue in front of us waiting for a table to clear was eight-time major winner Tom Watson who'd won The Masters twice in 1977 and 1981.

Unfortunately, my flag was in my bag in a locker back at The New Club ready for the next day's signing mission!

Note to Future Kev: Always Be Prepared!

This was an opportunity missed, and I wondered if it would present itself again. I knew Tom was guest of honour at The New Club that coming Saturday evening as he was being inducted as the Club's newest Honorary Member after the previous incumbent of forty-three years, Arnold Palmer, had passed away in September 2016, but I didn't have a ticket to that dinner. Ah, well, I still had three more days, and St Andrews isn't that big a place. How hard could it be to track him down again?

As we finished up our evening, Willie received a call which meant that he needed to head back to Aberdeen the next morning. He said I was welcome to stay at his sister's place until the Saturday when there were other guests coming in. If I was going to meet more Masters Champions, I would be doing it alone.

Let the Games Begin!

A MASTERS SAFARI

The next day, Willie dropped me at The Old Course Hotel. I wanted to try my luck again. How many more Masters Champions were staying there?

I took up my spot in the Reception on the leather chairs again and pretended to be working on my laptop, looking up every time footsteps approached. One hour passed, then two. No one.

I decided to head across to the Links Clubhouse directly opposite and hang out at the practice area.

As I turned the corner, the players were there. It was like a procession of Masters champions coming onto the putting green beside me. I remember someone once telling me they'd gone on a safari tour in Kenya and there had been nothing, then suddenly all the animals appeared one after the other. My friend speculated that the tour guides were in the bush, prodding these animals to appear on cue to keep the tourists happy. That's what it felt like here. Only this time the Golfing Gods were acting as the tour guides, sending first one Masters Champion out, then another, then another.

The Golfing Gods were testing me again, though. Would I pluck up the courage to speak to the players? They were working and making last minute preparations for their first round, and it just didn't feel right. This might be my only chance, though. My big boy pants needed to go on again.

Striding into the roped-off putting area came Vijay Singh, the first Masters Champion of the new century in the year 2000. Incredibly, there were just the two of us there, me on one side of the rope and Vijay standing yards away, head down, dropping balls onto the putting green. His caddy was away getting water. We hadn't been this close since that elevator in Augusta fourteen years before and this time I had my flag!

I watched as he went through his routine and, after ten minutes, as he went to walk away, I heard a little voice say, "Mr Singh?"

He looked up. Was there a flicker of recognition in his eyes?

Did he remember me as being Donald the Kilt's sidekick from that elevator in Augusta?

"Would you mind signing my Masters flag, please?"

Hesitation from Vijay.

"Billy Casper gave it to me and signed it and told me not to let anyone else, other than Masters Champions, sign it."

That seemed to do the trick; 'Billy Casper' was the password.

Vijay's face didn't move a muscle as he took the flag and sharpie pen from me across the ropes, scrawling his signature onto my flag and handing it back without saying a word, before walking away.

"Thank you, Mr Singh."

If he heard me, the three-time major winner didn't acknowledge me.

Next onto the putting green came Jose-Maria Olazabal, Seve's great pal and Ryder Cup partner. Jose-Maria was not tall in height, at least not compared to 6'2" Vijay, but he was large in presence, and he walked with an assurance that winning The Masters twice in 1994 and 1999 entitles you to walk with. I grabbed my chance as Olazabal stopped to chat to someone and then looked around at the beautiful surroundings.

"Mr Olazabal?" (not really that easy to say in a hurry) "Would you mind signing my Masters Flag?"

I didn't bother with the rest, as I thought it might get lost in translation.

"Sure, no problem," and he took it and signed it and handed it back, smiling before he moved back to his putting. He was a legend of the game, winning Masters and Ryder Cups and just oozed coolness and calmness. Some people are just born to be champions. I took the flag and wheeled round again. Who would be next?

The six-time Major winner was instantly recognisable as he meticulously checked his alignment and hit putt after putt after putt. As he completed his preparations, I plucked up the courage to speak. He was renowned for being aloof and I just wasn't sure how he would treat my request.

"Mr Faldo, would you sign my flag, please? Billy Casper gave it to me and ..."

Before I could finish, three-time Masters Champion Nick Faldo looked around and barked, "I don't see any Azaleas here!"

Oh no, I thought, He's not going to sign it.

Faldo stalled for a moment and then grabbed the flag from me and signed it. He had just wanted to show me that he hadn't lost his marbles and knew where he was. He was right, we weren't in Augusta in April, but in St Andrews in July!

Just then, Sandy Lyle sauntered over to me.

"Do you want me to sign that?" he said to me, having seen what I was doing.

"No thanks, Sandy, you've signed it already!"

Back in 2014 after the Ryder Cup Opening Ceremony at Gleneagles, I was heading back in a crowd towards the bus pick up point, when I saw Nick Faldo coming towards me and he was signing flags. Luckily, I had my Masters flag with me, and I pulled it out of the bag and waited as Faldo got to within twenty people of me. Then he stopped, and apologised, and said he had to be somewhere else. Disconsolate, I was walking away when I noticed a familiar figure coming towards me. No one else, though, seemed to have recognised his unassuming presence. It was Sandy Lyle, the 1988 Masters Champion. Best bunker shot and best birdie putt I'd ever seen under that kind of pressure.

"Mr Lyle, would you mind signing my Masters flag, please?"

Startled at being recognised, Sandy looked up from beneath his visor. "Of course, no problem at all," he said, looking genuinely pleased to be signing my flag.

Ten years after Mr Casper's solitary scribble, I had my second signature, and four years on from then, here I was in St Andrews turning down Sandy Lyle's request to sign my flag! Future Kev knew that Sandy and I would share an afternoon of fun with friends during the AIG Women's Open at The New Club in 2024, but Future Kev kept that to himself.

Happy with my afternoon's work so far, I headed from the practice ground to hear Paul McGinley and Tom Watson do a Question-and-Answer Session at the tented village. When they finished, I joined the throng waiting for Tom Watson and he began signing things. However, as he got near me, he announced he needed to be somewhere else and walked off in the direction of the R and A Clubhouse.

I decided to follow him as I was going to go back to The New Club anyway. As luck would have it, he stopped to sign for some more fans just beyond the R and A building. I waited in line with my Masters flag, watching as he edged nearer to adding his signature to my flag. As he got within two people of me, he apologised and said he needed to be somewhere else. He was a busy man! But I watched from a distance as he got in a buggy and headed towards The Old Course Hotel. He had to be staying there!

It was time for food, though, and satisfied with my couple of days, I decided to head to the Pizza Express restaurant just off South Street, before heading back to Crail that evening.

As I was finishing my pizza, sitting outside in the late summer sun, basking in the glory of the signing spree, a gentleman walked past me who I thought I recognised. Getting out my phone, I googled him to check the photo. I thought it was him, but the years had passed since that photograph, and I just wasn't sure.

I decided to take a chance and took my flag out of my bag and headed after him.

"Mr Mize?" I said uncertainly.

The gentleman turned round.

"Would you mind signing my Masters Flag, please?"

"Sure, no problem."

Now, part of me suspects there could be some American guy walking around the States, still telling his buddies how he'd been mistaken for Larry Mize in St Andrews in 2018. He'd been asked to sign a Masters flag by a crazy Scotsman, and they would still be laughing about it to this day. They may even have nicknamed him 'Larry' by now!

But I'm pretty sure it was the real Larry Mize because he signed it and then added a religious inscription below it; I discovered later that that was his thing. I wasn't likely to have bumped into Larry Mize again, so far from his home state of Georgia, so getting his signature was a real bonus.

I headed back to Crail and slept soundly after planning to head back to The Old Course Hotel the next morning to catch any final players. I still had Watson and Woosnam to get.

I woke the next morning to read on my phone that Ian Woosnam had had to withdraw due to injury and had returned home. Tom Watson it was, then, and hopefully I'd have more luck than the day before!

IN PURSUIT OF TOM

I'd decided to treat myself to a breakfast in the Road Hole Grill on the fourth floor of the Old Course Hotel which has incredible views across the Old Course and out to sea. The breakfasts there are amazing, with a choice of everything and then some. Pancakes with maple syrup, full Scottish, kippers, every egg every way you like them, fruit juices, champagne, smoked salmon ... the lot. I settled down to take in the menu and make my choice when I noticed Tom Watson sitting two tables away eating breakfast by himself. Oh, my goodness. Stay calm. We were almost breakfast buddies!

If I wasn't comfortable interrupting someone's day to get a signature, I certainly wasn't going to interrupt someone's breakfast for it, regardless of how important it seemed to me. So, I contented myself with a breakfast choice of full Scottish and some strong black coffee, sat back and googled 'Tom Watson'.

Tom had won the Par 3 Contest at The Masters earlier that year, beating Tommy Fleetwood and Thomas Pieters into second place with a six under par round to claim the crystal trophy. He'd accepted an invitation to become an honorary member of The New Club in St Andrews and the dinner was the next evening. I knew that already. Tom had shot a 69 in the first round of The British Seniors Open and the first prize that week was £240,000. Tom had won £46,000 for his last major win at The Open in 1983, so this was a big week for Tom, and he was playing well.

I also read that his wife, Hilary, was battling pancreatic cancer, having been diagnosed with it the previous October. She obviously hadn't made the journey across with him, as Tom was sitting breakfasting alone, consumed, I was sure, by a brain full of thoughts. How was Hilary doing, how should he play the Old Course today and what should he say at The New Club the next night?

He looked distant, but then I don't know what it's like to be that famous and to know everyone in the room is probably looking at you at some point during their breakfast. Maybe that was just his look, his way of dealing with that. It was definitely a good idea, though, not to approach him over breakfast to ask him to sign my flag!

I finished my hearty meal and headed out of the room, leaving Tom with his thoughts, figuring that the Reception was a good place for me to hunker down for the morning. I was sure that Tom had to come past the Reception on his way to the driving range ahead of his early afternoon tee time. I sat in the Reception for two hours waiting and watching the elevator doors opening and closing, monitoring who came out.

Finally, the man himself walked out, but instead of walking into the Reception, he turned left and disappeared. Where was he going?

I grabbed my flag, leaving my rucksack on the sofa, and went to investigate, walking towards the elevators, turning right and then left into a long corridor stretching the length of the first half of the seventeenth hole, from the conservatory all the way to the seventeenth tee. On that tee, the brave and the stupid would pick out the letter on the green painted sheds which they were going to hit over. The letters spelt out: OLD COURSE HOTEL.

The braver you were, the further to the right you would pick a letter. The 'L' in Hotel was the tiger line; with the right shape of shot, the ball would land almost beside the Jigger Inn, drawing looks and gasps of admiration from anyone sitting outside enjoying a drink in the garden area there. It could also land you with a bill from the hotel for a broken window if it all went horribly wrong.

Oblivious to anyone on the tee and what they were contemplating, I started my walk along that corridor, still unsure of where Tom could have gone. He didn't seem that fast a walker, but he was nowhere to be seen. He had disappeared into thin air. Until he was right there in front of me. It was almost like in a movie where someone knows they're being followed and hides and then jumps out to confront their stalker. But I wasn't a stalker. I just wanted Tom Watson to sign my Masters flag.

He didn't confront me or even challenge me. There was a small door to the left which he'd appeared from, maybe a bag store, and he just walked right past me giving me a small nod of his head. Had he just looked down there and seen my flag in my hand? It was bright yellow and was hard to miss.

As the brave and the stupid were deciding which shots to hit on the seventeenth tee, brave and stupid Kev was urging me to stop and turn back and was trying to engage my mouth with my brain. "This is your last chance. Kev, do it, do it now!" I turned on a sixpence and walked back the way I'd come. Tom had turned right.

"Mr Watson," I shouted.

He stopped and looked round. That was good. He hadn't started running away from me, at least not yet!

"Would you mind signing my Masters flag, please? Billy Casper gave it to me at the 2004 Masters and told me not to let anyone else other than Masters Champions sign it."

I had delivered my pitch, word perfect again. I was getting good at this and to using the 'Billy Casper' password. I held out my flag and my sharpie.

"I will not be signing your Masters flag, sir!" Were the words I heard come out of Tom's mouth.

What?!

"Billy Casper gave me the flag at the 2004 Masters and told me not to let anyone else sign it other than Masters Champions," I repeated, with a little less authority and with a touch of vulnerability thrown in too, hoping that mixing up the words slightly might do the trick this time. My mum, who was a drama teacher, would have been proud of my range of skills.

Watson looked at me long and hard, a look that a few journalists may have encountered over the years and repeated, "I will not be signing your Masters flag, sir," and he turned and walked away. I had joined the brave and the stupid all in the space of five seconds!

Like a punch-drunk boxer, I managed to make my way back to the sofa in the Reception and find some respite there as I gathered my racing thoughts. Why were his words so cutting? Had he already clocked my bright yellow Masters flag the day before during those near misses we'd had? Had he taken an instant dislike to me?

Normally, it took a little longer than that.

My head was spinning, but I wondered if Google might provide answers to my conundrum. I was probably clutching at straws; he just thought I was an arse! A grown man looking for a flag to be signed. Get a life!

Reaching for my laptop, I opened Google and typed in, 'Why would Tom Watson not sign a Masters Flag?'

There weren't too many straightforward answers thrown up, but reading between the lines, Tom Watson and Jack Nicklaus were very wary of who they signed for. There are people who go around tournaments collecting signatures on flags to put them on eBay or the equivalent or give them to charity auctions and take a cut from the sale proceeds. Professional autograph hunters. They will even give money to children to go and stand in line and get a signature from a player so that the player doesn't suss out the play. They have no back story to tell, no pride in prestige or provenance. They're just doing it for pure hard cash. Wow!

I sat back and reflected that no wonder Tom Watson hadn't signed. I'm not sure I would have either. I think you would feel used, wouldn't you? These people don't want a piece of history, they just want a piece of you to take and sell on.

I wasn't for giving up, though, and I searched Google again, this time for contact details for Tom. I came across tomwatson.com and after a bit of scrolling, right at the bottom of the page, I discovered a small, faint white-on-black Contact page. It didn't seem as if Tom really wanted to be contacted. Clicking on the link opened a Contact Page with a 'Send Fan Mail to Tom' message on the left-hand side and boxes for typing your message, asking for your Name, E Mail, Subject Matter and Message on the right-hand side of the page.

I certainly didn't qualify as a fan after what had just happened and Subject Matter? What would I write? I had a few choices …

"Why did you snub me??"

"How rude are you?"

"Billy Casper?"

That Friday morning, sitting in the Reception at The Old Course Hotel in St Andrews, where there are worse places in the world to feel let down and humiliated, I settled on the following Subject Matter and Message to Tom:

From: Kevin Davidson
Subject: Masters Flag

Dear Mr Watson

I approached you today at St Andrews Old Course Hotel to ask if you would sign a Masters flag gifted to me by Billy Casper at an hour-long meeting I had with him in 2004 at Augusta, organised by his son and my friend, Byron Casper. Mr Casper told me that I should only have the flag signed by Masters champions and he proceeded to sign it in the middle himself.

14 years on, this week I was attending the British Seniors and proceeded to obtain signatures at the Event from Fred Couples, Bernard Langer, Sir Nick Faldo, Vijay Singh, Jose Maria Olazabal and Larry Mize and tried to get your signature on the Thursday on a couple of occasions and then hung around the hotel for 5 hours on Friday before meeting you.

You said you would not sign my Masters flag but did not expand on why, even when I mentioned the fact that Mr Casper had given it to me.

I absolutely respect your decision not to sign it but I wondered if you might share with me why that was; if I offended you with my approach, I can only apologise for that.

I look forward to hearing from you at your convenience

Yours in anticipation

*Kevin Davidson
Scotland*

Happy with what seemed like the tenth draft, I pressed the black box that said 'Send Your Message', not expecting to hear back from Tom, but at least feeling better that I had done something. God, after all, loves a trier, or so people say!

That afternoon, I returned to Edinburgh where I was living, elated with the new additions to my flag, but deflated by the omission of Tom Watson's signature. I played golf at Duddingston Golf Club the following afternoon with my childhood friends, Ali and Niall. We'd been introduced at pre-school nursery in Ellon by our mothers, so these were my oldest friends, who I rarely got to hang out with, and we always had a lot to catch up on when we did.

I'd finished telling them about Tom Watson snubbing me and my email to him. I could see in their eyes that they wondered why I'd even gone to the bother of doing that. What chance was there of Tom Watson, with all that was going on in his life, even reading that, let alone replying to it? I probably shared their thoughts, but I like to live my life by the principle of 'I'm glad I did, not I wish I had' and I was glad I'd sent it.

On the twelfth hole, I was casually checking my phone when I spied a reply from tomwatson.com.

Mr. Davidson

Below please find Tom Watson's response to your email.

The email was from Tom's admin assistant, Kelly Fray. Tom must have checked in with his assistant at some point after his second round of 69 on Friday evening, with the time in Kansas being six hours behind, to be told that he'd received an email from someone he'd met earlier that day at the Old Course Hotel, who had a Masters flag he wanted signed. I could just imagine Tom's response to that! Kelly must have then read or forwarded the email to him, and this is what he wrote back,

Dear Mr. Davidson,

As I sometimes fail to discern properly who is going to sell the items I autograph or not, I will be happy to sign your flag if you present the opportunity again.

Sincerely,

Tom Watson

Kelly had obviously sent that email at 08:34 her time - Kansas being six hours behind - so basically, as soon as she got up on the Saturday morning, presumably so I could 'present the opportunity again' while Tom was still in Scotland. That was a very thoughtful thing of her to do, rather than leave it to reply until the start of the following working week, when her boss would likely be cruising at 35,000 feet, heading back across the Atlantic from his week's work in St Andrews. Thank you very much, Kelly. You are an asset to Mr Watson.

As we were walking up the twelfth hole, I read the email to Niall and Ali. They couldn't believe it. The thought of pushing a flag in front of people for their signature was alien to them, but not as alien as emailing an eight times Major Champion and then getting a response from them just twenty-four hours later!

"What are you going to do?" asked Ali.

"Simple," I said. "I'll head back to St Andrews tomorrow and I'll sit and wait for him at The Old Course Hotel again."

Ali and Niall smiled knowingly at each other. I read their minds. 'Aye, right, as if he'll show up!' I was more positive. As soon as I got off the golf course, I sent a response to Kelly's email.

From: Kevin Davidson
To: tomwatson.com

Many thanks for your speedy and kind response, Kelly/Mr Watson.

I am now back in Edinburgh but will make the trip back up to St Andrews on Sunday morning to the hotel again to try to get Mr Watson's signature as I'm not sure when the opportunity may arise again.

Hopefully, I'll catch Mr Watson sometime in the morning before he goes across to the practice ground ahead of his 14:00 tee off time.

With regards

Kevin

There was no response that night or in my inbox early Sunday morning when I awoke. I was half hoping for something along the lines of:

Dear Kevin

Mr Watson would be delighted if you could join him for breakfast on Sunday morning where he will sign your Masters flag, and he has also organised an 'inside the ropes' pass for you as his guest for Sunday afternoon's play round The Old Course. He has a reservation in the Road Hole Grill at 8pm after the Presentation Ceremony and is happy for you to dine with him and he will happily share some of his memories of Augusta.

Well, a man can dream! Instead, I found myself driving seventy-five minutes back up the road to St Andrews and parking in the car park outside The Old Course Hotel. I sat in the car looking at the hotel and wondering whether the security staff had all been issued with photos of me from the internet, with instructions not to let this man within fifty yards of the Reception, let alone Tom Watson. As I got out of the car and headed towards the front door of the Hotel, the sliding doors had a more formidable look about them this time.

Would the hotel go into lockdown as I approached? I wondered. Not even the red button at the side of the doors would open them, as the doormen and guests looked out at me trying to get in. Guests were asking the doormen what was going on and the doormen were pointing at me standing at the doors! I could see them mouthing the words 'Tom Watson' and 'that man'!

I tripped over an uneven stone, and it jolted me out from my daydream. The sliding doors opened as I walked towards them, and the doorman greeted me with a hearty "Good Morning!" I turned right and took my usual seat in the Reception, got out the Sunday papers and settled down to wait for Tom.

An hour passed. He wasn't coming. He would be exiting the hotel through the Grand Ballroom doors or via the Conservatory. Nipping over the wall, he would walk across the second hole of The Old Course to the Links Clubhouse. He would not have to sign my flag.

The elevator doors opened and out walked Tom Watson.

I got up, expecting him to veer towards the left again so that I would have to follow him along that same corridor, the scene of our last meeting where, this time, he'd be ready for me and show me his swing speed with his Driver across the back of my head! But no, Tom was walking straight towards me with a big smile on his face and his right hand out and there was no Driver to be seen.

"Good morning, Kevin, good to see you," Tom said. "Tell me the story of the flag again."

As I told him about Mr Casper in full glorious technicolour this time, he signed my flag along the top, with a very legible signature and with a big smile, listening intently.

I don't tend to do selfies with stars, and I wasn't about to start now. I just thanked him and wished him good luck and Cordial Tom was on his way ninety seconds after he'd arrived. Was it worth it? Hell, yes. Persistence pays off. The pursuit of this TW was over. Tiger Woods, though, might prove as difficult, if not more so, to pin down in the future!

Time would tell, but in the meantime, I'd kept my promise to Mr Casper, with eight signatures respectfully added outside his one, which still sat in splendid isolation in the centre of the logo. I would add ten more after moving to St Andrews, where my life and my golf handicap was about to change dramatically.

THE POSITIVE GOLFER

Part I

CHAPTER 5: MOVING TO ST. ANDREWS

After many, many years of playing the frustrating game of golf we all love, and love to hate, struggling to beat my handicap and trying to edge it downwards towards single figures, suddenly it tumbled from 10 to 1.5 in ten months! The secret to that dramatic reduction? There were a few things, but for me the main one was moving to St Andrews and breathing in the rarefied air there.

ALWAYS TAKE THE ROAD LESS TRAVELLED
I'd moved to Edinburgh from Aberdeen in 2018 and was renting a less than desirable two-bedroom flat in South Gyle, with a lovely natured, ambitious twenty-four-year-old entrepreneur called Pooja from Bangalore. We were trying to change our respective worlds, property and healthcare, using technology and as little money as possible.

Money was tight. Things were progressing ... but slowly. We were part of The Royal Bank of Scotland's Accelerator Programme and had free office space in their Entrepreneurial Hub at Gogarburn near the airport. However, in March 2020 COVID arrived and the world turned on its head.

I had sneaked away from Edinburgh on the Sunday morning to spend Mother's Day some one hundred and fifty miles north, with my Mum back in Ellon. Deciding to stay a second night, we watched TV as Boris Johnson announced sombrely that the UK would be going into full lockdown on 26th March with a review on 16th April. My brother Rory called right after Boris had exited stage right and asked whether I was going to head back to my gloomy room in Edinburgh or stay with Mum in her three-bedroom detached house with a garden in Ellon. It wasn't a difficult decision. I would stay with my mum, so that she wasn't alone. After all it was only for three weeks!

That decision helped change the course of my life. Eighteen weeks later, I emerged from the security of my 'Boris' imposed chrysalis, a different person from the one who'd arrived in Ellon. I had a new perspective. I was looking forward to a new beginning, a new normal and a new home to head to.

COVID was just the reset I needed, with my one hour a day release for exercise spent pounding the streets of Ellon from one side to the other and back again, retracing the same steps I'd taken as a hopeful, excited and uncertain fourteen-year-old, who had had to make the mile and a half trip to high school and back every day on foot. What untarnished dreams I had had back then!

Day by day, I grew closer again to the aspirations of fourteen-year-old Kevin who had wondered what the world had in store for him. Night by night, my Mum and I watched film after film, one night her choice, the next night mine, and I was returned to much more innocent times. No alcohol, daily walks and exercise helped my body get fit and my mind get positive. My Mum has always had a habit of being able to turn a bad situation into a better one with a positive turn of phrase and just being around her twenty-four hours a day made such a difference.

She lived now in a house overlooking the golf course in Ellon and every second day I would walk the eighteen holes there. Starting at the 11th hole beside her house, I walked up and down all the fairways, stopping at the eighteenth hole to stand beside the spot where I'd hit my three-iron through the trees and marvelling at what seventeen-year-old Kevin had achieved that day thirty-four years before. I could see my proud Dad again standing behind the green and I stopped to stand beside him, and we watched together as I made my two putt and took us to the Final.

I then crossed the road to walk the holes of the front nine and I sat on the memorial bench at the back of the sixth tee which the Club had situated there in memory of my Dad and the work he did for the Club. My one hour of exercise sometimes became slightly longer as I sat there, lost in thought.

However, my walks and memories on the golf course were interrupted towards the end of May, when golf courses were reopened for play ... but only for members and I wasn't a member of the Club anymore.

It was torture watching others get to enjoy the game and I could only reflect that my own Golf Club and courses were over a hundred miles away in St Andrews and travel that far was not yet allowed.

As the first Lockdown was coming to an end, we started discussing what I would do and where I would stay.

My Mum had seemed to really enjoy having me around, cooking and looking after me while I was working, bringing me pots of tea and snacks in her conservatory as I kept in touch with the outside world via zoom calls and emails. It was going to be hard for both of us when I flew the nest again, but as always, like every good parent, she put me first.

She helped me unravel the many thoughts about what was next, whether that might be buying a flat in Edinburgh, moving back to Aberdeen, staying with her in Ellon or, intriguingly, moving nearer to The New Golf Club in St Andrews.

It was my Mum who brought this last one up. Knowing how frustrated I was at not being able to play golf when others could, she mooted the idea of my moving closer to my own golf club.

However, property prices in St Andrews were insane and the rental prices were no better, so it looked like that wouldn't be an option. With encouragement though, I widened my search on the real estate portals and up came 'Leuchars', located six miles north and priced at around one third of St Andrews. It was worth a look.

Leuchars is a drive-through small town which used to house the Royal Air Force and was now taking care of the British Army. The train station is a hub for students and golfers alike and the start and end of term times resemble an ant hill with hundreds of scholars decanting from buses onto trains and vice versa onto the blue walkway bridge with trunks, cases and bags following behind with excited chatter about what the term or the holidays would hold ahead for them.

I found an ex-military three bedroomed terraced house in Warwick Close on the internet and at the end of June I broke the rules again by travelling further than five miles to go and inspect it. Needs must!

It was unfurnished, cold and devoid of any feeling of homeliness, but something, other than the low rent of £500 a month compared to £1200 a month for something similar in St Andrews, attracted me to it. I paid my deposit there and then to the estate agent and headed across to St Andrews for a quick nine holes on the Eden course to get my fix of golf. The sun was shining, and I had a feeling of calmness and a strange sense of wellbeing.

When I got back to Ellon, I immediately started ordering beds, sofas, white goods and electricals to arrive in time for the big move-in date of 20th July and I started to deal with the thought of leaving again. It was a real wrench to leave the security of what Ellon meant and head back to the outside world to a completely new beginning, but something was pulling me there.

I hired a van to take all my stuff to Leuchars and, after a highly charged emotional farewell with my mum in Ellon, I headed uncertainly down the A90 road, crossing over the Tay Bridge into the Kingdom of Fife. The left turn-off at the next roundabout was signposted for St Andrews and that's the road I would now be taking. I drove past Drumoig Golf Course and driving range and then past St Michaels Golf Course, both of which are well worth a visit.

In Leuchars, instead of turning right at the roundabout to St Andrews, I headed straight up the road past the butchers and the small Spar convenience store which would become so familiar to me over the next thirty-three months. I drove past the beautiful medieval St Athernase Church which dates back to 1185 and headed towards my desolate, mid-terraced living quarters for one.

Warwick Close ... with triple glazing installed in all the windows by the air force to deaden the noise of the aircraft from the nearby airbase flying overhead on their training missions at Mach 2. Oh, what joy!

Almost immediately, though, these air exercises brought a thunderous sense of excitement for me. From the back door of the house, I watched two 'Typhoon' planes tear over the house and out to the hills beyond in less than a couple of seconds, giving me my own personal flyover to welcome me to the area and wish me all the best for my golf that coming week!

After I'd unpacked and closed the front door, I relaxed. They say that home is where the heart is and that was back in Ellon, but this place would reach in and grab a piece of my heart too over the coming years. Although I was uncertain about what the future held, I loved the fact that this was my new beginning and something just felt right. I couldn't know at that point just how right it was going to turn out!

CHAPTER 6: 10 TO 1.5 IN 10 MONTHS!

NOW THAT'S MAGIC!

Five days later, in my first competitive round of golf for over four months, I shot a net 64 over the New Course and won the medal. I knew I'd made the right call. The 'magic' had started to kick in! No flyover that day, though. Very disappointing. Maybe they didn't work weekends?

Over the next ten months, as my handicap tumbled, I toyed with writing a book called *'10 to Scratch in 10 Months'*.

Here's how my handicap went:

2020
End of July   9.9
End of August   7.7
End of September   7.7
End of October   6.3
End of November   5.7
End of December   5.3

2021

End of January	5.4
End of February	4.5
End of March	3.6
End of April	2.2
Mid-May	1.5

I was within touching distance of scratch with two weeks to go. The book was going to get written!

Throughout the previous ten months, I had concentrated on the positives and there were lots of them, without one golf lesson and with the same set of golf clubs I'd had for over twenty years. So, if it wasn't a change in technique or equipment, what was it that had helped get me there?

The Positive Golfer, that's what.

By the end of May, though, instead of being at scratch, I was back up to 2.2!

As I'd edged nearer to scratch, I started concentrating on the outcome rather than just on my game. I'm sure that we've all done something similar at some point. We're on a good score with three holes to play and then we let our mind wander and suddenly, wham bam, we finish badly. However, it was a good lesson for me going forward.

I think in golf you can choose to be a Positive Golfer or a Negative Golfer and maybe that mirrors life too. I had told an acquaintance of mine about the idea for the book in March when my handicap was 3.6 and still on its way down. After May had passed and my handicap sat at 2.2 instead of scratch, he took great delight in telling anyone who would listen how I'd fallen short of my goal. He was concentrating on the negatives while I was looking at it in a much more positive way and that the drop from 10 to 1.5 was amazing.

He took the positive narrative and turned it into a negative narrative and was trying to drag me down into a negative place. It wasn't going to happen, though.

I'm always keen to make people feel good about themselves on the golf course and pass on the positivity. I hope that some of the following learnings from my golf journey from 10 to 1.5 may help others in theirs.

CHAPTER 7: MY EIGHT PILLARS FOR POSITIVE GOLF

MY LEARNINGS FROM THE LINKS

My learnings from St Andrews Links helped me in my downward trajectory from 10 to 1.5 in 10 months. They worked for me then and they continue to work for me now. Some of them may seem like common sense, but until I looked back and analysed my journey, I didn't really understand how such a dramatic reduction in handicap had occurred (without maybe some positive help from The Golfing Gods!)

One learning was as important as another for me and doing one without the other wouldn't have worked. I call them my eight pillars.

MY EIGHT PILLARS FOR POSITIVE GOLF

Playing positively was key for me to play good golf. I could have had the best technical swing in the world, but if I played negatively, then that swing wasn't going to help me play my best golf on any particular day.

In Greece, at the top of the Acropolis in Athens, sits The Parthenon, which was built to worship Athena, the goddess of wisdom. Its pillars have endured for over two thousand five hundred years. My Learnings from the Links created my own enduring pillars of wisdom for positive golf and formed the foundations for my improvement.

My Physical Pillars
Be Prepared
Play Competitive Games Regularly
Seek Continuous Improvement
Look After My Body

My Mental Pillars.
Keep The Brain Slumbering
Be Positive & Stay Positive
Set Goals
Enjoy Myself

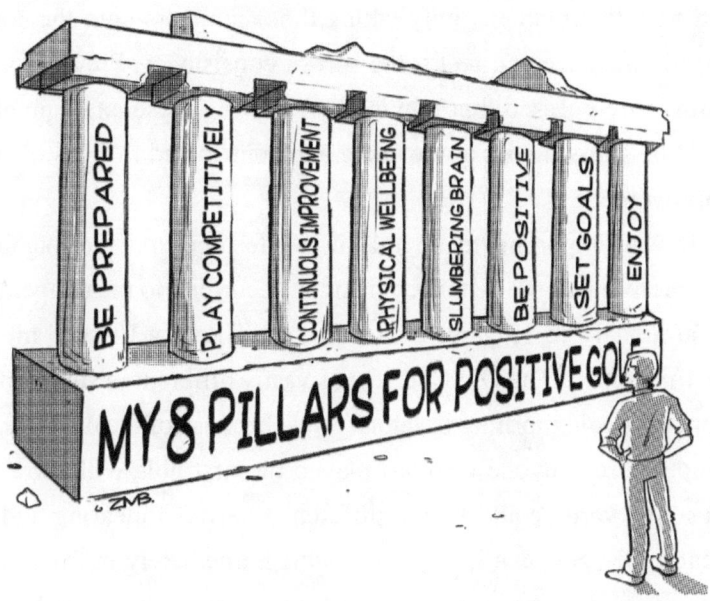

Warning: I'm a very methodical thinker and like to go into detail. That may not be for everyone, so feel free to jump straight to Chapter 8 if detail isn't your thing.

Read on if it is.

MY PHYSICAL PILLARS

Pillar 1: Be Prepared

KNOW MY YARDAGES
With a world class driving range at St Andrews Golf Academy and ball tracking technology, it was a no-brainer to spend time there. I used the technology to track my yardages and monitor the height I hit each of my clubs.

From Sand Wedge to Driver, I would hit ten balls with each club and note the numbers, only taking those numbers onto the course once I could see and feel some sort of consistency. Previously, I'd really only guessed, but now really knowing these exact numbers took the guessing out of the game and contributed to an immediate improvement.

It was important to do this in wintertime and then again in summertime, as the distances changed according to the temperature by around 10 to 15 yards a club for me. The shot I would hit into the first hole of The Old Course was vastly different in summertime from on a cold morning in January, just because of the difference in temperature. Anyone who has played the first hole will know that those ten yards could be the difference between clearing and not clearing the Swilcan Burn, which runs immediately in front of the first green. Having to take a penalty drop and play over the burn again in front of your amused playing partners can be an even more nerve-wracking test.

Knowing My Yardages helped make those adjustments and meant that I didn't land in the burn very often.

There was nothing dramatic in my numbers and in my mid-fifties was probably about right for me, especially when I compared myself to others around my age, height and ability. What did stand out though, was that the distances were evenly spaced between clubs, allowing me to have certainty when standing over a shot. If there were huge gaps between club distances, then it might have been time to get fitted for new clubs.

My Summer Numbers

Club	Carry (Yards)	Total Distance (Yards)
60-degree wedge*	48	50
58-degree wedge	57	60
56-degree wedge*	66	70
54-degree wedge*	75	80
52-degree wedge	85	90
50-degree wedge*	95	100
Pitching wedge	100	105
9-iron	115	120
8-iron	130	135
7-iron	140	150
6-iron	155	165
5-iron	165	175
4-iron	180	190
5-hybrid	195	205
3-wood/metal	205	220
Driver	235	260

*I didn't carry these clubs in my bag.

ALWAYS WARM UP BEFORE PLAYING

I made my first ball off the first tee my sixty first shot, not my first shot of the day. I warmed up with a bucket of sixty balls, or at the very least thirty, to get the muscles warmed up and my back ready to make those alien movements that only golfers make.

Warming up also allowed me to know when I was ready to play the courses. If I wasn't achieving my optimum ball speed, then I knew that I wasn't loosened off properly. I also discovered that I needed to hit sixty balls during a warmup to be completely ready to head to the first tee.

How many times do you see people rocking up to the first tee and hitting the ball like they were ninety years old, with an 'ooh' or an 'ahh', as if they'd just put their back out? It takes them six holes to warm up, which, when you count the shots on their card, is probably around thirty shots. Then they moan about their score and their handicap and wonder why they never have a decent round!

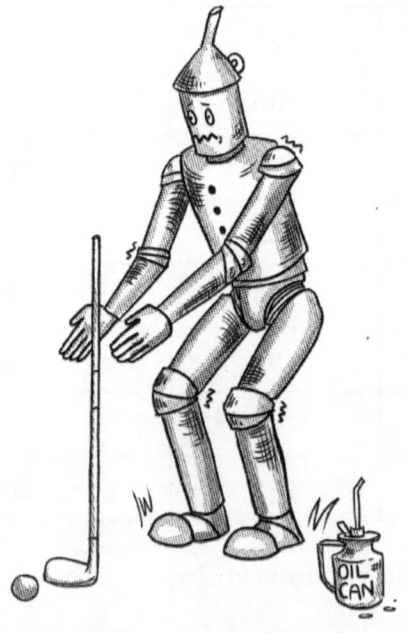

"I WISH I'D WARMED UP!"

If they'd only set aside twenty to thirty minutes to warm up their muscles on the range or in nets, they could chop two to three shots off their score and their handicap almost immediately. I can't imagine that if they played any other sport like football, rugby or even cricket, that they would pitch up and start the game without a proper warm-up. Why should golf be any different, especially with the range of muscles used when making a swing? Miguel Angel Jiminez has a great stretching routine before he hits any balls on the range and any golfer, whatever their age, would do worse than look it up on YouTube and copy him.

The ball tracking technology at the driving range also allowed me to see how the wind that day would affect my ball. The feedback helped me understand whether the wind was pushing a ball five or ten yards left or right and helped me work that into my calculations and alignments on the course. Without that, I had no way of knowing and would have been trying this out in real time on the course for the first couple of holes and potentially dropping shots. I tried to do all my preparation for the round ahead when I was warming up at the driving range.

USE A LASER RANGEFINDER

I didn't have to guess the distance to the flag anymore after investing in a laser rangefinder. For anyone who watched the Peacock/Sky Atlantic series 'Day of the Jackal' starring Eddie Redmayne, you will recall him shooting a target 3815 metres away! The Jackal knew the exact distance to the target and had also factored in the wind and other conditions to work out what was required to successfully extinguish his victim. If he had used rough estimates, The Jackal would have been renamed The Jackass!

Before I got a rangefinder, I was working off a watch for front, middle and back distances to the green. However, with the greens at St Andrews being so huge, that could be the difference of twenty yards from front to centre and centre to back and the same from side to side. In fact, the 5th green on The Old Course is one hundred yards from front to back and sixty yards from side to side, so you can see the problem.

I thought like The Jackal and lasered the flagstick to get the exact distance to it, starting my calculations from there. Then I worked out the wind. Was it hurting or was it helping? Was it a 1-club wind, a 2-club wind or even a 5-club wind, as we sometimes have blowing over St Andrews? I then translated that into 1 club = 10 yards, 2 clubs = 20 yards and so on. A 140-yard shot may play 165 yards into the wind and 110 yards with the wind, and I committed to the new adjusted number and hit the shot. (I was told by a higher handicapper recently when we were playing a Texas scramble that this was a new way of calculating things for him, but it certainly helped him look at things differently when he played shots into and with the wind.)

I'm sure everyone will have a slightly different tactic, but the important thing is to have a tactic and not just leave it to chance.

PRACTICE WITH PURPOSE FOR 'GAME DAY'

There was no point in just swinging a golf club for the sake of it. Not even if I was just warming up. Even then, I needed to be concentrating on a particular set of muscles.

At the driving range, I was either warming up or working on some part of my game. The sixty balls I hit to warm up before I played were for just that, warming up and to make sure I was ready to go out on the course to play. No thoughts or attempts to work on my game when warming up or on the course when I was playing unless it was a practice round.

A practice round was just that … I was practicing on something.

I didn't care about my score or any match. If I was recording my score or playing a match, then I left my practice behind and I let my swing take over, untouched by technical thoughts.

This was 'Game Day' and I had to rely on my practice to make a difference. For me, practice was there so I got to do it again and again until I got it right and meant that on 'Game Day' I could rely on practice to deliver. (Can you imagine watching your favourite sports team make a mistake during a match and then ask the referee to stop the game so they can try it again? Not a chance. They're all playing with their 'Game Day' heads on.)

Just before I walked from my car to the first tee, I would say to myself, 'Let's go, it's Game Day, Kev," to let my brain know there was a difference that day.

TAKE A TIP FROM BRUCE LEE

I'm not a golf coach, and I'm not qualified to teach a swing, a grip or recognise when something looks wrong with another player's swing. I leave that to the professional teachers who are brilliant at spotting the slightest thing that's gone wrong and whose approach can be tweaked to help players of all standards improve.

For me, Practicing with Purpose meant working on a particular technique, shot shape or trying to recreate pressure. I'd watch YouTube videos of top professionals talking about their shot making, I'd read books on putting, chipping and mindset but ultimately, it was me who had to pick up a club and try and hit the shots.

Bruce Lee famously said, "I fear not the man who has practiced 10,000 kicks once, but I fear the man who has practiced one kick 10,000 times."

In my mind, that's what practice was all about. It was going to the range and using ball tracking technology to try and hit the left to right shot, which I needed to play into a right-to-left wind and had beat me up the day before, or trying to hit the 100 or 150-yard sign using a selection of different clubs from 5 iron to PW. It was about imagining myself in a 'Wham!' match (see Pillar 2) with Ian and Colin and Hector watching me hit a shot or make a putt to win the game.

Without practicing with purpose for 'Game Day', I'm not sure what it's all for, if it's not all about improving your game and lowering your scores? Some may say that it's just for the enjoyment and it's for the fresh air and the exercise and that they don't like playing competitively with all that entails. However, I was competitive. I wanted to beat the golf course, and I wanted to be as good as I could be. I firmly believed that enjoyment and the joy of golf followed from the joy of improving, the joy of scoring and the joy of playing well.

PUTTING PRACTICE FOR GAME DAY

Two things helped me immensely during my journey from 10 to 1.5 in 10 months: Bob Rotella and a green-reading YouTube video.

Bob Rotella

Bob's book *'Putting Out of Your Mind'* is a great book and will have something for everyone in it to improve their putting.

For me, it was a simple 'Take your stance, look up at the target, look back at the ball and then roll the putt'.

I just practiced this for an hour or so and let my mind and body work out how hard to hit it and get comfortable with it. This technique changed my putting.

Green Reading

I came across a series of short videos called 'The Lost Art of Putting Masterclass' by Gary Nicol[3] and loved what he had to say about Green Reading and Low Side Reading.

This helped my putting enormously. I went and practiced with purpose and came out the other side a much better green reader. This in turn meant that my putts would follow the break of the greens so much better and leave the golf ball inches away from the hole rather than feet away. The result: shots off my handicap and matches won.

Lining Up My Putts

Finally, I lined up my putt using a line on the ball. It was my personal preference, but it worked for me. I got immediate feedback on whether I had read the putt correctly and it let me forget about the line and just concentrate on rolling the ball to the hole at the correct pace.

All these little things helped me get marginal gains and added up over the months.

3 https://www.nationalclubgolfer.com/video/the-lost-art-of-putting-masterclass-episode-17-a-green-reading-tip-to-help-with-longer-putts/

Pillar 2: Play Competitive Games Regularly

THE MONDAY FELLOWSHIP

When I moved to St Andrews, I was told about The New Golf Club's Fellowship[4] and I signed myself up for it. Basically, around thirty to fifty golfers, who are either retired or between jobs, got together every Monday and played in organised fourballs on the Links. Each week was a different fourball so that you got to meet and play with different members of the Club.

A 'Fellowship' is defined as a 'friendly association', but as well as playing for Stableford points in a race to be crowned Fellowship Champion, each fourball played a match. These matches were fiercely competitive, the prize being loud bragging rights in the bar afterwards. Having to sink putts to half or win holes every week helped get me into game shape for when I needed to make putts in medals and competitions to lower my handicap or to win a hole in match play for real.

FRIDAY 'WHAM!' MATCHES

I also played 'Wham!' matches on a Friday with Hector the Tinkerer, Colin the Metronome and Big Ian, an excellent plus handicap player.

The matches were called 'Wham! vs. The Spies'. Hector and I (Wham!) had a penchant for wearing shorts as soon as the temperature rose above ten degrees, while Ian and Colin (The Spies) were ex-military. (You may recall that Wham! were an eighties UK pop band known for wearing shorts on stage). Unfortunately, that was the only link Hector and I had to the eighties pop group, but the 'Wham!' name stuck.

[4] Every Club should consider running a Fellowship, as well as a Seniors Section, so as not to exclude those who are perhaps off work on a particular day or are between jobs, rather than just retired. The New Club has one on a Monday and another one on a Wednesday, where no trophy is played for, but the matches are just as competitive. It's a great way to integrate new members into the Club, meet new people and sharpen your game to boot.)

The matches were always fiercely contested and the score updated in our WhatsApp group after every game - Wham! 1 vs. Spies 0, Wham! 3 vs. Spies 4 and so on – with whoever won that week also having have their photo added as the profile photo until the next match.

Both the score and the photograph would serve as ample incentive to the other team to raise their game for the following week. That, and the constant abuse in the WhatsApp chat during the week from the winning team. The further added incentive was that the losers at the end of the year would have to buy the winners Christmas lunch and drinks in The New Club.

These regular games helped sharpen all our play, with The New Club's Winter Handicap Team of eight golfers frequently being made up from three quarters of our 'Wham!' match via Hector, Colin and myself, with Ian being a mainstay of the Scratch Team, who were recently crowned league champions.

Our weekly 'Wham!' matches helped all of us get used to having to make shots and putts when it counted.

Pillar 3: Seek Continuous Improvement

MEASURE MY GAME

If I didn't measure my game, I couldn't measure my performance and, in turn, I couldn't track areas of improvement and for improvement.

In an excel spreadsheet, I recorded lots of data including how many fairways in regulation, greens in regulation, the number of one putts, three putts, and total putts per round. In addition, I recorded eagles, birdies, pars, bogeys and double bogeys or worse. Finally, I noted the score at each hole by way of colour coding, orange for eagle, pink for birdie, green for par, blue for bogey and red for double bogey or worse.

What did I discover from all of this? I discovered I had to eat. The colour coding helped me instantly recognise patterns and, early on, I noticed I was on the 'bogey bus' over the last four to six holes, as a run of blue bogeys brought my rounds to an end. Being able to see this clearly from the colour coded boxes, I was then able to reflect that perhaps I was getting tired and needed more energy. I packed energy snacks and bananas into my bag and started grazing on them every three or four holes to maintain my energy levels.

I also made sure I had a bottle of water with me to ensure my body and my brain remained hydrated. It seemed to work as my scores improved during the last six holes or so, helping me maintain focus and push on to a good score.

MY SCORECARD HIEROGLYPHICS

This may all sound like a lot of hard work, but I simply recorded these things as I recorded my score on my scorecard. For example, in the last box of the score card, I record '112'.

The first '1' is for Fairways in Regulation; if I don't hit it, then it's a '0'. The next '1' is for Greens in Regulation, and if I don't hit it, then it's a '0'. The last '2' is for the number of putts taken, remembering that putts from off the green are not counted in these figures. For me, the best number was 110, if I chip in, and the worst was 003. Hopefully, I don't have more than a 3 putt, although I did once six putt the par 3 8th green on the Eden course from the front of the green up to a pin placed just at the top of the hill! Oops!

DRAGGING MYSELF OUT OF MY PIT OF DESPAIR

After a round when I got home, the first thing I did when I got in the door was excitedly open my laptop and transfer the captured hieroglyphics to my spreadsheet.

I say excitedly because it was at this point that I marked the various areas of my game out of ten. Although I may not have scored well, and felt I played poorly, I boosted myself back up by seeing that my driving was a 9, as were my long irons, and, in fact, the root of the problem that day was the chipping or the long putting which only merited a 5 or a 6. My overall game total gave me a further boost and normally dragged me out my pit of despair.

Without this immediate brain dump from scorecard to laptop, I would be too hard on myself, and I wouldn't know what I would have to go and practice.

Measuring my game definitely helped improve my game.

Pillar 4: Look After My Body

MARGINAL GAINS

With all those alien movements we make as golfers, it was no wonder that my body needed looking after. The twisting, the turning, the exasperated throwing back of the head in disgust at a missed putt, the tutting, the neck craning to see where the ball had gone when it disappeared over the horizon towards a tree or a bush, tender loving care towards my body could add up to marginal gains that could help me gain a stroke or two a round.

MY BACK

Before I arrived in St Andrews, I used to go to a chiropractor only when my back was causing me discomfort. This was normally like clockwork every eight weeks. I would attend one of those chiropractors who holds your neck and then twists and 'cracks' it to within an inch of its life. I'm told that is called 'Diversified Chiropractic'. It always caused me great consternation. Did they know what they were doing? Were they about to leave me playing wheelchair golf for the rest of my life?

After I moved to St Andrews and started playing much more regularly, I found Chiropractor Kate, who practiced a different type of chiropractic, called 'McTimoney'. It's much gentler with lower force adjustments, using what seemed like a series of strange flicks and taps. I was sceptical at first after the rough manipulations I'd been used to. How could these little slaps to the skin surface have the same effect? They did, though, and instead of attending reactively when my back had almost passed its point of no return, I was booking in for sessions every four to five weeks to get what they call proactive treatment to correct the slight misalignments that the previous month's golf or sitting at a desk at work would throw up.

It was amazing just how much difference that proactive approach made to my golf. I was virtually pain free and able to swing freely, which made a big difference to my scoring. I sensed when my back was beginning to seize up and most of the time I could get an appointment at short notice.

However, on one occasion this didn't work for me. I woke up on the morning of an important Club Championship match and felt that something was wrong with my back and needed tweaking. Unfortunately, I couldn't get an appointment with Kate before the match and because I couldn't fully turn, my body felt out of sync, and I was well beaten in my match. I never let that happen again, hence the reason for my proactive schedule with Kate. I wanted to win or lose matches based on my ability, not my 'disabilities' for that day or week, and felt that prevention was the key.

So many back problems are preventable and don't need to be endured. Regular proactive sessions made such a difference to my golf swing and to my game in general.

I'm truly amazed at the number of golfers I play with who suffer from back spasms and stiffness. A session with a chiropractor would have them swinging freely again and knocking shots off their scores and their handicaps.

Proactive Chiropractic = Marginal gains.

YOGA

Yoga works all the same movements as golf. Prime video has a few free yoga videos to stream. Twenty minutes for three times a week in the privacy of my own living room helped keep my back and my body flexible and helped add a few more miles an hour to my swing speed and yards to my shots.

MY FEET

My feet were the only things between me and the big ball called Earth and golf put them under all sorts of pressure. The twisting action of the golf swing caused callouses and corns which, if left untreated for five or six weeks, became quite painful to the point that they distracted me during a round of golf. This had an impact on me both physically and mentally, resulting in my not being able to swing optimally.

Those distractions could cost me a shot here and there, so once a month I scheduled a trip to my foot professional, Andrea. She worked her magic, getting rid of the seed corns and ensured that the health of my feet were good enough to play my best golf the following month, without the foot distractions.

Proactive Podiatry = Marginal Gains.

MY FACE

I now always wear Factor 50 sun cream on my face all year round when I'm golfing. The winter sun and wind caused as much damage to my face as the summer sun.

I played golf with a skin specialist in St Andrews who put the fear into me, after which I went and got a very small blemish on my nose checked out by my GP. I was told that I had pre-cancerous cells, and I was prescribed a cream called Efudix™, which I had to rub around the affected area every night for four weeks.

There was no change for ten days, then quickly after that, my previously invisible damaged cells, which were being targeted by the cream, started to redden and crust for the next two weeks. My nose looked like I had been in a fight with a gorse bush. After a further week or so, the crusting disappeared, the skin healed and the cancer clock on these areas was reset. However, if I'd left these untreated, then there was a high chance it could have developed into skin cancer.

I completed another bout of cream application on my cheeks to blitz any pre-cancerous cells there too. The change and look was startling but was well worth it. In fact, I posted my 'before' and 'after' photos on my social media channels and was surprised by the number of comments and questions from friends who then went to get themselves checked out. One unfortunately discovered cancerous cells and is receiving ongoing treatment but was thankful they went to get checked out when they did.

As golfers, we forget how long we spend in the sun. It's vital to apply suncream before we play, and reapply at the 10th tee, on our face and on our ears too. If you don't think this applies to you, then check out my before, during and after photos on my website at www.kevindavidsonauthor.com and then decide.

If you only take one thing away from reading this book, let this be it.

IT'S GOOD TO TALK

I played with several 'older' golfers in their sixties, seventies and even into their eighties and my conversations on the golf course moved over the years with fellow golfers from 'going out, girls and playing football' to 'getting up in the middle of the night to go the toilet, prostates and watching football"

Men of a certain age don't tend to share their thoughts or feelings, but on the golf course something happens, and all sorts of ailments are shared. Sometimes, it's like sitting in the waiting room at the local medical practice.

I think it's a great thing to be able to share in a safe place, knowing that only you and your three playing partners (then the rest of the Fellowship, and then the full membership!) know about your ailments. Sharing helps others speak about things and even go to make an appointment. Stripping back the mystery of these diseases saves lives and helps give people an outlet.

It's good to talk!

"ITS GOOD TO TALK!"

IT'S GOOD TO WALK

A recent visit to a wellness check-up confirmed what a lot of us know; walking is good for you. I just didn't realise how good it was until the health professional confirmed that walking three times a week can lower the blood pressure top number by up to twenty points. This number measures the pressure your blood is pushing against your artery walls when the heart beats, and a number below 120 and above 90 is optimal. Given that a number above 130 is in the high range, then a drop of twenty points seems to be very meaningful.

As well as being out on the course improving my golf game and getting my fix of regular social interaction, I was also improving my health too.

Golf truly is a magical game!!

MY MENTAL PILLARS

Pillar 5: Keep The Brain Slumbering

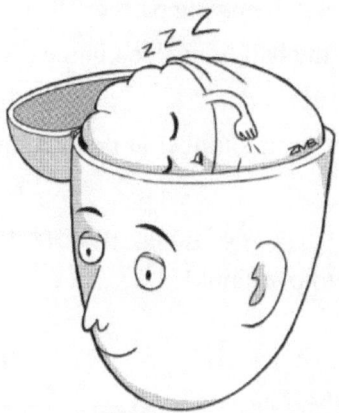

"THE SLUMBERING BRAIN"

What do I mean by this? It's probably easier if I share some stories of not keeping the brain slumbering.

'DIVOTGATE'

Hitting a fantastic drive up the 11th hole on the Jubilee course, I left myself a full pitching wedge into the green. The only issue was that my ball had landed in, and nestled down in, an old divot. As I write this, there has been no edict from the powers that be that a ball can be lifted out of a divot and placed within 6 inches, no nearer the hole. So, I had to play it out of the divot.

As a fully paid-up member of the KYBS-Keep Your Brain Slumbering-movement, I didn't flinch or say anything out loud as I walked up to my ball, which, from only twenty yards away, looked like it was in the perfect position. I was not about to make the fatal mistake of bemoaning my bad luck. I walked up as if I didn't have a care in the world, as if I was going to play the simplest of 100-yard pitches onto the green.

My brain was slumbering. I wasn't about to change that and give it any reason to wake up and add its tuppence worth to the situation. I surveyed the land and calmly decided on the shot just as my fellow 'Wham!' match playing partner Hector walked up beside me, took one look at the ball lying deep in the divot and exclaimed, "Oh, that's unlucky!"

My brain woke from its slumber at the commotion to check out what was unlucky.

It checked out what was going on, spotted the divot and immediately started to overthink!

 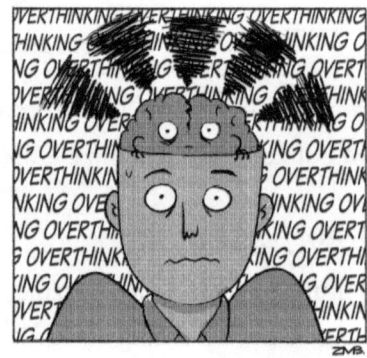

My 'Paddington' stare towards Hector told its own story as I tried to make him rue his words.

I steadied myself over the shot, but the damage had been done, and I thinned my shot out of the divot and through the green.

Note to Self: Try and play any difficult shots before my playing partners get anywhere near me and pass on their own unhelpful comments.

Keep The Brain Slumbering!

'JUBILEEGATE'

I won't embarrass the individual by naming them, but during The New Club's Founders Day Trophy, I was playing with him on the Jubilee Course where he scored an exceptional twenty-three Stableford points on the front nine. He walked off the 9th hole and should have been confident because he was playing supremely well for anyone, let alone for his course handicap of twelve.

However, what he said as we were standing on the tenth tee about to tee off, astounded me. He blurted out, "And now for the hardest nine. I hate the Jubilee back nine. Three times I've stood on the tenth tee, never having been more than one over par and three times I've not broken my handicap by the end of the round."

I couldn't believe what I was hearing. Why would you externalise your thoughts and wake up your brain, which until that point had been slumbering, as you put together a one over par front nine!

He walked off the back nine with seventeen Stableford points, which still wasn't bad, although he'd scored zero points on two holes. On the par 3 13th hole he carelessly missed a six-inch tap in putt and, on the long par 4 16th which was into a cold one-club wind that day, he hit two balls left into the gorse, never to be seen again.

Unfortunately, he was pipped into second place by another player who'd also scored forty points. I say unfortunately, but I knew from the moment he'd woken up his slumbering brain on the tenth tee, with firstly his own thoughts and then with his words to the rest of us, that his name was unlikely to be on the prestigious club trophy this year.

This wasn't a one-off, though, as it happened again in a fourball Club match when he and his partner were four up after nine holes on the Jubilee course. He and his partner were beaten on the last hole. Somehow, I think he managed to infect his playing partner with his negativity!

Keep The Brain Slumbering!

'EDENGATE'

A playing partner of mine in a competition looked at his card on the par 3 15th tee on the Eden course and remarked that the first five holes of his second nine looked very much like the first six holes of his first nine when he shot all pars, but that his next two holes were bogey, double bogey!

Astonished, I said to him, "Why would you externalise that?"

He looked at me and said, "But there's just the two of us here," and he asked what I meant.

I said that he'd just let his brain hear what he had just said. He looked at me as if I was insane. He then shot a double bogey on 15 and a bogey on 16 and said to me as we walked off the 16th green, "You were right about that stuff, eh!"

No Shit, Sherlock!

Keep The Brain Slumbering!

My slumbering brain delivers what I say or think or what someone else says to me … if I let myself be influenced or manipulated. I've got to be able to switch off and manipulate my own mind. If I can calm down my brain after a misplaced comment, then I can still salvage the situation. I've got to recognise it, though, and know how to deal with it.

Personally, I walk away ten yards, then walk back towards my ball as if it's the first time I'm approaching it. I try and fool my brain and send it back into its slumbering state.

Pillar 6: Be Positive, Stay Positive

NO TIME MACHINE

This may seem obvious in a book written by The Positive Golfer, and it does tie into the previous Pillar, but I don't allow myself to have negative thoughts or use negative language. My brain is listening to me.

As an example, how many times have you thought to yourself, "Don't hit it there," and you hit it exactly there! Our brains don't appear to hear the word 'Don't' and just hear "Hit it there"!

I use positive language or just ask myself what a scratch or a plus handicap golfer would do. More often than not, I find the answer and take my brain away from its negative 'Don't' thoughts.

I also remember that sometimes The Golfing Gods have a different path in mind for me. That bounce or that missed putt have been sent to challenge me and see what I am made of. No time machine has been invented to let me go back and replay that shot. No Delorean from the 'Back to the Future' movies about to roar down the fairway to transport me back to play it again. I have to accept it, stay positive and move onto the next shot.

DON'T LEAVE PUTTS SHORT

The difference between low handicap players and mid to high handicappers is that the low players make more birdies. They only do this by being aggressive and rolling putts to and beyond the hole. 100% of short putts do not go in, so I started being more aggressive and more often than not I started watching the putts drop.

STAY CALM AND NEVER GIVE UP

I've lost count of the number of times I see players start a game badly and then watch as their game goes from bad to worse, resulting inevitably in a No Return or a non-contribution in a match play situation because they've got so down on themselves early on.

I've started bogey, bogey double bogey to be four over par after three holes, only to buckle down and finish four over par. My mindset is that each hole is a new hole, each shot a new shot. The game never ceases to amaze me and just one great or even one good shot can get a round going again.

I keep my head up and remember that I can't get into that time machine and go back and change the past. All I can do is affect the future with my mindset. I have to be able to forget ... forget the bad shots and start again with the next shot. Go through the routine and try and kick start my round.

Sometimes my body is just out of sync, though, and I have to be able to recognise that and look forward to the next round. Tomorrow is always another day.

BE MY OWN CADDY & CHEERLEADER

I've played golf on a few occasions with a caddy, and I'm always amazed at how well I play when I take a caddy. I think it is because they do all the thinking and working out for me and then just tell me what club to hit. All self-doubt and confusion is removed, and I just tend to hit the club and trust the caddy.

Without a caddy, I talk myself through the shots – out loud works best - but I just try to keep it in my head if I think that my playing partners may go reaching for their mobile phones and contact mental health services.

When I hit a great shot, I am my own cheerleader and give myself a slap on the back and say 'Well done' to myself. If I hit a stinker of a shot, I'm not hard on myself. I just asked what my caddy would have said to me. They certainly don't let me dwell on the negatives; they just start getting me ready to hit the next shot. I have learned to do the same for myself.

Pillar 7: Set Goals

AIM FOR THE STARS

Some people don't like setting or sharing goals as they fear looking stupid if they fall short of them. However, I'm happy to share the ones I've set myself since moving to St Andrews. They were all written before the start of that particular year and the goals with the asterisks beside them have since been achieved:

2021

1. Get to scratch handicap
2. Win a tournament*
3. Qualify for scratch club championship*
4. Shoot under par on one of the St Andrews courses*
5. Shoot in the 60s on one of the St Andrews courses*
6. Fire 6 birdies in one round*
7. No bogeys in a round
8. Have ten rounds in a row in the 70s
9. Play Pebble Beach* and Sawgrass
10. Play in the Dunhill Links

2022

1. Play in the Gold Medal competition in May
2. Get to +1 handicap
3. Win a tournament*
4. Qualify for scratch match play championship*
5. Shoot under par on all the courses in St Andrews Links
6. Shoot a gross 65
7. Get 8 birdies in one round
8. Have 10 x 1 putts in one round*
9. Have no bogeys in one round
10. Have 10 rounds in a row under 75
11. Hit all fairways in regulation*
12. Hit all greens in regulation

2023

1. Get to plus handicap
2. Win The New Club Scratch Club Championship
3. Play in The Gold Medal

2024
1. Handicap down to +1
2. Qualify for New Club Champs Scratch Match Play and Win it
3. Qualify for Gold Medal and play afternoon round
4. Golf Holiday abroad*
5. Qualify for Monthly Medals Final*

2025
1. Greater consistency with ball striking
2. Cut down the number of double bogeys
3. Cut down the number of three putts
4. Qualify for Monthly Medals Final
5. Win a Club Trophy
6. Win The New Club Scratch Club Championship
7. Qualify for The Gold Medal
8. Handicap to plus handicap
9. Finish & Publish Book *

Some have said that I'm insane for sharing my goals, but I say aim for the stars and sometimes it's alright to land on the moon.

When I was working as a labourer during the summer every year earning spending money for University, I received the best piece of worldly advice I've ever had from a joiner I worked with. I'd come into the yard one morning, aged sixteen, disconsolate, having just opened the brown envelope containing my 'Higher' exam results. To become a lawyer and take my first steps to University and study law, I needed at least 3As and 2Bs to get in the next year. I opened the envelope to 2 Bs and 3 Cs which was not good enough, leaving me wondering what the future held for me.

Joiner Bill asked me what was wrong, and I told him.

"What did you aim for?" Bill asked simply.

I had no answer. I hadn't aimed for anything. He asked why I hadn't aimed for 5 As and, even if I 'd fallen back slightly, I would maybe have got the 3As and 2Bs I needed. Simple! The following year, I resat several subjects and opened the brown envelope that summer to 5As, which allowed me to take up my conditional offer at Aberdeen University to study law. That piece of advice opened my career in law and a lifetime of friendships from University, all thanks to Joiner Bill.

I still follow that advice in everything I do, including golf. Even though I haven't yet achieved all the goals I set every year, they're still there as a bar for me. I'm not afraid to continue to set them, even if I fall short, because it's still not a bad view from the moon … until I reach the stars!

Pillar 8: Enjoy Myself

It's a frustrating game but above all else I've got to remember to enjoy myself.

If I am having a bad game and getting down on myself, I simply sit on one of the golf benches dotted around the courses which are inscribed with plaques dedicated to someone who had obviously loved the game of golf. It doesn't take long to jumpstart my mind back to a positive state, remembering that that person would trade places with me in an instant.

I look around at the scenery, take in nature and breathe in the fresh air. I watch the birds, the kites, the walkers and I see life being enjoyed.

I interact with my playing partners and enjoy hearing about their lives and their golf stories and observing their swings and listen to their stories.

I remembered the picture hanging in my house which says:

'A bad day golfing beats a good day working.' How true that is. Why else does getting up early for golf never seem to be a problem compared with getting up early to travel or go to work?

I try to kickstart my round by playing a good shot or landing a good putt in an effort to find the key to my game again.

I remember that I am about to complete 13,000 steps and the health benefits of that.

I remember that there is nowhere else I would rather be. There is no point in club thumping, club throwing, swearing, sulking, tears or tantrums; I chose this game, and I love this game. It's frustrating at times, yes, and it's exhilarating and debilitating all within five minutes.

Golf is a four-letter word, but I love it, and I enjoy it, even when things aren't going well. Whenever my golf takes a downturn - and it invariably does - I revisit my eight pillars to check what might be missing.

THE EIGHT FOLLIES

As a quick aside, the opposite of pillars are follies. Follies are mostly used for purely decorative purposes and don't have strong foundations or have a need to be load-bearing. Check out the opposites, I call them the Eight Follies. If I was The Negative Golfer, I would have had these all at my fingertips.

Do you have any Follies you commit which could simply be changed into Pillars?

> You aren't prepared
> You don't play competitive games regularly
> You don't measure your game
> You don't look after your body
> You don't keep your brain slumbering
> You aren't positive
> You don't set goals
> You don't enjoy yourself

CHAPTER 8: CHIPPING WOES AND WINNING WAYS

CHIPPING WOES

Just in case you were thinking that everything was rosy in the garden with my golf game during this period, let me reassure you that chipping was causing me major problems.

For as long as I could remember, my chipping had never been great and was a source of much merriment for a lot of my playing partners over the years, as ball after ball would sometimes land further away from the hole than the shot before it.

I'd developed a great long game to compensate for my chipping faux pas, and my long putting was acceptable, but when I missed a green, I could feel my heart start to beat through my chest from the moment I started walking up the fairway to where my ball had nestled down at the side of the green.

I'm not sure what happened to my mind or my hands, but they both turned to mush, and I'd manage to thin or chunk nearly every chip through a variety of concocted club positions as I tried everything to cure my issues.

I stood on one foot, closed one eye, closed both eyes, hummed, counted internally, counted externally, recounted spiritual incantations and tried everything short of throwing the ball and my club onto the green in a final act of desperation.

These all contributed to bogeys or double bogeys, an immediate seeping of confidence and a growing anger and frustration at myself, which boiled inside me and had me close to tears on more than one occasion.

Hopefully, you get the picture of how bad my chipping was. The tight links turf of St Andrews did nothing to help and probably made it worse. My better rounds invariably came about because I was hitting a good number of greens in regulation, and my chipping was kept to a minimum.

My regular 'Wham! vs. Spies' match on a Friday morning meant that my chipping would come in for stick and intense scrutiny, which only increased my anxiety every time I tightened up and hunched over a chip. It didn't help that Hector was a Master Chipper, Ian played off + 2 and Colin tended to say the wrong thing quite frequently without meaning to.

Everyone tried to give me helpful advice. No one could understand how I could make such a hash of chipping every time ... and it was every time!

It was like getting an electric shock any time I went near a ball. Practice sessions and practice swings were fine, but *'Edward Scissorhands'* would suddenly appear when I was due to hit the shot. It was like a virus had burrowed deep inside my body and would crawl out for a look as soon as it could sense my ball was within twenty paces of the green.

For anyone who has had the putting yips, they'll be able to identify with what I was going through. I tried everything to fix it. I watched videos, I read books, I got lessons, I listened to everyone who ventured an opinion and there were lots of opinions ventured. I practiced chipping incessantly. I could practice for two hours without problems and then come onto the golf course and thin the first chip on the first hole, destroying all the good feelings and memories built up. I resigned myself to the fact that I had the chipping yips and there was little I could do about it.

One thing I didn't do, though, was give up or let my head go down. I worked round it by avoiding chipping whenever I could. I knew I was a plus handicap player in every other aspect of my game and my catastrophic chipping wasn't stopping my handicap from tumbling further, so I just accepted it and tried to play round it even though I chipped even worse than an absolute beginner. It was truly embarrassing. I had to remain positive and not let it stop me trying to achieve some of my goals. After all, the rest of my game was good and kept on improving. It had to improve, to compensate for the chipping!

WINNING WAYS

With a new-found handicap and a hopeless chipping technique, I helped The New Golf Club's Winter Handicap team win the Cup for the first time and retain it the following year. I also helped the Scratch Team to retain The Bute Trophy against arch-rivals St Andrews Golf Club.

Individually, I got through to the Scratch Club Championship for the Thistle Club, St Andrews second oldest golf club, despite taking a ten on one of the holes in the qualifying round ... which probably involved a few chips!

My first match play round found me six down after eight holes, but I followed my Eight Pillars for Positive Golf and didn't give up. Remarkably, I won the match 2 and 1.

My next match had me four up after ten holes, with my opponent having to then retire with a bad back. (I gave him Chiropractor Kate's number after we'd finished!) A semi-final slot awaited against a plus two handicap player. This would be a test, as my handicap had crept back up to 5.1 during the summer. Playing off scratch, I brought my 'A game' and, without having to chip, I triumphed by two holes. Next up in the final was a plus three player. Surely, I would just be making up the numbers?!

SCRATCH CLUB CHAMPIONSHIP FINAL

The Final was a special occasion with Honorary President George Cunningham seeing us off on the first tee and the Vice-Captain of the Club, Bill Donaldson accompanying us as match referee.

My excellent tee to green golf continued as did my poor fringe to green play but, thankfully, I kept my misses to a minimum, masking how bad my chipping really was.

I was ahead for most of the match and my opponent was growing so frustrated with his own golf that I wondered whether the Golfing Gods might deliver a rebuke to him at some point.

I came to the 18th tee, one up with one to play, with a memorable win lying just three hundred and fifty yards away. I could see Bill checking his watch. It was coming up to 9 o'clock at night and it was time he was at home for his tea. Kevin had this in the bag. One more good drive, a good second shot and the win was his.

However, much to Bill's dismay and mine, I managed to hook my drive out of bounds, and we were heading down the first hole again to play extra holes. Bugger! Bill's tea would have to wait. Sorry, Bill.

Both our drives fired straight down the middle of the first fairway, but when my opponent got to his ball, it was, unfortunately for him, sitting down in a divot.

Rather than keep his brain slumbering, he exclaimed loudly

what bad luck that was for him and how it was just typical of his day! I knew then that if I remained calm, I'd win the final, with his brain having been woken from its slumber.

Predictably, he thinned his second shot into the bunker at the back of the green, chipped out to five feet and missed the putt. I'd managed to pitch (not chip) my second shot to twenty feet and rolled the putt to four feet.

Now, I just needed to go through my routine and forget that the outcome was a first Club Championship win.

I let my brain slumber and rolled in the putt to win the Final. Captain Bill could now go home for his tea!

It was a very proud, emotional moment to become a scratch club champion in St Andrews and, doing it in the way I did it, following my Eight Pillars, made it even more memorable.

'THAT ROUND'

"What did you score, then?" said Vice-Captain Andy, as I walked past his table at lunchtime. He was having a pre-round beer with some buddies as I was taking a seat with my playing partners, having finished my round in The New Club's Summer Meeting on The Old Course in June of 2023.

The New Club gets the Old Course all day on four Saturdays a year in March for the Winter Meeting, May for the Spring Meeting, June for the Summer Meeting and August for the Autumn Meeting. The Summer Meeting is always the largest field as the days are longest in June. First tee off is 6am and last tee off is at 5pm, with over two hundred and ten players taking part.

"I shot a 67," I replied to Andy.

"Good score," came the reply from Andy.

A couple of minutes passed. As our drinks were being served, Andy, who'd obviously just checked the app for the scores, interrupted our conversation.

"You didn't say that it was a gross 67," he said in disbelief. "That's an incredible score off a handicap of four. Gross 67 around the Old Course off the back tees. Congratulations!"

It had been an incredible round. One of those 'Caddyshack' rounds when everything went in and nothing missed, however hard I tried to miss. Putts would be going wide of the hole, hit a small piece of grass and realign, dropping into the hole, as if there were a magnet in the hole and one attached to the ball, and I swear there wasn't!

Seven birdies - the 3rd. 5th, 7th, 8th, 10th,12th and 18th - with the last one in front of a small, gathered crowd around the green and drawing some enthusiastic applause in the sunshine. Two bogeys on the 4th and 9th and the rest all being pars. It was a scorecard worthy of a framed place on my living room wall for evermore.

No chips required. I putted in the dry conditions from everywhere, including an outrageous eighty-foot putt from right of the 14th green to two feet for a par. David, my playing partner, just shook his head. I laughed; I could do no wrong.

Someone asked me afterwards when I had started to get nervous and I answered honestly; not once did I get nervous. I was completely in the moment, moving on from each hole, focusing on the next and trying to make the best score I could. I guess these rounds don't come around very often. Maybe the Golfing Gods were rewarding me for all the hard work I'd put in and the emotional turmoil they'd put me through with my chipping! Whatever it was, it was a fun, unforgettable round which will live with me forever.

I won the scratch prize and the handicap prize with a net 63, by four shots in each case. £200 was added to my membership card and a further £15 for my two on the 8th hole. I'd never won such riches before on the golf course and I wondered if I'd have to give up my amateur status with the vast fortunes coming my way!

As well as the money, I won the R and A Quaich too for the lowest nett score of the day, but the best thing was that text after text, day after day for the following week or so, came in from fellow members congratulating me on 'that round'. I couldn't come into the club without being stopped to discuss 'that round' for a couple of months afterwards. Even now, two years on, I can be playing in a medal with someone who mentions 'that round'.

There was definitely something in the air that day.

REUNITED WITH MR WATSON

'That round' also qualified me for the 'Tom Watson Trophy', which was donated after Mr Watson was made an Honorary Member of the Club back in 2018 and is played for by the top four qualifiers from each of the Summer and Autumn Meetings.

I negotiated my way through the Quarter Final and Semi Final, both of which were played on The Jubilee course and booked a date in the Final on The Old Course, my favourite, for an early evening tee time on Friday 6th September 2023.

The only issue was that I was playing a twenty-two handicapper, and with my handicap having tumbled from 4 to 1 in one fell swoop, thanks to 'that round', I was giving away 20 shots!!

Somehow, I managed to win 2 and 1, despite giving my opponent two shots at the 14th. Hole. He'd managed to carve two balls out of bounds right on the 14th and the 16th (easily done) but made a par with his second ball on 14 leaving me having to make a birdie to win the hole.

The Golfing Gods obviously wanted me and Tom Watson, albeit the trophy, to be reunited and this time there was no chase required.

Hey, I still couldn't chip properly but I'd managed to win a few things, and I couldn't help wondering what I might be able to do when I finally could chip!

I was to find out ... eventually.

THE MAGIC IN ST ANDREWS
Part II

CHAPTER 9: ST ANDREWS BEACH TO PEBBLE BEACH

A DREAM DESTINATION

For most golfers, St Andrews is their preferred dream destination, but when you live in St Andrews and play the seven links courses as often as residents do, then for a lot of us, Pebble Beach is our dream destination.

I'd seen the Pro-Am every year on TV and, much like The Masters from Augusta, the green of the grass and the blue of the ocean were etched in my mind as wonders of the golfing world and it was a goal of mine to play there one day.

I'd only ever been to the east coast of the States before and COVID had made international travel a lot less enticing, so I reckoned I would forever have to content myself with just tuning in every February for my annual fix of the sights and sounds of Pebble Beach.

I hadn't reckoned on how the 'Magic in St Andrews' would deliver me to the Monterey Peninsula, driving along 17-Mile Drive past The Lone Cypress Tree, all the way to Pebble Beach Golf Course.

THE AMERICANS ARE COMING

Despite the travel ban being lifted by the UK Government on 17th May 2021, travel to the UK was not made easy by the many COVID rules still in place that Autumn.

The United States had been on the United Kingdom's green list since the beginning of August, meaning that anyone arriving here from the USA had to be fully vaccinated. Before boarding their flight to the UK, they also had to show evidence of their vaccination, together with evidence of a negative COVID test taken no more than three days ahead of the flight. Then they had to complete a Passenger Locator Form on the inbound flight, detailing where they would be staying, which also allowed them to input their Day 2 post arrival COVID test booking reference number. No booking reference number, no entry to the UK!

These post arrival COVID tests were being provided in the car park at Edinburgh airport by approved providers, at a cost of around $100, and had to be taken within two days of arrival, so most transatlantic travellers headed to the car parks immediately after they landed, took the test and waited up to twenty-four hours to get their results back. If they failed the Day 2 test , then they had to self-isolate for ten days in accordance with the rules in Scotland.

Easy eh!

CASPER IS COMING

Byron Casper (Billy's son) and I had been back in touch on Facebook in 2010 and had remained in touch since then.

In March 2021, Byron messaged me to start discussing a trip to St Andrews later in the year to play The Old Course and the excellent new Dumbarnie Links. At the time, we were locked down in Scotland, with all bars and restaurants closed until the end of April at the earliest, so I didn't rate his chances of making it across particularly highly. We started planning, though, and he passed on the details of his two other travelling companions, Dean and Doug. Their plan was to stay four days at the Old Course Hotel and then four days at Turnberry Hotel. Nice!

On 29th July, Nicola Sturgeon, Scotland's First Minister at the time, announced that the country was going to allow double vaccinated US citizens to enter the country from 2nd August, without having to quarantine. I messaged Byron right away. We were going to meet again in person for the first time in almost twenty years on 8th September 2021. While he was doing his pre-arrival COVID test, I would be entering the Old Course Ballot for the four of us.

On 6th September, two days before their arrival, we were exchanging updated travel details as countries opened and closed their borders to travellers on a whim and without much notice. As quickly as borders were closing, Byron and his pals seemed to be able to change their flights. This was an alien concept to me as I was used to simply booking a flight and paying for it; it was then fixed and non-refundable. However, I would find out how they did it and be the recipient of their 'travel witchcraft' myself in the months to follow.

I'd managed to book The Castle Course for us and paired it, the following Wednesday, with the recently opened, highly impressive Dumbarnie Links, which we would play after their trip to Turnberry. Zig-zagging three hours across country and then back for a game of golf just didn't seem to bother them at all.

Now all we needed was The Golfing Gods and The Links Trust to look after us, by drawing us out of the Old Course Ballot for Thursday 9th September.

On 7th September at 16:15 I messaged Byron: "Guess what?...... We have 14:40 on the Old on Thursday."

Nothing from Byron. That was very strange. Normally, I would get cartwheel emojis back from people drawn out of the Ballot.

Maybe Byron had played it that many times before that the news wasn't that exciting.

That wasn't it, though!

CASPER ISN'T COMING!

Twelve hours after my jubilant text to Byron, at 04:30 UK time on 8th September, the day before we were due to play the Old Course, I received the following message from him: "I tested positive on the PCR COVID test, and I needed that to travel outside the US. I'm vaccinated so I can't believe it. Dean and Doug are still on their way to Edinburgh. I'm bumming hard right now. Dean and I have talked about this trip for over a year. I'm sorry I won't be able to play golf and catch up."

I was so disappointed for Byron at being denied entry back into the country he'd called home for years and at not being able to play golf at some of the country's top courses with his buddies.

I texted him how sorry I was for him and that I would still meet and play with Dean and Doug and would head to the Old Course Hotel that evening to meet and chat things through with them.

Byron texted back: "Btw, Doug's daughter, Katie, is with him. I don't know her, but I hear she was a decent college golfer Originally, she was only going to play once or twice during the trip but since I'm not there, hopefully she can take my spot on the Old Course?"

Byron's unfortunate run in with COVID and his latest text meant that he was going to be responsible yet again for another unforgettable golfing trip to the States, this time playing Pebble Beach in less than five months' time.

MEETING THE DOUBLE DS

I walked into the Old Course Hotel Road Hole Bar the next evening to meet Byron's 'Byronless' friends. Dean was there to greet me, and Doug and his daughter Katie joined us shortly after.

We exchanged pleasantries about Byron and journeys, my fifteen-minute trip from Leuchars five miles away and their circuitous five-thousand-mile trip from San Francisco airport via Frankfurt into Edinburgh, which had begun the evening before and had ended with us all sitting there in the comfy leather pot chairs overlooking the most famous course in the world. Fate and golf have a strange, but fun, way of throwing strangers together.

We discussed timings, plans and courses for the next few days, but jet lag was getting the better of them and we agreed to meet at The Starters Hut at The Pavillion by the first hole of the Old Course at 2 pm the next day.

The Double Ds, Doug and Dean, were instantly likeable, as was Katie.

TRANSATLANTIC TRIPS

Here follows a quick potted history of what happened over those next six days.

We all played The Old Course on the Thursday afternoon and The Castle Course on the Friday morning. We all played the Old Course again on Saturday afternoon and headed out for a bite to eat on Saturday evening.

I dropped everything else I was doing for those few days as homage to the missing Byron. This was my first interaction with international visitors in St Andrews since I'd moved there the year before and I wanted to host them as best I could. It wasn't hard, though, as they were all easy to get on with and their love of golf was as strong as mine.

Dean, Doug and Katie departed for Turnberry Hotel on Sunday to stay and play there and I met up with them again the following Wednesday to play Dumbarnie after which they headed home to

San Francisco the next day.

Lifelong friendships were made for all of us during those few days.

Katie had mentioned that she was between jobs and had time on her hands and, as a fan of the TV series 'Outlander', wanted to travel to the Highlands of Scotland. Just after she returned home, she messaged me to say that she'd booked her flights and would be arriving at the start of November, just over seven weeks away. Wow, that was commitment to the 'Outlander' cause!

As the eager host, I took some time off work to act as her tour guide of the Highlands. It's a mesmerising, late autumn drive up the A9 at that time of year with the leaves on the trees mixing and matching incredible oranges, reds and yellows, and left us in awe of this part of Scotland.

Loch Ness was as breathtaking, and the visit to the vast, cold 'Culloden' battlefield, where some of the 'Outlander' series was set was moving for Katie, but even more moving for me as a proud Scotsman. Incredibly - and embarrassingly - it took a visit of a fan of a fictional TV series from California to have brought me to a place which was only ever a two-to-three-hour drive away for me. The things we miss in our own country because of other priorities in our lives!

As she was preparing to leave, there came the invite of all invites. Katie remarked that she had been discussing matters with her dad, and it was my turn now to come across to California if I fancied it. This was an intriguing invite as I was now the one between jobs and had time, but not a lot of money, so I wasn't really in the mood to splash the cash on flights, and I felt I wasn't able to accept their kind invite.

They weren't taking no for an answer, though.

Doug travelled a lot and had built up millions of air miles. He was an elite member of one airline, had a private hotline to their bookings desk and could chop and change flights to suit. Now, suddenly those last-minute changes from back in September made sense.

Doug was more than happy to use some of his miles to help secure my flights to San Francisco and back again and the 18th of February 2022 was set as the date for my own transatlantic trip.

'DOING A DOUG'

What I didn't know was that Doug had secured first class tickets for my trip with his airmiles. A lie flat seat at the front of the plane, 1A, which was Doug's own favoured seat of choice for his travels. OMG! Thank you, Doug.

It was his 70th birthday while I was going to be over there, and I got him some whisky glasses from the Old Course Hotel. That would make up for his generosity - not! I resolved instead to do my bit going forward for others in future in whatever small way I could ... I called it 'Doing A Doug' and I've since managed to 'Do A Doug' for a few friends and acquaintances in meeting, greeting and hosting them or their friends in and around St Andrews.

CALIFORNIA DREAMING

The flights were booked and, unbeknown to me, a few extra surprises lay in wait. We would be staying and playing at Pebble Beach on the fabled links on the Tuesday if I wanted to play it.

Let me check my diary ... funnily enough it's clear that day! I felt I was about to wake up from a dream and that it would be the morning before Byron was due to arrive in September and COVID hadn't struck him down, a bit like the famous shower scene in the popular US soap 'Dallas' from back in the eighties when Pam wakes to find Bobby in the shower, revealing that the entire previous season, including Bobby's death, had been her dream.

Thankfully, this wasn't a dream, and Pebble Beach was going ahead, along with a round at Spyglass Hill on the Wednesday and a game at The Olympic Club with the Double Ds on the Thursday!

THE WEATHER GODS

There was snow on the ground as I left Edinburgh airport on the morning of 18th February, and near hurricane force winds at Heathrow airport, which delayed the flight by more than two hours as the roof of the terminal felt as if it was about to be blown off, exposing the poor souls within to the ferocity outside. There was some consternation that the flight was going to be cancelled, but the Golfing and the Weather Gods were on my side, and we finally took off, albeit a couple of hours late and into an alarming head wind, heading for sunnier climes where layers weren't a consideration.

February is traditionally the coldest month on the Links of St Andrews. A chill wind would blow in off the north sea to make the temperature feel like one or two degrees below freezing. There is no such thing as bad weather, though, just the wrong clothes, and I was used to wearing five layers and still swinging a golf club using my 'winter swing'. I would be so restricted and constrained by my clothing that seeing my feet over all the layers of clothing was a problem, let alone swinging the club. This was golf in winter in Scotland, though, and I'd got used to it and loved it. I remember the days before St Andrews, when I would play golf until the end of October and then put the golf clubs away, only to bring them out again the following year after The Masters in April. Five months without golf ... outrageous. I struggle to go five days without a game of golf now.

ESCAPE FROM ALCATRAZ

Flying over the horizon, I could see the sun setting beautifully in the evening sky over San Francisco. I had been to big cities in the US before, but this one was filling me with a real sense of excitement. The Streets of San Francisco seemed a long way from the Streets of St Andrews, even though our bridge was as famous as their bridge, at least in golfing circles!

I had a day to myself before catching up with everyone and took full advantage with a solo trip to Alcatraz Island. This was a strange experience, with couples and families chattering all around me on the boat across. I couldn't help thinking how every prisoner felt being taken across to the island, lost in their thoughts and wondering what was ahead of them.

For me, though, there was an Escape from Alcatraz and a round of golf at Pebble Beach to look forward to. For them, there was no such reward, other than maybe for the three who allegedly escaped from the prison.

There was no mention in the walking audio tour of whether the escapees were golfers and whether desperation for a game had finally made them crack and escape from the notorious prison, risking being shot or drowning, all for a one last crack on the fairways.

People will go to some extremes for a game of golf you know! Maybe they had a pre-booked tee time at Pebble Beach the next day. Did anyone even think to check the tee sheet for the missing men only to find the Anglin brothers, Morris and West playing fourball?

PALO ALTO, BABY

I was collected from my hotel and taken to the family home in Menlo Park which was thirty-two miles south of San Francisco and was a place I'd heard about during my entrepreneurial accelerators in Aberdeen and Edinburgh.

Facebook and Google were based nearby in Palo Alto, and most tech start-ups were funded by venture capital funds based in Menlo Park where we were heading. We drove past the coffee shops of Palo Alto where students and start-ups were imagining changing the world. The embers of my own entrepreneurial spirit lit inside me again and my entrepreneurial and golfing worlds momentarily fused.

I couldn't have been made to feel more welcome by everyone

and we played golf at Sharon Heights, their local country club, where I bumped into fellow Scot Kathryn Imrie who was a teaching professional at the club. Kathryn had been one of Catriona Matthew's vice-captains at the Solheim Cup six months before, as Europe won the Cup on American soil for only the second time. She'd also been a member of the same Curtis Cup team as a solicitor colleague of mine, Elaine Farquharson from Aberdeen, and for five minutes we chatted about golf and Scotland thousands of miles from home on American soil.

The Golfing Gods seem to have a habit of placing us Scots all over the world, spreading their golfing gospel.

PEBBLE BEACH

I didn't know what to expect as we left Menlo Park on the Monday to make the 100-mile trip to Pebble Beach.

A gated entrance awaited and, after every corner we turned, I expected to see a sign for the golf course, but we kept driving round more corners. Finally, we made the last turn and in front of us was Pebble Beach Golf Course, with an armed guard standing at the hut with its sign saying 'Welcome To Pebble Beach'. We had arrived. We were staying on site at Casa Palmero and not playing until the next day so had a chance to explore the historic surroundings which included the Tap Room, The Lone Cypress and The Links at Spanish Bay where we caught the lone piper at sunset.

WARMING UP ... QUITE LITERALLY!

The next morning, I thought I'd been transported back to Scotland as we headed to the driving range to warm up. The cold morning caught me off guard. My concerns about sunstroke had been misplaced. The guys escaping from Alcatraz would have been warmer in the icy waters around the island and I wish that I'd packed my winter mitts.

I'd let Hector and Colin, from my Friday 'Wham!' game, know I was teeing off at 09:40 and they tuned into the Golf Cam online at 17:30 their time. I could see their messages on the WhatsApp group as I sauntered onto the practice green ten minutes before.

"Is that Kev?" texted Colin.

"It looks like Kev," texted Hector.

"Yes, it is Kev - I recognise his blue New Club Team top," replied Colin.

Putting on the large practice putting surface doesn't really prepare you for putting on the small greens that Pebble is renowned for. I'd seen the image showing that nine of Pebble's greens could fit into the 18th green at The Old Course and it was so true.

Our caddy, who didn't say much, took both our bags, one over each shoulder. I hadn't seen this done before, but he was getting double paid, and we were getting to walk and enjoy the sights and sounds of the course.

Katie was still a newish returning golfer and was expecting us to just be playing in a two ball, but as with all these courses that wasn't going to happen. The tee times are maximised, and we were paired with two singles, one of whom was Eric, who I keep in touch with, and who I recently helped 'Do a Doug' for one of his clients, when they were coming to St Andrews.

FIRST TEE NERVES

Nothing ever settles your nerves before you tee off the first tee of a course like Pebble for the first time. You're keen to make par, but you also just want to make contact with the ball off the first tee.

There are lots of people milling around the starters hut and pro shop who stop and watch the golfers on the tee. They could see I was a golfer as I was dressed like one, but was I 'all the gear with no idea' or was I a player?

These are the thoughts that go through every spectator's head as a player practice swings on the first tee. The player standing on the first tee knows the spectators are thinking that and the spectators knows the player knows they are thinking that.

Nerves abound, but what do you do with them? Succumb to them or embrace them?

Rather unhelpfully, my brain sent out a fleeting recollection of my first ever shot on The Old Course when I topped it twenty yards off the tee! Where had that come from? I hadn't packed that memory in my 23kg suitcase.

I was a different player now, though, and I was able to handle these big occasions, I told myself.

Then another thought was fired into my brain, as I took my final practice swing. Hector and Colin were watching on the live link, along with countless others tuning in from all around the world, dreaming of playing the course some day or just reminiscing about their own previous round over a coffee and morning snack in front of their laptop while their bosses weren't looking.

Ok, so now in my head thousands of golfers were watching and it wasn't helping.

I looked at my club chart I'd prepared from the online stroke saver and from watching on TV. Three wood was my club of choice to stay short of the bunkers. It was a small head, though, and I yearned for the big head of my new driver. I couldn't miss the ball with it, but I could with this small headed imposter. I couldn't go back to my bag, though. My caddy already didn't look happy for some reason.

Smallhead it was, then. I took one more practice swing and noted that the sound wasn't so much a swoosh but a whimper. On no, was Smallhead ready for this challenge?

I aimed up the left and swung. Smallhead did rise to the challenge and sent my brand-new Titleist ProV1 two hundred yards up the fairway, albeit slightly left and not far enough to make the second shot into the green an easy one, but I'd avoided the bunkers as planned, so the outcome was good. A happy Smallhead was handed back to my caddy, to start the boast with my other clubs of how it had stepped up to the mark and what could the rest of them do now?

BUNKER TERROR

Bogeying the first did nothing to settle my nerves and they weren't eased further when my second shot went into a bunker to the left of the green. When I got there, the view I had from the bunker was a near pin and the Pacific Ocean crashing onto the rocks directly behind the green. Welcome to Pebble Beach. Hopefully, not literally, though, as I didn't fancy the clamber down the rocks to get my ball if I didn't execute this delicate sand shot properly. I wasn't a bad bunker player, but this was a whole different shot.

Or was it? Just take the stance, open the clubface and hit the sand an inch behind the ball. It would depend on the sand, though. Was this good sand or bad sand? I would imagine it was good sand here. It felt like good sand. Soft and looking forward to welcoming my 58-degree wedge into its midst for the first time. Swoosh, full swing and the ball popped out, bouncing and landing five feet from the pin. "Good shot," said Katie and Eric. Nothing from my caddy!

To be fair, my caddy sussed out my game quickly and, when he advised me to hit a 5-iron uphill to the tenth hole and I nailed it to twelve feet, I thought I would get something from him, but not a thing! After I birdied the par 3 twelfth hole to go to two over par, I still got nothing from him. He wasn't for cheerleading, so I would have to cheerlead myself if I was going to break the course record. These Pebble Beach caddies are hard to get excited. Then again, he had seen me bogey the famous par 3 7th hole and the 8th hole, so he was probably right to keep his obvious growing internal excitement to himself.

JORDAN'S CLIFF

That 8th hole was indelibly imprinted on my mind from two weeks before when I'd sat glued to the television during the pro-am and watched frozen as Jordan Spieth took his life in his hands and played a shot from around three feet shy of the cliff which split the fairway and the route to the green. He and his caddy, Michael Greller, took an age debating whether he should play the shot or take a drop far back from the sixty-eight-foot drop cliff. Jordan overruled Michael's sensible protestations about life being more important than golf and stepped forward to play the shot. The golfing world waited with bated breath, wondering if they were about to watch the most horrific moment ever seen in the history of the game with Jordan Spieth falling to his death live on primetime television.

Jordan swung, connected with the ball and leapt back five feet all in the same motion. The ball soared towards the green, Jordan soared backwards. He'd survived, but later apologised to Michael, his family, and future players of Pebble Beach (me included) for his gross stupidity and recklessness.

I was still traumatised from the incident when my drive came to rest ten feet short of the same cliff. I was struggling to even go that close to play my shot. The full extent of Jordan's recklessness only became evident from the 8th green looking back up towards the sheer drop of the cliff.

(Search for Jordan's shot again on YouTube and be prepared to be terrified.)

I BLAME BING

Anyway, back to my non cheerleader caddy. How right he was, as I proceeded to double bogey 13, 14, 15 and 16.

I don't blame myself for starting that run of bogeys on the 13th hole. Oh no, I lay the blame firmly at the door of one Bing Crosby, the American actor song writer responsible for such classics as *'White Christmas'* and the golfing song *'Straight Down The Middle'*.

I was far from 'Straight Down The Middle' on the 13th hole. My ball was drawn to the right of the fairway with my drive, towards Bing's house, leaving me one of those awkward chips that I always hope to avoid. My ball was obviously star struck and wanted a quick glimpse of the house where the crooner used to live.

I was left with a difficult chip with my little white sightseeing friend, oblivious to the churning going on in my stomach. I tried to pull off one of those shots I hated, in front of my already clearly unimpressed caddy, Katie and Eric, who, up until that point, thought I was a decent golfer. I was, after all, sitting two over par. Unfortunately, another titan of Hollywood, *Edward Scissorhands*, decided to make a guest appearance and I thinned my chip across the green, almost taking out my caddy in the process, who'd moved to the back of the green and was getting ready to draw my putter from my bag.

Silly him. It would be a couple of shots more before we would be needing that now. Katie and Eric tried to hide their amazement, but I could see the obvious surprise in their faces. My caddy had seen this type of thing many times before. I was disgusted at Bing and at the ball, but I tried to contain my growing anger at them both as I horsed across the green, embarrassed, enraged and cursing the success of 'White Christmas', a film and a song which I'd loved to watch every festive season when I was growing up.

The bubble was well and truly burst as I double bogeyed 13, 14, 15 and 16 and, although I parred the iconic par 3 17th and the par 5

18th, the course and the greens beat me. I just couldn't get my head round some putts that looked downhill but putted as if into treacle.

The sights and sounds of Pebble were immense, though. It's a place everyone should try to play at least once in their lives.

TOMORROW IS A NEW DAY

As golfers, we can put things right the next day and that's what I did. With a cheerleader caddy, I shot two over par round Spyglass Hill which is a more difficult course, and I think if that caddy had been with me the day before at Pebble, I might be telling a different story about Pebble.

A positive caddy or playing partner can make such a difference to other people's games and I try to pay the positivity forward whenever I'm playing or caddying with other people. That all comes from the two days I had with those two very different caddies.

The Olympic Club

Tuesday at Pebble Beach, Wednesday at Spyglass Hill and now Thursday we were playing The Olympic Club. It was some three days for a golf nut!

Dean was a member at The Olympic Club in San Francisco and had booked a time for himself, Doug, me and a pal of theirs, Andy, but all that would be after lunch in the Clubhouse.

As we drove into the car park, I could see this wasn't just any clubhouse. This was an institution, sitting proudly atop the hill overlooking the 18th green of the Lake Course, where six golfers had been crowned major champions, the last of whom was Yuka Saso in 2021, when the US Womens Open went to a play off.

The 2033 Ryder Cup will be held there, the first time since 1959 that a Ryder Cup will have been held on the west coast of America, so expect a lot of noise around the Club ahead of that. Before that, in 2028, the US PGA Championship will be played there for the first time, so it was clear to me that the Lake Course was a major tournament course, and I was about to test myself against it.

CASPER THE CHAMP

As I wandered through the marble entrance, I stopped to look at the history of the Club and saw a face on the wall I knew. It was Mr Casper. He'd won the US Open here in 1966 when he'd clawed back a seven shot final round deficit to tie the one and only Arnold Palmer and force a playoff. Mr Palmer was trying to win his eighth major, but Mr Casper had other thoughts and won the eighteen-hole playoff and walked out of The Olympic Club with his winner's cheque for $26,500.

Mr Palmer wouldn't win another Major. Mr Casper would go on to win The Masters in 1970 and it dawned on me just then that his victory in 1970 was the reason I was now standing there looking up at the walls of The Olympic Club.

Mr Casper's win at the US Open in 1966 was also notable as there was a 'continuous putting' rule in place for the tournament to speed up play. A player wasn't allowed to mark their ball when on the putting green unless it was to lift and clean the ball and had to continue putting until they holed out. I couldn't help thinking that this rule would help in certain tournaments nowadays where slow play is a problem.

A GIFT FROM A STRANGER

Fresh from my musings about Mr Casper, I walked into the beautiful dining room, ready for lunch. The high ceilings and mahogany beams were something to behold and the arches and long flowing ceiling to floor curtains were complemented by the white tablecloths throughout. This was a special place, and I felt very privileged to have been invited here as a guest of Dean. All I'd done for him was get him on the Old Course ... twice!

As I walked in, I met Big Andy, our fourth player who greeted me like a long-lost friend with a warm handshake. He reached down to his side and handed me a framed photo of four titans of the game siting on the Swilcan Bridge in St Andrews - Raymond Floyd, Arnold Palmer, my old friend Tom Watson and the Golden Bear Jack Nicklaus. It was titled Arnie's last British Open, and it was signed.

Wow ... what a thoughtful gift! Knowing that I'd travelled all the way from St Andrews, Andy, who was involved with sports memorabilia, had picked out one that would mean so much to me and it did.

TEQUILA FOR BIRDIES
(AND PARS, BOGEYS AND DOUBLES!)

Andy was a big guy with a big personality and had a heart of gold. He loved his golf, and he loved his tequila, and for the first time playing golf I discovered the two could be undertaken together. In fact, in Andy's company, it was frowned upon if they weren't!

I managed to refrain from the tequila until the 'Hot Dog Bills' stand on the back nine when I savoured my first 'Burger dog' and succumbed to a tequila from Andy's five litre dispenser which had been full when we started and was looking very bereft of liquid by the time I indulged.

To be fair, I probably needed more of it for the Lake course. I'd been cajoled into playing off the back tees by and with Andy, as word had reached him about my two over par round at Spyglass Hill the day before. So, in a testosterone-fuelled moment, which was to be further fuelled by tequila, I had a testosterone and tequila fuelled round at The Olympic Club. The only winner, though, was The Olympic Club.

I've never played so many three metal shots uphill for my

second shot on so many holes in my life and I still wasn't getting close to the green. This was a monster course, even off the Blue Tees which were just in front of the championship tees. I say, "just in front of", but the blues were 6,626 and had a slope index rating of 134 and the championship tees came in at 7,214 yards and had a slope index of 143!

I was used to playing The Old Course Black tees at 6,670 yards, slope rating 136, but somehow the two just didn't seem to compare. Maybe when I've played Olympics' Blues as many times as I've played The Old Course it may not seem so tough, or maybe the haze from the tequila made more of a difference than I gave it credit for. I did manage to beat Andy, though, even with a few tequilas in me. It might have been because Andy had a few more in him, but a win was a win for all that!

In fact, perhaps the USGA could consider an amendment to their rules for the 2028 PGA Championship to counter low scoring. It's just a suggestion, but one I hope they may take time to consider carefully with their membership.

For every birdie made, the golfer and his caddy must take a shot of tequila served by Tequila Andy and his buddies situated strategically behind each green with their five litre dispensers. I think that you'd see a lot more putts shave the hole rather than drop in and that scoring will be nearer par than many under par. Either that, or you are going to have a great last few holes as players stagger up the fairways, high fiving the fans, plus a potentially very entertaining winner's speech.

BAMBI, BORIS AND BYRON

As well as Spyglass, Pebble Beach and The Olympic Club, we managed to fit in a game at the spectacular Meadow Club, Alister Mackenzie's first American-designed course, located way up in in the hills above San Francisco about half an hour's drive from the second most amazing bridge in the world, The Golden Gate Bridge.

I also got to play TPC Stonebrae with Tequila Andy, where twenty of my golf balls found their final resting place. Doug also let me drive his prized car there and back and over the Golden Gate Bridge. I didn't stop for photos on it, though!

Doug's 70th birthday party was a blast, and I managed a quick chat with former Bond girl, 'Bambi'. You may recall her as being the lady with the thighs that nearly suffocated Sean Connery in the 1971 Bond movie 'Diamonds are Forever'.

My trip finished with a sightseeing weekend in Los Angeles with Graham, a friend of mine, who had recently moved with work to Long Beach from Edinburgh. Having really only packed for golfing, my golf fashion wasn't appreciated by LA's glitterati at a rooftop hip hop bar where Graham had taken me. One girl point blank asked me 'just what was I wearing?! My instant response that it was a chocolate noir classic gilet by 'Under Armour' did nothing to calm her and instead seemed to heighten her agitation. We made a hurried exit from the club much to the relief of LA's fashion police and my pained eardrums.

My journey back home to Scotland came via England, where I bumped into then Prime Minister Boris Johnson on the train from London Euston Station to Liverpool. I played Hillside Golf Club and Royal Liverpool with the 'Hoylake Heroes' from St Andrews (Brian, Andy and Dr Jim) against our host and a member of The New Club, John and his friends. A formal lunch upstairs afterwards in the magnificent clubhouse at Hoylake, scene of thirteen previous Open Championship was a marvellous way to end an incredible three weeks.

All in all, a very eventful and memorable trip thanks to Byron unfortunately catching COVID. Thanks again, Byron, Dean, Doug and Katie. Lifelong memories made with lifelong friends. It's what this wonderful game of golf is all about.

Thankfully Byron did finally make it across to St Andrews the following year, when we met face to face again after nearly twenty years, and got our game together on the Old Course, albeit with a slight mid-round thunder and lightning delay.! Things just never seem to run smoothly for us, do they Byron?!

HOME AGAIN

I finally made it back home to Leuchars on 14th March 2022, almost a month after leaving with trepidation, returning with a mind full of special memories.

Golf stops for no one, though. The Castle Course was open again after its winter break and The New Golf Club had a Handicap Cup to win in a few weeks' time.

There was also the small matter of the 150th Open coming to town in a little over four months and this would produce a great championship, an unlikely champion and a host of memorable moments for me, including partying with the winner into the wee small hours at The Old Course Hotel.

Bring it on.

CHAPTER 10: THE 150TH OPEN COMES TO TOWN

PART 1: THE BUILD UP

LOSING THE OLD COURSE, LOSING MY GAME

The build-up to the Greatest Show on Earth seemed to take so long. I remember posting an image on Facebook from the car park at Leuchars Railway Station in January 2021 in the depths of yet another COVID restriction saying,

"Less than eighteen months until the world comes to town"

The infrastructure started going up around April 2022, a full three months ahead, and playing the Old Course with the massive stand running from the first tee to Grannie Clark's Wynd (the tarmac road which splits the first and eighteenth fairways which must be played off if you land on it) was something special, giving us amateurs a tiny glimpse of what it's like to play in front of championship stands.

There was a massive amount of disruption to the St Andrews golfer's natural habitat during the Open year. The Old Course closed from the middle of June. There were reduced and composite courses and the nine-hole Balgove Course was also requisitioned for parking.

We also lost our driving range from the end of April for the massive, tented village where The Open Shop was to be located.

Some handicaps in St Andrews went up during that period from the end of April until the end of August, until we got our practice facilities back again. Mine certainly headed upwards, climbing from 3.7 at the end of April to 5.8 during August, before heading downwards again after the driving range reopened.

In fact, if The 150th Open hadn't provided me with such a lifetime of memories and experiences, I would have been sorely tempted to submit a small claim for compensation to the Links Trust and the R and A that autumn, for the distress and injury to reputation caused!

LET THE SHOW BEGIN
SUPER SATURDAY (9TH JULY 2022)

The Saturday before The Open started was a remarkable day. The course was still available to walk as if it was a Sunday in St Andrews. The Old Course is normally closed, when humans can roam freely whilst dogs and small children can cause havoc in the bunkers!

The sun was shining, and with a two-club wind, I decided to walk all eighteen holes myself that afternoon and video it, before the fences and the ropes went up the next day and kept the public at a safe distance from the professional golfers who were here to try and claim golf's greatest prize at golf's greatest arena.

The New Club had been assigned two holes to provide marshals for… at the 2nd and the 17th. I was disappointed initially not to be positioned on the iconic 17th hole, but by the end of the Open week

I'd become a £100,000 marshall, featured on Sky TV's coverage, had players chatting to me and held up The Open for ten minutes. So, all in all, the second hole turned out a brilliant place to be.

Back to my walk ... I stood at the announcer's table on the first tee where the world's finest male golfers would be introduced and then wandered up the golf's widest fairway to the tee at the second hole which would be my hole for the week. In amongst the golden eagles, the sniffer dogs and the drones flying overhead, I managed to grab a sneaky peak inside one of 'The Players Toilets' behind the second hole, not quite sure what to expect. Would there be gold trimmed taps and quilted toilet tissue? Nope ... it was just a toilet cubicle, the same as any of us get when we go to an event. No mirror, no aftershaves, no concierge services and definitely no bidet. Presumably, the R and A didn't want to make it too opulent just in case it slowed up play.

'Tee, pee and play' appeared to be the thinking from the powers that be.

THE STARS COME OUT
VIKTOR

As I continued my walk around the course, I finished the loop around 7,8,9,10 and 11 and started walking back along the twelfth hole in towards the town again. Across on the seventh tee, I could see the distinctive branded 'J Lindeberg' clothing of one of the world's best golfers. It was Viktor Hovland, one of the favourites for the championship this week and he was hitting drives off the seventh tee. Astonishingly, it was just him and his caddy, with no one else around them. He looked just like an everyday golfer, standing there hitting drive after drive with different clubs.

Fast forward just over a week, when Viktor would end up sharing the lead after three rounds, going out in the last group with fans favourite Rory McIlroy amid the pandemonium of the final day of the Open. Was Viktor envisioning that moment standing there on the seventh tee this Saturday afternoon? Was he seeing into the future and imagining playing shots under that sort of pressure?

Whatever he was working on, arriving early in St Andrews paid off for Viktor. He left without the Claret Jug but tied for fourth and almost £525,000 better off.

PHIL

Looking forward, I could see a small crowd ahead on the 14th tee, which had been moved so far back onto the Eden course to make the 14th a monster 605 yards.

I recognised the distinctive languid swing of Phil Mickelson who was playing his second shot.

A six-time major winner, Phil was in town early as well, trying to add the Open to his US PGA win the year before, when he became the oldest man ever to have won a major at the age of fifty at Kiawah Island in South Carolina. He had defected to LIV from the PGA tour earlier in the year, but had lost none of his popularity, judging by the crowd that was following him.

Phil was a three times Masters winner including in 2004, when he spoiled my chance of a Masters After Party With Ernie Els. I wondered if I might get close enough to have words with him about that! More importantly, would I get close enough to him to ask him to sign my Masters flag. I'd brought it with me just in case there were any Masters winners dotting about St Andrews and as luck would have it ...

I followed Phil down the fairways, walking at a respectful distance behind him, not once shouting out "Hey Phil, you're a party pooper."

I'd made my plan. When Phil finished his round at the 18th green, I figured he would probably sign some autographs at the bottom of the steps beside the R and A Building, so that's where I needed to be. I was just hoping this wasn't going to be another episode like my pursuit of Tom Watson. I didn't have time for that this week. I had marshalling duties and if I managed to sneak a few signatures too on my flag then great, otherwise Phil's signature would have to wait for another time.

As Phil completed his round, one of his security team told the waiting throngs that Phil would be signing at the bottom of the steps and would try and get round everyone so just to form an orderly queue. I got my flag out of my rucksack just as I'd done so many times before and waited. Luckily, I'd casually spoken to Phil's security detail on one of the fairways earlier and had chatted about my flag, so he was primed and miraculously the queue started right beside where I was standing!

Phil walked up and I asked him if he would mind signing my Masters Flag. He was busy and others were waiting, so I didn't dive into my Billy Casper story or rebuke him for his first major win spoiling my chance of an afterparty. He took my flag, signed it and handed it back to me. I thanked him and wished him luck for this week. He smiled and moved on.

It was a great end to my walk round The Old Course on Super Saturday and a great start to my flag signing journey that week. Signature Eleven was on my flag.

SIGNATURE TEN

Signature Ten had been added forty-four days earlier by two-time Masters Champion Gary Player who'd won it in 1961 and 1974.

Gary had been playing the Old Course as part of the sponsors week ahead of The 150th Open, but not content with playing every day as part of his contract, he decided to play the Jubilee course with his manager. Only the two of them and just for the love of the game.

By chance I'd seen him tee off the first hole earlier in the day and headed back home to get my flag and wait for him to come in at the 18th hole, three and a half hours later. Eighty-six years old, the nine-time major winner was still as fit as fiddle and his enthusiasm could be heard from a hundred yards away!

As he came off the green, his caddie said that Gary would be over in a moment as he wanted to go across and have a chat to a young couple who were just teeing off on the first hole. Nobody he knew, but they'd stopped to watch him putt out on eighteen and he just seemed to love talking to anyone.

As he walked over, I got my flag out and he signed it as he was talking to everyone around us. A group of American golfers had gathered round the starters box where he was signing and sensing a larger audience Player finished signing and started engaging. Asked by one of them which was the hardest course he'd played, he didn't hesitate when he said Carnoustie and with a shout of 'Viva La France', he launched into a story about Jean Van De Velde and his overzealous play on the 18th which cost him the Open in 1999[5].

ADAM

Adam Scott was playing just behind Phil Mickelson and having won The Masters in 2013 I needed to wait around at the R and A steps for Adam to get Signature Twelve. There I was with a gaggle of ladies who all seemed to be taken with Adam's good looks.

Adam didn't disappoint as he putted out and moved over to his adoring fans. Standing 6 foot tall with piercing blue eyes, the man wouldn't have looked out of place on a catwalk. Thankfully, I managed to get his signature before he was engulfed, and I escaped from the side of the scrum towards the safety of The New Club for

[5] Check it out at my YouTube Channel at https://youtube.com/shorts/K_qZONA1DKU

a bite to eat. Good luck Adam, not just for this week, but also for escaping that melee.

A SIGHT TO BEHOLD

I was walking back towards The New Club when I saw a sight at The Swilcan Bridge that I'd never seen before in St Andrews.

A lady was manoeuvring what looked like a pristine white buggy up and onto the Bridge. She was strapped in though, and it looked as if it may have been an electric type of wheelchair, but there seemed to be a set of golf clubs attached to the left-hand side of the buggy.

I was intrigued and headed beyond the rear of New Clubhouse towards the bridge. I watched as she first headed forwards onto the bridge but then realised that the photo of choice was facing towards the 17th green with the backdrop of the R and A Clubhouse and The Hamilton Grand behind.

I admired the lady's resilience as she managed to reverse back up the bridge to allow her to get the photo with her and her female companion. They were quite a sight, embracing each other on the Swilcan Bridge in the sunshine with the famous backdrop behind them. She then drove back down, turned and headed forward, up and over the bridge pausing on the top, with her companion making sure that her tyres fitted neatly between the sides of the bridge.

I hadn't realised that she'd played a tee shot from the 18th tee, before stopping for that photo at the bridge. I'm not sure how, as it was only players who were allowed out on the course today and surely only males too? I was very confused!

The distance of her drive would have made some of my Monday Fellowship players green with envy. I edged onto the 18th fairway to within a respectable distance of where she was about to play from.

Who was this lady in the strange looking contraption playing the 18th hole of The Old Course, which had been closed for the last four weeks to the public, ahead of the 150th Open?

I marvelled as the seat of the buggy moved upwards and forwards to lift the lady from her seated position into an upright position. She took her stance and placed the club in her right hand and then swung it one handed at the golf ball. Slow away and with a smooth swing, the ball was propelled forwards into the Valley of Sin. There in two. Not bad at all!

She didn't seem to be that happy with it, though, and dropped another two more balls and hit them with two separate clubs. She was practicing, but what was she practicing for?

TIGER AND JUSTIN

I was distracted by a few people walking up the first hole surrounding a couple of players. It was 7 o clock. Who could be coming out at that time of night?

I strained to see who it was amongst the crowd of forty or so people, all milling around the two players who were chatting to each other.

Tiger Woods and Justin Thomas appeared through the throng carrying only three clubs each, as their security team managed to hold back the growing crowd at a respectable distance.

That crowd was soon joined by me and my Masters flag as we all walked up to the first green. The security people continued to keep us all well away from the two of them and after they'd putted from various areas on the green, they headed across to the second hole.

I'd had enough walking for the day though. Tiger and my flag would have to meet some other time. A comfortable seat and a pint of Tennent's in the world famous 'Dunvegan' pub had my name on it, and I retired there to reflect on a great day and mingle with excited locals and visitors alike.

****

PART II: MEETING MONIQUE

SLIDING DOORS SUNDAY (10TH JULY 2022)
TEE BOX SPECULATION

My first shift as a marshal was on the practice Sunday. It was a lot different from the following Sunday in terms of numbers and atmosphere.

I was on the second hole tee box, but there weren't many players out and about at that time of the day. The four marshalls there were just getting used to the area, marvelling at how far back this tee was compared to where we'd normally play this hole from, immediately to the right of the first green.

The R and A had moved the tee to the back of the 'Himalayas' next to where the Swilcan Burn meanders out to sea. They must have added another eighty yards to the hole to lengthen a course that most people didn't think could be lengthened.

My fellow marshals and I speculated on where the line would be from this tee to avoid 'Cheape's Bunker' which was hidden from sight behind a gorse bush perched on a hill about 150 yards ahead. In fact, the line was exactly where a marshal was sitting with a green and red flag to let players on the tee know when it was safe to hit their drive down the second fairway after the players ahead had played their second shots.

The highlight of the morning had been putting on the official marshal's uniform for the first time. White and grey jacket, grey cap and sunglasses and shorts. Good weather was forecast all week, and the designers of the jacket, 'Boss' had thought of everything as the sleeves zipped off allowing us to enjoy the sunshine or zip them back on if the weather took a turn for the worse. In Scotland? Never!

AT THE RANGE

My four-hour shift ended without incident, and I headed to the practice range to see what was going on there. The first and eighteenth holes of the Jubilee course had been requisitioned for The Open and there was a massive net about 150 feet high protecting the greenkeepers yard about 350 yards away for the big hitters and on the right as well to protect the road users from wayward shots. Players were tinkering there before heading out onto the course later in the day.

Viktor, Phil and Adam had been joined by others now and their coaches, their caddies, their psychologists, their wives and some of their friends. Each bay resembled a small house party which had ended up in the kitchen with everyone huddled into that small space. It was difficult to pick out the player in the throng until a glint of silver appeared above someone's head as they swung so smoothly to a target in the distance.

I stood and watched for a while and marvelled again at the lady in the buggy from the day before evening who was also hitting balls, right beside former Open Champions Phil Mickelson and Darren Clarke.

I saw Phil and Darren both casting a sideways glance towards her as she manoeuvred herself to place her tee in the ground, then rose in her chair to standing height by virtue of the mechanics of the buggy, steadied herself on the grip handle with her left hand and swung the driver with her right hand. They too were marvelling at the distance she could hit the ball like that. She later described the feeling ...

"like standing, but you are also hanging, as if you are standing on ice skates on ice and swinging a golf club."

Wow, it's bad enough standing on grass and trying to swing a golf club!

I think that she would have been Champion Golfer of The Year over anyone in the field that week if they'd tried to do the same from her chair. No coach, no psychologist, no caddy-just her friend standing beside her, chatting and laughing with her,

They disappeared down to the chipping and putting area and intrigued I followed them down, wondering how the perfectly manicured greens would react to what looked like quite a heavy piece of kit. The wheels were wide, though, and didn't seem to leave any indentations due to the ingenuity of the design. I found out later it was a Paragolfer™ which had been designed by Anthony Netto, founder of the Stand Up and Play Foundation (https://standupandplayfoundation.org)

I watched for a few minutes as she went through the same routine for chipping and putting one handed. Maybe I should try one handed chipping and see if that could improve it. It couldn't be any worse. I'd try anything!

LEE TREVINO'S IN THE HOUSE

At that, I went for a wander round the course, when I came across superstar golfer Lee Trevino, sitting in a buggy chatting excitedly to some folks who'd gathered around him.

He was a six-time major champion, but The Masters was the only one which had eluded him. My flag remained steadfastly in my rucksack. It wasn't coming out for a non-winner regardless of how many other majors he'd won. I stood and watched as he held the gallery in the palm of his hands with his stories and his hand gestures. I wondered if this week's Champion Golfer of the Year would be having the same impact on fans in fifty years' time. (Trevino won the second of his Opens at magnificent Muirfield further down the east coast of Scotland in 1972).

MY 'SLIDING DOORS' WALK

I headed up the third hole, across the 16th and stood behind the grandstand at 17 looking at the daunting shot that awaited the world's best golfers. Moving on through the tented village, and around the Old Course Hotel, I came back out at the 17th green where drama would undoubtedly unfold in a week's time.

Some players were practicing out of the Road Hole Bunker. It shouldn't come into play for the winner, whoever that may be. Their golf would be so sublime, and I was sure that they would have their golfing satnavs turned on and tuned in that week to avoid such a potential card wrecker. The Champion Golfer of the Year here should also turn out to be the champion course manager of the week.

I decided to head back across to the practice facilities to see if any more Masters champions might be there.

My whole week at The Open changed at this point.

MEETING MONIQUE

On my way back to the practice ground, I came across the buggy lady's companion.

"You look a little bit lost," I said.

"I've lost my friend," the lady replied, in English with a slight hint of a Dutch accent.

"The lady in the wheelchair buggy?" I asked.

"Yes, that's right," she looked a little surprised that I knew that.

"I saw her earlier at the practice range hitting balls, but I haven't seen her since. If you don't mind me asking, what's she doing here this week?" I enquired.

The lady replied "She's been asked by The R and A to play in the Celebration of Champions tournament on Monday, so she's just getting familiar with the surroundings. She's struggling with the links turf a little and with knowing where she's supposed to be hitting to.

My ears pricked up.

"Has she not got a caddy?" I asked

"They've allocated one to her I think, but that's not until the day of the tournament.," came the lady's response

"I've played the Old Course over a hundred times if she would like some help," I mentioned casually.

"She would be interested in that. By the way, I'm Deborah"

"I'm Kevin," shaking Deborah's hand.

Just then Monique came round the corner of the Caddyshack in her Paragolfer™ and looked quizzically at Deborah.

"Monique, this is Kevin. He's played the Old Course over a hundred times and has said he'd be happy to help you ahead of the tournament.," said Deborah

I was secretly hoping that Monique's caddy hadn't been allocated yet and that I could be part of the Celebration of Champions tournament which was going to be a big thing.

"Hi Kevin. Nice to meet you. I'm Monique. Would you like to join us for a bite to eat? We're just heading to the Players Clubhouse just now. I'd love to hear your thoughts on The Old Course. First, though, would you mind taking some photos of us please?"

And just like that, I became a photographer, an Old Course Consultant and a friend, all over a delicious buffet in the Players Clubhouse.

I got to know Deborah and Monique, immediately warming to them both and their easy manner. I answered questions about St Andrews and the Old Course, and we agreed to meet the next morning, before my marshalling shift, to walk the four holes of the Old Course she would be playing during the Celebration of Champions tournament. She'd been drawn to play with former Open Champions Bob Charles, Gary Player and my old pal Sandy Lyle.

Monique had shared that she was really very nervous, as tennis was her game and that she'd only recently discovered and fallen in love with golf. She didn't want to make a fool of herself, so would welcome any tips I could give her ahead of the big day.

I hoped I had set her mind at rest that I could assist her and I said my goodbyes to them. I looked to my left on my way out. There on the practice putting green below was a Masters Champion with his caddy and a very recent Masters Champion at that.

SIGNATURE THIRTEEN

Caddy Ted Scott was setting up some round the clock drills for that year's Masters winner Scottie Scheffler. It was 8 o clock at night. It looked like Scottie meant business.

Heading outside to the green, I watched and waited. Just Ted and Scottie on the practice green and me the only spectator. Scottie was lost in concentration, and Ted was collecting and resetting balls. Four tee pegs four feet away, four more eight feet away then four more 12 feet away. Each ball had to be made before Scottie could move onto the next ball.

I watched mesmerised as Scottie made all twelve balls twice in a row and then finally missed one of the eight footers on the third time round. He immediately went back to the four-foot putts and started again. He took as much time over each ball, bending down and lining up the line on his ball to match the line of the putt, then went through his pre-putt routine on every ball as if it was to win the tournament here in a week's time. It was a lesson in preparation which I gorged upon. This was the type of practice which major champions put themselves through. I stood and waited for an hour. Scottie didn't let on that he knew I was there. He was the picture of concentration.

Finally, he stopped and Ted pulled out the tees. I grabbed my chance and asked Scottie if he would mind signing my Masters flag. No problem. He signed it and handed it back. Signature Thirteen had been added and I'd got a putting masterclass to boot. One hour to wait for a signature-was I mad?

No, I was just keen, and I had nowhere else to be that evening. That paled into insignificance with the three hour wait I had for the next signature later in the week.

AN AMAZING LADY

If you google 'Monique Kalkman', Wikipedia will provide you with the following information:-

'Monique Kalkman-Van Den Bosch competed at the Paralympics in 1984, 1988, 1992 and 1996 for the Netherlands at wheelchair tennis and wheelchair table tennis, winning Olympic Gold at Barcelona in 1992 in the singles and doubles and in 1996 Silver in the Singles and Gold in the Doubles.'

She is Paralympic Royalty.

Monique was inducted into the International Tennis Hall of Fame in 2017 along with Kim Clijsters and Andy Roddick. Her husband and coach Marc Kalkman's emotional speech as he presented her with the award is well worth watching on YouTube. He said she had a lot of D's-Dedication, Determination, Devotion and Discipline and (Long) Days of hitting 1,000s of forehands, backhands, serves, returns, volleys and then it was time for lunch.

"Each and every day has a story. Each and everybody has a dream. Some people chase their dreams, and some people chase their dreams even if disrupted by events," he said.

Monique's own dreams of being a world class tennis player, following in the footsteps of her idols Chris Evert and Martina Navratilova, had been disrupted when she was just fourteen years of age, when she was diagnosed with cancer. Although she was cured of cancer, she was left paralysed from the waist down and 'confined' to a wheelchair.

She was not confined though. She flourished in her wheelchair as she first found wheelchair table tennis, then wheelchair tennis six years later after finding new heroes, wheelchair tennis icons Brad Parks and Randy Snow.

Monique speaks of 'her glass always being half full' and 'aiming for gold but being thankful for anything less'.

Little was I to know that Sunday evening just how this incredible lady was about to impact my own week at The Open.

MONIQUE MONDAY (11TH JULY 2022)
CADDYING ON THE OLD COURSE

I got a text to say that Monique had been given a tee time at 1045.

I was excited to be able to walk the Old Course, albeit just four holes, on Championship week. I checked in through the main gates with my marshall pass and headed down the side of the 18th fairway and along Grannie Clark's Wynd.

Disaster though! Monique had been given an earlier tee time and was just teeing up on the first tee. I watched from Grannie Clark's Wynd as Monique hit her shot, to a round of applause from some practice day spectators sitting in the large stand running alongside the first hole. Deborah was looking around at the stands and the scenery and caught my eye. She motioned to me to join them. I hesitated, before walking onto the turf and up the hole I had walked so many times before.

I waited to be rugby tackled by security, but the tackle didn't come. Deborah shouted over to Monique "Kevin's here," and Monique stopped and waited for me to join them to discuss her second shot into the first hole.

It was one of the most feared shots in golf with the Swilcan Burn right in front of the green, waiting to gobble up any errant shots. A game of caddy ping pong followed.

"What should I do here?" Monique asked me.

"It's 180 yards to the pin-which means you need to carry 160 yards. you have 10 yards of wind with you, so you need to carry it 150 yards. Can you do that?" I replied.

"I can, but I'd prefer to lay up and pitch on to be safe. What's the number to lay-up?" Monique asked

I liked her style and her course management. No ego, just sense.

"It's 120 yards to be safe.," I said.

"So, 110 metres, yes?" she said looking for clarification.

"Yes," I came back.

"Ok I'll carry it 85 yards then to leave it short safe," she said.

She reached beside her for her five wood, pressed a button and raised herself to a vertical position, as if she was standing on ice skates! She reached for her grab handle with her left hand, and she took a smooth practice swing with her right arm. Now just repeat that swing.

I held my breath, hoping my calculations without my laser finder were right, relying on the disks in the fairway which read to the front of the green and on my eyesight as to how far beyond the front of the green the pin was. Monique sent a smooth shot up the fairway, landing it thirty-five yards short of the Swilcan Burn, her golf ball jumping forward another ten yards.

Perfect. She knew her numbers, but of course she did. She was a world class Olympic winning athlete, whose preparations would be meticulous in everything she did, whether that was tennis, table tennis or golf. I was working with a professional here.

Correction, this third shot was one of the most feared shots in golf. So near yet so far to the fabled first green, with just the Swilcan Burn left to negotiate. Up and down for a par on the first hole. Easy.

Unfortunately, not for me with my *'Edward Scissorhands'* chipping, but I had to hope Monique's chipping was more like my pal Hector's than mine, or her ball would soon be in a watery grave.

Before I'd had a chance to say anything, Monique was at her ball, had reached into her bag and was practice swinging with one of her wedges. it looked quite lofted, and the turf was tight. I held my breath. I felt the tightness and anxiety I experienced whenever I chipped. The club went back and came through, clipping the ball beautifully and sending it up and over the Swilcan Burn to land ten yards over rolling to within eight feet of the hole. Monique was a master chipper! I was envious, but what a shot. Fearless.

"Great shot," I said, and we all headed over the small bridge to the right of the green where four of my fellow marshalls, including my friend Skip, were standing beside the second tee. I'd seen them out of the corner of my eye standing in amazement, mesmerised as Monique, in her Paragolfer™, had played her two shots into the first hole and had all clapped in unison at her chip. This was as good as any of us had seen on The Old Course before, bar none.

They were a little surprised to see me with my backpack on and my white marshal jacket on, walking alongside her and I could see them nudging each other and looking towards me.

"Morning Skip," I shouted over.

A large smile came over Skip's face as he realised who it was who was greeting him.

"How did you manage to get this gig?," he said to me, as we walked past.

"Magic, Skip! I winked at him and proceeded onto the green.

Monique and her Paragolfer™ were a unique sight on the first green. Remarkably, the wheels of the vehicle did not leave a mark on the manicured surface, so good was the design of it.

I gave Monique the read for her putt, and she stroked it towards the hole. I'd love to say we parred it, but it grazed the right edge of the hole and missed on the high professional side. Good stroke from

Monique, bad read from me.

As we walked from the first green to the second tee, I was grateful to the R and A for showing some mercy to the Celebration of Champions players. They had moved the tees forward, so we could at least see 'Cheape's Bunker' up ahead. It was still a daunting drive, but with the right advice, it could be navigated. Now I just had to give Monique the right advice!

My fellow marshals gathered behind Monique as she teed up the ball. Curious and expectant, they were keen to see how this played out. They watched as she bent down to put the tee in the ground, raise herself up to vertical with a press of a button, hold onto the grab handle with her left hand and swing the driver back in a beautiful arc to almost the perfect angle, and then release forward. That was just the practice swing. Monique turned to me and checked the line again.

"Just at the right edge of the bunker," I said, drawing agreement from the marshals who nodded.

Monique set herself again and swung. The ball obeyed and headed off to the right of 'Cheape's Bunker' garnering a round of applause from the marshals and the small crowd who'd gathered to see how what Monique was doing was possible. Monique smiled, lowered herself back down into her chair, picked up her tee and drove forward.

As we proceeded past The Old Course Hotel, Monique pointed out the room on the ground floor that the R and A had put her in for the week. The flowers in the window boxes outside the hotel were in full bloom, the sun was shining, and I was caddying on The Old Course during Open week. Life was good!

We navigated Monique's second shot to the front right of the second hole, just short of the two bunkers. Both bunkers were armed with small tv cameras to capture stray balls landing in there and the skills and the agony as players tried to make their par from there.

Monique had one of those chips again to a pin just over the bunker!

Sitting in the stands behind the green were four more marshals, one of whom was Hector. I hadn't had a chance to mention to him that I'd met Monique, let alone that I was acting as her caddy during Monday's practice round. The wind carried Hector's voice across the green as he said to one of the marshals,

"That looks like Kev! It is Kev! Just as well it isn't Kev trying to chip that shot. It would definitely finish in the bunker"

Laughter from the other marshals, who'd all witnessed my chipping capitulations at some point over the last couple of years.

I looked up and reached behind me into my rucksack, taking out my 'Quiet Please' sign from my rucksack, holding it up towards the stand where Hector was sitting. More laughter from the marshals. I decided to carry that sign in my golf bag for our Friday 'Wham!' matches.

`Monique was not afflicted by my chipping disease though, easily negotiating the shot up and over the bunker. Another round of applause. Oh, how I dreamt about getting a round of applause for a chip! Maybe one day but today was about helping Monique. On the green, I read the putt for her, and she slotted it home ... yes! As Monique hit some more putts from all around the large green getting used to the undulations, I sauntered over to Hector and the other guys.

"How did you manage to get involved with her?" Hector asked.

"Magic, Hector. I'll tell you all about it later. I've got work to do here."

Hector would meet Monique later that day on Links Place just beside the 18th green where he would introduce himself as Kev's pal and ask her for a selfie. His next selfie after that with Monique would be with Cam Smith and the Claret Jug!

Monique, Deborah and I were getting set to cut across and play the 17th hole, when one of the R and A officials came over to us, radio in hand. Had he seen that my accreditation badge did not allow me on the course? Was I about to be thrown off the course in front of Hector and the grandstand marshals? Oh no!

"I'm so sorry," he said "but the greenkeeping staff are doing some final prep work this morning on the fairways here. They didn't expect any players to be passing through until after 12 noon."

Of course, most of the players teeing off at the first hole in the morning would be playing the front nine and then coming past that spot again two to three hours later, not just playing 1,2,17 and 18 as Monique was doing, These were the only holes she needed to play, as these were the only holes she was going to play during the Celebration of Champions Tournament. Well, at least, I wasn't being thrown off the course.

It was a pity that was my stint caddying at The Open over. One and a half holes and my player was one over par. Not great, but not a disaster. We'd negotiated the Swilcan Burn twice and bunkers galore, well three anyway. I could retire my imaginary caddie's bib into my own Caddy Hall of Fame in a cupboard back home.

"Well, that was fun," I said to Hector as I walked back past the grandstand behind the second green.

"We thought you'd just been thrown off the course," said Hector.

"You wish!" I smiled and headed off back down the second hole to start my marshalling shift. I had Rory McIlroy and Harry Diamond to see off from the tee in less than twelve minutes.

THE CELEBRATION OF CHAMPIONS TOURNAMENT

I finished my shift just as The Celebration of Champions tournament started at 3pm allowing me to follow Monique round all four holes.

Twenty-five Champion Golfers of the Year were taking part,

along with fifteen other invited champions from various other fields. The R and A had allocated Monique her own caddy for the four-hole extravaganza, but he wouldn't know her game like I did!

Gary Player did what Gary Player does and talked and told stories. Sandy Lyle and Bob Charles made up the fourball and they all tried to ease Monique's nerves, but this was the Old Course, and golf was not her first sport. Monique was used to Flushing Meadows or Wimbledon, but this was a whole new ball game-quite literally. She said she loved every moment of it, though, and being able to showcase what was possible, despite certain limitations, to a worldwide audience was a massive thrill for her.

Monique was an inspiration to a whole new sporting audience today and the photograph in front of the Swilcan Bridge with Gary, Sandy, Bob and herself was a special memory of the week for her as was Tiger waving across to her group as they went down the 18th hole, as he walked up the 1st fairway with Rory, Lee Trevino and Georgia Hall.

WONDERFUL WEDNESDAY (13TH JULY 2022)
CHAIRLIFTS AND CHARIOTS

That lunchtime, Monique christened the newly installed chair lift in the New Golf Clubhouse with her being one of the first to use it. She gave it a glowing review on her way up to meet our Vice Captain Peter Ferguson in the Peter Thompson Suite overlooking the Old Course. Monique, as most people do, loved The New Club.

That afternoon, Monique was due to give a golf demo at the Tented Village and had to meet First Minister Nicola Sturgeon there. I was marshalling at the Grandstand behind the 2nd green, so we went our separate ways.

When we met up again much later to exchange tales from the day, Monique showed me videos of her giving youngsters a ride with her on her Paragolfer™ chariot and I showed her the three other signatures I'd managed to get on my Masters Flag.

SIGNATURES FOURTEEN, FIFTEEN & SIXTEEN
HIDEKI

I waited for Hideki on the practice ground for three hours, long into the evening after all the other players had gone.

Just Hideki and his caddy on one side of the ropes, with me and another guy, who introduced himself as Ian, on the other side.

It turned out that Ian was one of those professional memorabilia people that Tom Watson avoided signing things for. He'd travelled up from Yorkshire for this week, so he could get numerous different flags signed. He had a rucksack full of flags-Masters flags, US Open flags, Open flags, PGA flags and Ryder Cup flags-basically a flag for every major golfing occasion. Whenever he saw a player, he would pull out a piece of paper, run his finger down it and bring the relevant flag out to be signed. It would then be sold on quickly, to ensure that the money kept coming in. It must have been worthwhile, given that he was here in St Andrews for three days with the cost of accommodation, food etc.

"Have you managed to get Tiger's signature?" I asked Ian.

"Oh yes, but I think he knows me now, so I've got to find different ways to get him to sign, but most of the time he does. I'll even pay a kid to go and get a flag signed if I've got to.," Ian rasped out.

Ian and I waited for a full three hours for Hideki to finish his practice session. We had no way of knowing that he was going to be that long, but after you've stood for an hour and a half, it's difficult to leave. Hideki finally finished and came walking towards us. I hoped that the presence of Ian wouldn't lead to Hideki snubbing me. I jumped in first and said politely,

"Mr Matsuyama would you mind signing my flag, please?"

Without even looking up, the 2021 Masters Champion took my flag, signed it and handed it back. He signed Ian's too. I wondered how long Ian held on to his flag and how much he got for it.

PATRICK AND DUSTIN

LIV golfers and Masters Champions, Patrick Reed (2018) and Dustin Johnson, (2020) were the next signatures on my flag. With a little bit of help from my friends, I came face to face with them, on the course during one of the practice days, and whipped out my flag for them to sign. Both obliged and went on with their practice. Signatures 14, 15 and 16 had been secured.

PART III: THE TOURNAMENT:

SLOW PLAY THURSDAY (14TH JULY 2022)

The first day had finally arrived. All the practice was done, and the crowds arrived to be marshalled. It was game day! Golf crowds in general are knowledgeable and polite, and it was a pleasure to interact with them, so I was sorry when my shift finished.

Tired, though, from standing for four hours, I decided against venturing further out onto the course, and I retired to The New Club to watch the remainder on tv with a beer. What stood out in that first day was that the afternoon rounds were taking so long . The Old Course suffers from several cross-over holes which holds up play, as players wait for each other to play them. Seven and Eleven, Eight and Ten and with the wind blowing in a certain direction, players were having to wait on the par 5 fourteenth. Tiger Woods teed off the first just before 3pm and finished his round just after 9pm. Six hours for a man with a dodgy back!

I heard from one of my other marshal pals that Tiger stood for forty minutes on the 14th tee waiting and he just looked ahead the whole time., not saying a word to anyone, not engaging with marshals or players, just staring ahead.

Was he managing the pain he was in, or was he reflecting on past glories on these links? He'd won here in 2000 and 2005, but it didn't look as if he was going to be the first golfer in history to win it three times at St Andrews as he was on his way to a first-round score of 78.

I'm not sure if the R and A have plans to avoid this happening again in 2027? Maybe some gaps in between tee times depending on wind direction? They are meticulous in their planning for everything else, so I'm sure this will be on the agenda for the organising committee, together with how to control the crowds around the Swilcan Burn on the final hole on the final day.

FRANTIC FRIDAY (15TH JULY 2022)
CUT DAY

Friday is Cut Day. Make the cut and you're in the money as a player. Miss it and you're going home. Your week has cost you money, which hurts a professional golfer. It hurts them in the pocket, and it hurts their pride.

My Friday job on the second hole was marshalling the crowds trying to cross from one side of the course, from our Hole 2 to Hole 17. As players drove off the second, we had to hold the crowds in the middle of the two fairways until the players had walked past the crossing point and on towards 'Cheape's Bunker' on the left side of the fairway, which most of them safely negotiated with a controlled fade leaving a relatively short iron into the green.

THE £100,000 MARSHAL

If you've ever wondered what the value of a good marshal is, I'm going to let you know ... it's just over £100,000.

I was chatting to the gathered crowds in the holding pen, while they were stopped there and letting them know what would happen after the players went through. Keep to the left and those coming the opposite way would do the same and chaos would be avoided. The message just didn't seem to drop for some people, though, and chaos would normally ensue. However, we kept repeating the message every time we pulled the rope across, taking bets amongst the marshals whether this time would be the time the crowds would follow our instructions.

Whoosh! Over our heads fired Chris Kirk's ball from the tee, landing in position A1 just right of 'Cheape's Bunker'. Next up was US golfer Kevin Kisner. His ball whooshed over us with a different sound though. It was the sound of a slice. I was following the ball all the way from tee to fairway and saw it dive into a gorse bush on the right-hand side of the fairway, about 50 yards right of A1.

As the players walked through and we were about to release the rope, I could see the ball spotters milling around a gorse bush about thirty yards further on from the one where Kevin's ball had dived into. I handed the rope to one of the other rope marshals and headed over to the head marshal and said that I'd seen where the ball had landed, and it wasn't where the ball spotters were looking.

"Could I leave my position and head 150 yards up the fairway and show them where they should be looking?"

The head marshal gave me the go ahead and I jogged up the fairway, passing Kisner and his group on the inside and called the ball spotters back to the gorse bush thirty yards behind them.

KEV'S BUSH

We all started looking in the bush and were quickly joined by Kisner and his caddy, who let us know what type of ball he was playing.

"You only need to identify it," said a rules official who had arrived onsite. "You don't have to retrieve it."

One minute passed. Nothing. Another minute. Still nothing. Then success, as one of the ball spotters pulled back a branch far enough to see a ball and Kisner was able to identify that it was his ball. He couldn't get to it to retrieve it, but he didn't need to. He took his penalty drop under the line-of-sight rule, as far back as he wanted, keeping the flag and the original ball in his line and he hit his third shot onto the green and two putted for a bogey five.

Kevin Kisner made the cut right on the mark that evening. His one-shot penalty instead of a two-shot penalty for a lost ball meant he was playing at the weekend and would be in the money. There was certainly Magic in St Andrews for Kevin Kisner that afternoon or was it just a Magic Marshal?! Kevin earned £100,448 for eventually finishing tied 21st after a scintillating 65 on Saturday and a closing round of 70 on Sunday. You're welcome, Kevin!

Hey, I'd have done the same thing even if his name wasn't Kevin! And no, he didn't send on a percentage of his earnings to be spent behind the bar at The New Club, but Kevin, if you're reading this, I will gladly see you back in St Andrews for a selfie at Kev's Bush and a beer at The New Club in 2027.

TIGER'S FAREWELL TO ST ANDREWS ... NOT QUITE!

The Friday was also memorable for Tiger's Farewell to The Open at St Andrews. The only thing was that Tiger hadn't read the script. The world's media were waiting for Tiger to cross the Swilcan Bridge and do what every other retiring player who is playing their last Open here does by standing on the bridge, taking their cap off and saying a farewell and thanks for the memories.

Excitement was growing. Tiger hadn't shot a 66 to make the cut at 144 and at 3pm during my shift on Hole 2, I saw Tiger play down the 17th hole and knew that he'd be making that walk in a short time.

The crowds around the second hole also knew this and were stopping in the walkways to get a glimpse of this historical moment. We marshals were not popular as we repeated our mantra to keep to the left and keep moving.

Five minutes later, Tiger crossed the Swilcan Bridge. He didn't stop to acknowledge the crowds or the photographers. He just kept walking and doffed his cap. In his mind, he was coming back for his farewell another time.

Maybe he'll get himself primed and ready to win his third Open at St Andrews in 2027, a feat unlikely ever to be matched. I wouldn't put it past him, but time will tell.

I was captured by the television cameras in the background of Tiger's moment on the Bridge, albeit very much in the background. In fact, you'd really have to take a snapshot of the tv screen, blow it up and know that it was me.

I knew it was me and so did my mum and that's all that mattered!

FLAG DAY SATURDAY (16TH JULY 2022)
BRINGING THE OPEN TO A STANDSTILL

The day had finally come. I was in charge of the green and red flags on my shift. Everything had led to this, and it was quite a responsibility. One wrong flag and some of the world's top golfers may become casualties and I didn't fancy becoming the first marshall to be frogmarched off the course for gross misconduct.

Players playing their second shots into the second hole were waiting for those on the green to finish. Players on the tee were waiting for the red flag to turn green. Like F1 racing drivers they waited for the lights to change, so they could continue to hopefully a memorable round.

Musing over a birdie at the first or a ball which had spun back into the Swilcan Burn, they were lost in their thoughts as I looked back towards the second tee and then looked forwards towards 'Cheape's Bunker' to see if it was safe for them to play.

Only I could decide when they could be transported out of their minds and back to their game.

Only I had the power to change the red flag to green. With great power comes great responsibility. I just had to make sure that the week so far didn't catch up with me and nod off. Can you imagine? Sky Sports coverage having to stop, as a tower crane camera zooms in to see what the issue is at Hole 2, only to see me sleeping beside my bush, green flag still in hand!

Thankfully, despite my tiredness I was a professional, and things moved well. That was until Bryson DeChambeau appeared on the 17th hole. He'd fired his tee shot further down the hole than anyone else had done, but it had carried a little left of perfect, and he was standing just left of the line of the drives from the 2nd tee.

I had a decision to make. Change the flag from red to green and risk Bryson being brained by a wayward tee shot or keep the flag red. On the tee was Lee Westwood, one of Bryson's LIV Tour buddies and his playing partner David Carey from Ireland. I could see Lee pacing about chatting to his caddie asking why the flag hadn't changed to green yet. His caddie couldn't answer his query. Only I could.

What I didn't know was that Bryson had just four putted the 16th green and then ballooned his drive left into the rough on 17 and had to wait for a rules official to get relief from the grandstand behind the first hole-that's how far left Bryson had gone. As with all of these things, it takes a little while to get a ruling and Bryson and his caddy and the spectators following him weren't for moving from that spot.

What should I do? Red to Green or just keep it red. I was all for caution and I kept the flag red. Five minutes passed. Still Bryson hadn't played. Finally, a ruling and he got relief, played his shot and moved off. Ten minutes had passed since Lee Westwood had arrived on the second tee.

I reached for my green flag, and a small cheer went up from the spectators either side of the walkway. They'd been penned in there for around ten minutes and looked like they were plotting to storm the bastille, which was my little hill, if the flags hadn't changed soon. They had golf to watch and couldn't see much from where they were stranded.

Thankfully, I'd sensed the possible rebellion and had already sussed out the gorse branches which could be detached quickly and easily to defend myself with. I was twitching as Bryson was swinging and quickly changed my flag from red to green. The rebellion was quashed.

Swoosh. Lee Westwood's ball shot perilously close over my head. Then he started walking with purpose towards me past the spectator walkways. The spectators were released just after Lee walked past them. Would they join him in flogging the flag bearer?

Lee walked close by and shouted over to me ...

"Was that Bryson holding us up?"

"Yes, it was," I replied

"You should have knocked him out," Lee shouted back.

"He's a little bit bigger me than me Lee and I didn't fancy being the news story of the day," I said.

Lee laughed and walked on. I'd escaped the wrath of Lee and of Bryson, all in the space of ten minutes and no one from the R and A had stopped by to question why The Open had come to a standstill for that amount of time.

Result!

SENSATIONAL SUNDAY (17TH JULY 2022)
MASHED POTATO HEADS

I arrived outside The New Club for my early shift and did a short walkthrough video in the Club at 9am, capturing the atmosphere there[6].

My shift on the small standing platform to the right of the second tee started at 11am and finished at 3pm, just after the leaders had passed through the 2nd hole. My biggest challenge of the day was staring down the 'empty headers' shouting "Mashed Potato" and "Light The Candle" just after players hit their tee shots. I'm not sure what possesses people to do that, but I'd love to see these idiots thrown out of the tournament and guessed that so would the majority of the disgusted genuine golf fans standing around them, tutting and looking for someone to have them ejected. It wasn't within the marshal's remit though, but it isn't tolerated at The Masters, and it shouldn't be at The Open. Personally, I'd mash their heads and light a candle up their backside. Enough ranting though. Back to the golf!

EVERYTHING HAS LED TO THIS

The final round of the 150th Open included a star-studded leaderboard with the final group containing Rory McIlroy and my previous Saturday afternoon course buddy Viktor Hovland. Viktor's early arrival and preparations had obviously paid off. Both had shot 66's on Saturday to lead The Open by four shots from Cam Smith and Cam Young. It all looked set for a sensational Sunday, with a win for Rory being what the fans in town that Sunday were hoping for.

Jack Nicklaus had famously said,

"If you're going to be a player people will remember, you have

---
[6] Here's the link: https://youtu.be/vslE4pzAUvw

to win the Open at St. Andrews"

Rory McIlroy was a lover of the history of the game and knew the significance of winning at St Andrews. Was it written in the stars for him to win this most monumental of anniversary Opens?

Neither Rory nor Victor could spark off each other though. Victor shot a two over 74 and although Rory shot a two under par 70, he didn't have momentum on his side and could only birdie one of the last nine holes and was unable to force a play-off against an on-fire Cam Smith. Cam Smith fired 6 birdies in the last nine holes to rip the Claret Jug away from Rory.

Hector The Tinkerer had decided to stay with me that evening in Leuchars and we watched the drama unfold from the Peter Thomson Suite on the second floor of The New Club. We watched on TV as Cam Smith, dressed in a distinctive 'magenta' polo shirt, with ice in his veins, putted thirty feet from just off the 17th green. It doesn't sound that hard, but factor in the following:-

He was one shot ahead of Rory

The Open Championship was on the line

In his line lay the most feared bunker in golf, The Road Hole Bunker.

A bogey here would draw him back level with Rory and give Rory more than a glimmer of hope of lifting the Claret Jug with two holes to play.

Most professional golfers would have reached for a wedge and tried to do the expected and spectacular, sending it up in the air and landing it on the right edge of the bunker and watched it roll down to two feet for an easy par. Golfing snobs would turn their noses up at using a putter from off the green ... that wasn't how the game should be played. Professional golfers are magicians with wedges, and the public are used to 'oohing and ahhing' as their wedge skills beggar belief.

Cam was an artist too, but he had been putting like a god. He reached for his putter. The crowd in the giant stand overlooking the green held their breath. This putt needed to be pinpoint accurate or else he could putt into the bunker, which would be a tad embarrassing.

No practice putt. Cam just rolled the putt. The ball, sensing its own chance of golf ball immortality, rolled perfectly end over end, three steps right of the dangerous bunker, not even stopping to give it a look, continuing its perfect journey onto the green, snaking left then right and ending ten feet from the pin which was tucked in behind the bunker. Ten feet. Surely Cam couldn't knock this one in, willed Rory's fans. Rory had a chance again.

They didn't reckon on 'Ice-Cool Cam' though. He rolled in the left to right putt for possibly one of the best two putts in major history. Cam was still one shot ahead, although Rory did have two holes still to go.

Rory continued his birdie-free run on the 17th and could only watch as Cam made birdie on the 18th, leaving Cam on 20 under par and Rory two behind waiting to tee off on the final hole. Rory's fans knew Rory had more than enough power to get up to the 18th green with his drive. If he could leave an eight-foot putt for eagle, then the dream was still alive. Come on Rory. It was only 356 yards.

The message below the second tier of the grandstand behind the 18th green shouted out to Rory as he looked down the hole,

'EVERYTHING HAS LED TO THIS'

The message wasn't wrong.

The fans watched lined up both sides of the widest fairway in golf, the world watched on television and Hector and I watched from The New Club, as Rory cracked his driver off the tee.

Rory shouted "Go, Go, Go," to his ball, a shout he would use again at the 17th hole in the final round at The Masters in 2025.

We could see his ball land soft and short, just shy of the 'Valley of Sin', around thirty yards short of the pin . Rory would have to hole his second shot to tie 'Ice-Cool Cam'. If anyone could do it, then Rory could do it. After all, everything had led to this moment and Rory, the generational talent, was meant to win the 150th Open in St Andrews, wasn't he?

It seemed like most fans wanted to see Rory do it. Crowds jumped dangerously over the Swilcan Burn onto the 18th fairway behind Rory and his caddy Harry. Rory kept looking back at the melee or was he looking back wistfully at the back nine, which had not yielded one birdie to him that afternoon? One now would not be enough. He needed a bigger bird. He needed an eagle. Would one swoop down in the next few moments and help Rory wrestle the Claret Jug from Cam Smith's hands?

Rory opted to chip the ball rather than putt it.

Despite hitting a clean crisp chip which landed exactly the right distance, Rory's ball bounced one foot left of the pin and came to a stop 15 feet past the pin.

Ice-Cool Cam Smith was The Champion Golfer of the Year. Not just any year, though; this was the 150th Year and this was at St Andrews. Cam Smith, with the mullet hairstyle and laid-back attitude hadn't been written into the final script of this most special of Opens. However, Cam had decided to gatecrash the party and was now getting ready to party.

Little did Hector and I know at that moment, as we looked out on the presentation ceremony of The Claret Jug to Cam on the 18th green, that we would be joining his party in just a few hours' time and that we too would be holding the coveted Claret Jug.

MONIQUE MAGIC - PARTYING WITH CAM

We watched the presentation of the trophy from the windows of

The New Club Suite upstairs. We laughed as fans milled around afterwards trying to become background tv stars as Sky Sports and other channels were completing their analysis on the 18th fairway of what had unfolded. We were all slightly deflated as we'd wanted Rory to win this one.

Our work was done, the 150th Open had been won. Monique was going to join us at The New Club but texted to say that she was tired after a full week and was going to stay at her hotel. I had arranged to play golf with her on The Eden Course on Tuesday so would see her again then before she headed back home to The Netherlands.

Eventually, Hector and I left the scene of the crime where Cam had made off with the Claret Jug. We walked past 'The Dunvegan' bar, which was rammed inside and out, with people spilling out right across the other side of the road, excitedly recounting their tales of the day with a beer or two in hand.

Greyfriars Inn was quieter, and we stood at the bar and reflected on our week. What a week it had been. We had been part of the history of The Open as marshalls and Kevin Kisner was £100,000 richer as well! We'd received our stylish grey 150th Open caps, grey and white jackets and £15 of vouchers a day to spend in The New Club or in Auchterlonies. And we had our memories. What more could a marshall ask for?

A text had just come through on my phone. It was from Monique. "Guess who is in the party," ... alongside a photo of a guy in a white t-shirt with a baseball cap on back to front drinking from a trophy.

"Who is that? (Me).

"Are you kidding?" (Monique)

"I can't see." (Me)

"There is only one person in this world with the real claret jug now. He's from Australia." (Monique)

There was a laughing crying emoji below it, which I think meant are you for real!

"If you want to see him you have to come." (Monique)

Monique was staying at The Old Course Hotel for the week, courtesy of the R and A and Cam and his entourage were staying there too.

"I can't get in…no pass," I responded sadly " And Hector is with me too" instantly regretting inviting Hector to stay at mine. One person in maybe, two people-not a chance! Not in Open week.

Within thirty minutes we were transported into the lift in The Old Course Hotel which led to the Road Hole Bar. I can't disclose how, suffice to say that the 'Magic In St Andrews' had delivered again. As the lift door opened, I could see a glint in the distance. It was The Claret Jug. I like to play it cool, and I turned left and headed straight to the bar. I knew this place like the back of my hand. I had been here many times before. I ordered two large red wines for Monique and myself and a beer for Hector.

Where was Hector. He had been in the lift with me just seconds before. I felt a tap on my shoulder and looked round. Hector was standing there with Cam Smith and The Claret Jug.

"Cam this is my pal Kev, do you mind if we get a photo please?"

Hector loves a celebrity selfie. He has posted many before from his golf trips. Charley Hull, Dame Laura Davies. Monique Kalkman. When the lift doors had opened, Hector had seen the glint of the Claret Jug too. There was no playing it cool from him though. He was off like a greyhound out of the traps. And here he was, standing in front of me, with his reward. A Champion Golfer of the year and his Claret Jug.

"Hey, Cam," I said "Congratulations on today. Would you like a drink?"

"No thanks mate," Cam replied, looking as if he'd had several already. Media reports the next day would confirm as much.

Hector handed his phone to Monique and asked her if she would take a photo of Cam, me and Hector. Monique obliged. Hector them asked Cam if he would take a photo of Monique, me and Hector with Cam's Claret Jug. Cam obliged.

That was enough now Hector. I settled into a chair to chat with Monique and some of Cam's Aussie pals.

I could see Hector scurrying about on the other side of the room phone in one hand and Claret Jug in the other. Cam had just handed it over to him and Hector had grabbed the opportunity with both hands. Photos of just Hector in front of the bar, Hector and Cam, Hector and Adam Scott who was there celebrating with Cam too, Hector in front of the Open logo. Finally, he brought it over and took one of Monique and me together and then he handed it back over to Cam, reluctantly it must be said.

Well done though Hector for doing all that. As well as the memories, we have the photos of that night, and it wasn't long before they were plastered all over our Facebook pages for everyone to wake up to the next morning. It did feel like a scene from 'The Hangover' film, though, as we checked our phones the next morning to see what had gone on the night before.

PLAYING GOLF WITH MONIQUE

I finally got to play golf with Monique on the Tuesday after the Open furore had subsided. We played the Eden Course on the hottest day of the year when the thermometer hit thirty degrees Celsius. Monique was a fourteen-handicap golfer, and she could play to it. Her short game was immense. I was jealous. She knew about my chipping woes as Hector had alluded to it enough times during the last week. I marvelled at how Monique manoeuvred herself into position on her buggy, steadied herself with one arm and swung the club with the other.

What an inspiration.

And with that my week with Monique was over. I cherished my week with this inspirational lady, and I cherished the message I received from her as she was sitting on the plane waiting to leave

"Ready to go! Thank you so much for being part of this very special week and making magical memories. Wishing you good luck in creating the right balance between golf and work you desire. Thanks. And pls stay in touch!"

'The Magic in St Andrews' had brought us together. What a week. What a story. From Strangers to Good Friends in less than a week, all thanks to golf.

Little did I know that I was about to meet another very special person in less than four days' time, as the 'Tinder Gods' were about to work their magic.

CHAPTER 11: FINDING LOVE ON THE LINKS

    Heart I: Meeting Magic

    Heart II: Tinder Magic

    Heart III: Making Magic

    Heart IV: The Magic of Golf

    Heart V: The Magic of Learning

    Heart VI: The Magic of Golfing Together

    Heart VII: Seeing Magic

    Heart VIII: The Magic of Bobby Jones

    Heart IX: The Magic Of Friendship

    Heart X: For The Love Of The Game

Heart I: Meeting Magic

YOU CAN'T HURRY LOVE

During COVID, whilst staying in Ellon during Lockdown, my Mum had asked me whether I was still looking for love. Previously, I'd involved her in almost every emotional moment along the rocky road of my four-year marriage from the wedding in Barbados in 2007 to my eventual divorce in 2012.

I was surprised, then, when she brought up relationships as we were getting ready to choose a film one evening. I think my penchant for rom-com movies might have given her a clue that I was really a hopeless romantic at heart, with *'Four Weddings and a Funeral'*, *'Notting Hill'* and *'Love Actually'* featuring amongst my choices every second night.

"What would you be looking for in someone if you moved to St Andrews?" my Mum said.

"Someone who can play golf would be ideal and then we can hang out on the golf course and go on golfing holidays," I replied.

I was moving to 'Disney for Golfers', so I was allowed to dream big but with the benefit of hindsight and knowing what I know now about the Magic in St Andrews, I shouldn't have been surprised that I was delivered what I was looking for.

Although neither of my recent long-term encounters had been long term successes, deep down I still secretly hoped that someone special was out there. My days of partying and going to bars and clubs were well behind me, so my only hope of meeting that someone was on the golf course.

However, having never really gone out in St Andrews, I didn't know what to expect. The students were too young, and I didn't know any lady golfers. I was starting from scratch, or in fact a handicap of fifty-two, which was my age at the time, so I was having to leave it to fate as to who and what was in store for me. My barber McGiff, based in the town, was my resident romance consultant after I arrived in 2020 but as it turned out, it was the Tinder Gods who would take control of my life, delivering love, a home for me in St Andrews and meetings with golfers from all over the world.

Not before I found a different type of love on the links, though.

A PERFECT MATCH

In September 2021, I'd finally decided to change my golf clubs. I'd got down to a handicap of 1.5 in May and then headed from there back up to 4.6 by the end of August. Some drastic action was needed.

Rather than tinker, I decided I would go for a full-scale change of clubs to help me achieve my golfing goals.

I didn't like to rush in, especially for a life-changing decision like this. My golf clubs and I, we lasted! I'd had my previous set of clubs for over twenty-five years. My King Cobra irons and my Ping G2 driver had seen off several other relationships. The odd disappointments, yes, but no arguments and no silent treatments. We'd stuck together through thick and thin. We were a constant in the maelstrom of life.

So, it was with heavy heart that I travelled to Swanston Golf Club in Edinburgh at the beginning of September for my three-hour fitting for woods, irons and wedges at SGGT. I almost turned back home a couple of times, but after sitting in the car park for a few minutes, I finally plucked up the courage to go through with the appointment which would bring an end to the beautiful connection.

'If it ain't broke, don't fix it', I was always told, but now was the time. I thrashed ball after ball and tried club after club. Nothing seemed to match. Much like my love life!

I began to despair that there wouldn't be a right fit for me, when suddenly I was given a Taylor Made 770 seven iron. Oh, my goodness. It felt perfect, it looked perfect, and it hit perfect.

Bob Rotella wrote a book called 'Golf Is Not A Game Of Perfect', but what did he know? He'd obviously never picked up a Taylor Made 770 iron before he wrote the book. I'd found my perfect match.

I hit the other clubs from eight iron to pitching wedge and from six iron to four iron, each one of them connecting with the ball in a moment of tender but passionate embrace, before the ball eased up the grooves of the club and shot out into the hot summer's afternoon, landing softly, dreaming of being swiftly collected again to be reunited again with its sensitive new soulmate.

I was in love. The birds were singing, the sun was shining, and the world was a beautiful place. I said a silent thank you to the designers at Taylor Made as I placed my order with Ross the fitter. He'd succeeded where others had failed before him. The clubs and I were made for each other.

"Do you want them 'pured'?" he asked. (Puring is a process that aims to optimize the performance of a golf shaft by aligning its most stable orientation with the golfer's swing, which potentially leads to more consistent and accurate shots.)

As far as I was concerned, they were already as pure as the driven snow, but Grant, a buddy of mine, had told me that his shafts were pured and he played off scratch. If it was good enough for him, then it was good enough for me, as I now intended to try to get from 10 to scratch in twenty months!

"That'll be another £560, then," said Ross.

"F**k you, Grant," I said under my breath and "Thank you, Ross," I said a little louder to Ross, as I signed up for 'Puring'.

Maybe the clubs needed to be cleansed after their X-rated encounter with those golf balls in the bay?! Whatever it was, it was going to take eight weeks for them to be delivered to me. I wasn't sure I could wait that long and felt a sense of loss as soon as I left the building. I packed my old clubs into the boot of my car. Another divorce was looming!

It was a long, silent car journey back to St Andrews with my old King Cobra clubs sitting sullenly in the back of the car, plotting ways to sabotage my game over the next few weeks before they were cast aside in favour of my new Taylor Mades. I'd had my head turned and I couldn't wait to be reunited with my new clubs.

Finally, I got the call. My clubs had arrived. When could I collect them from Edinburgh? I was in the car with mobile in hand before the caller could finish their sentence. I couldn't wait any longer. I arrived and picked up the clubs within ninety minutes of receiving the call.

In the back of the car, I unwrapped the long sleek cardboard box. The clubs were gleaming, beautiful and untouched. I headed straight back to St Andrews to the driving range and set about getting to know each one of them intimately. I had a trip to Pebble Beach to get ready for and my Taylor Mades were coming with me. I'd found my perfect match on the course. Now I was ready to meet my perfect match off it.

Heart II: Tinder Magic

THE TINDER GODS WORK THEIR MAGIC

I'd been 'swiping right' on my backswing and 'swiping left' on my downswing all my life, but Tinder was serious swiping. Instead of hitting a ball in between swipes, there were photos of a host of women on my Tinder app. You either swiped right or left, and you didn't have to communicate with or meet them if you didn't want to.

Tinder was quite literally a whole new ball game, and days had changed indeed from my previous dating life in the early 2000s. Then, I'd had to pluck up the courage in a bar to make the long walk over to speak to someone I found attractive.

I never knew whether my walk was going to be worth it or wasted. Was I going to have to make the embarrassing walk of shame back to my waiting friends, after being turned down by said attractive one? Would I have to shuffle slowly back over to the drooling pack of dogs, desperate to know how my latest turn down had unfolded, laughing and ribbing me for the next hour or so, until my next tentative shuffle across the bar? Even then, on the dating scene, I employed my sixth pillar of "Be Positive, Stay Positive."

For those not familiar with the Tinder app, you upload photos of yourself, purportedly looking your best and living your best life. The purpose of these photos is to attract another person to spend some time with. For some, it's just a coffee, lunch or dinner. For others, it might be for the night. And for a few, it might be for a lifetime.

I'd never used it before and had heard all the stories about it just being for one-night stands. That wasn't for me. I was simply intrigued that I could lie on my sofa at home and the world of Tinder would present me with photos and opportunities to engage and gasp at some of the photos people considered to be their best self!

If I wasn't attracted to the person, then I'd swipe left on the photograph. I did that a lot. Some of the photos just didn't do it for me ... washing hanging up behind them, rabbit ear filters, selfies with celebrities and one with an apple in their mouth posing provocatively!

If I did find someone attractive, I would swipe right on their photo and if they'd done the same then 'IT'S A MATCH' would come up right across the screen. The rush of adrenaline was palpable when that happened and was the best part for me. There was no plucking up courage, no shuffling across the floor and no walk of shame. Perfect!

But then you had to communicate with your match, and I wasn't sure I wanted to communicate. I was happy with my golf and my life. I think I'd become too selfish to share my life with someone else. Would 'Sheena' or 'Davina' let me play as much golf? Would 'Hannah' or 'Anna' want me to go on long walks in the countryside? What was the point of a long walk without golf clubs?

Life was good. On second thoughts, maybe swiping right wasn't such a good idea, but I liked the interaction with the 'outside world' through the app - matching without the hassle.

My answer was to become a mute right swiper. All the excitement of the match, without the chat afterwards. I wasn't rude. I did say hi, but made my chat so boring that my match would 'unmatch' and so it would go on. Match...Mute...Unmatch!

TINDER FOR GOLFERS ... NOT!

My own set of Tinder photos had a golfing theme. Me in front on the first tee of the Old Course with the R and A Clubhouse behind me. Me in full swing action shot driving a ball over the sheds on the 17th hole of the Old Course. Me standing all alone on the Swilcan Bridge, subconsciously seeking a golfing partner to join me on the famous bridge. I looked a little like Princess Diana in her famous staged solo photo in front of the Taj Mahal.

I'd gone full-out golf in my photos, so it was unlikely I'd be attracting anyone who didn't like or have an interest in golf.

My profile

'Not looking for anything serious too soon, just someone to share some great experiences with.'

My Filters

Female, Age 45-55

Location - within 20 miles, which changed quickly to within 50 miles, and then changed again to within 100 miles as I got 'swipe left finger' when my Tinder game yielded less and less matches as the weeks went by. Would The Tinder Gods ever deliver?

KERRY THE GOLFING GODDESS

Finally, they delivered Kerry. A beginner golfer and a goddess, who was two years younger than me and located sixty miles away in Edinburgh.

Unusually for me, the Tinder Mute, we'd been messaging online for around five weeks, but our diaries hadn't allowed for a physical meet up. I was on holiday in Tenerife with my Mum, then had the small matter of the 150th Open and Kerry was dealing with her own busy life. Finally, we managed to get a date in the diary.

This was to be my very first 'in person' Tinder date. I'd messaged one or two girls back and forth on Tinder, but no one I'd wanted to meet up with in person, so I was a little nervous but also a little nonchalant as I'd grown quite attached to my solo golf-oriented life in St Andrews.

Having to travel to Edinburgh for a date with someone who lived over an hour away from me just didn't seem to have any point or any future. I'd arranged to meet Long Beach Graham, who was back from the States before the date, though, , so it was a good opportunity to see him, and I asked myself what I had to lose by meeting Kerry when I was in the capital anyway. It would only be for an hour at most and I could have a large glass of red wine too as I'd taken the train!

It was exactly one week after I'd partied with Cam Smith. With the sun still shining, I arrived at our date in my shorts and my 'Boss" grey and white 150th Open marshal's jacket. In hindsight, I hadn't really made much of an effort, but I figured that this was what I was comfortable wearing in the heat, and I was too long in the tooth to be dressing for someone else. Subconsciously, in fact, I'd brought a little piece of St Andrews with me.

As well as being attracted by Kerry's looks, I'd also been drawn in by a couple of photos of her swinging a golf club on a golf course.

Her set up and swing looked good. Bingo. She was into golf.

Kerry was as beautiful in real life as in her photos and her smile and eyes lit up the room as soon as she walked into 'Juniper' bar on Princes Street. Our first date went very well. Kerry was enchanting, conversation was easy, and she was like no one I'd ever met before. If her golf was as good as her chat, then I'd found my mixed open partner for life.

I got the train back to Leuchars with a spring in my step.

THE 'KEEPER OF THE GREENS' MEETS THE KEEPER

Our second date would come ten days later, but this time it was on my home turf in St Andrews.

I'd planned a great day to impress Kerry and show off St Andrews. First was lunch, but as we walked into the Links Clubhouse, the fire alarm went off and everyone was evacuated.

Strike One.

Next, we headed to 'The Himalayas' for a spot of putting. I'd read that it was originally a well-known late 19th century courting spot where the daughters of R and A members would play and potential suitors would hold their cards and remove the pin flags. Many a long-term relationship started there, and I hoped that the Magic of the Himalayas would rub off on us. We turned up at the 'shelter' as it's known, with our own putters and balls and I asked to pay for two.

"Have you booked?" said the person at the window.

"No, I haven't," I said sheepishly. "I didn't know we needed to."

"I'm so sorry, but we're fully booked today," said the starter.

Strike Two!

Kerry was chilled, though, and didn't seem bothered, and we walked on past the undulating hills of The Ladies Putting Club, full of happy putters.

As we continued, I was racking my brains where else we could go. Finally, after five minutes walking round the back of the first tee of the Old Course, it came to me ... I would show Kerry the cemetery. I was just an old romantic at heart!

I hadn't been there before and I'm not sure what possessed me to think that a graveyard in the middle of the day was a good place to take someone on a second date, but something had possessed me.

Thankfully, the graveyard was open and, as we walked in and around the grounds, I marvelled at the graves of former Open champions and wondered where the magnificent memorial to Young Tom Morris was located.

Venturing further into the grounds, we finally came across it and Old Tom Morris's grave located close by. I stopped and stood in silence, paying my respects to the grandfather of golf, Old Tom, the Keeper of the Greens and a four-time Open Champion (1861, 1862, 1864 and 1867) and his son Young Tom, the only player in history to win The Open four times in a row (1868, 1869, 1870 and 1872). We were in the presence of golfing greatness.

Strangely, though, Kerry seemed unmoved. I learned later that she'd told her friends who'd asked how our second date had gone that it was great, but that I'd taken her to see some graves of some old golfers! She did feign interest very well, though, and I would never have known until she told me. She was a Keeper!

We visited The Dunvegan and The Road Hole Bar in The Old Course Hotel where I regaled (or perhaps bored) Kerry with tales of the 150th Open and partying with Cam Smith.

Notwithstanding the initial setbacks, we chatted and laughed throughout the day. I even took her to my second home in St Andrews, The New Golf Club, where we bumped into my 'Wham!' opponent Colin The Metronome and his family. Despite that, we left agreeing to have another date in Edinburgh!

LIVING SEPARATELY EVER AFTER

The following week, I managed to win the Thistle Club Championship and Kerry texted good luck and well done before and after every match, showing great interest as I updated her with my wins of 2 and 1, 3 and 1, and 1 hole after extra holes. She didn't have a clue what any of these weird combinations of numbers and letters meant, but she seemed genuinely delighted I'd won.

Our relationship blossomed and love soon came calling. Neither of us had been looking for anything serious but, as is often the way, when you're not looking, love finds you. We shared a love of golf and a love of 'Abba'!

Neither of us wanted to get married again, both enjoyed living on our own and had no intentions of changing that, so we decided to live separately ever after. Kerry in the centre of Edinburgh and me in Leuchars.

However, that didn't stop us buying a house together within six months of meeting each other as a 'project' in St Andrews.

When you know, you know!

Heart III: Making Magic

THE HOUSE OF GOLF

When we first viewed the house in St Andrews with a real estate agent in November 2022, it looked more like 'The House of Horrors' than 'The House of Golf'.

Overgrown trees and bushes swamped the property as the previous owner, who'd recently passed away, had valued his privacy and undervalued the amenity of the rest of the neighbourhood. The décor inside hadn't been touched for forty years, which may have been the last time it was cleaned too.

Kerry is a creative genius, though, and as soon as she set foot in the grounds and in the house, she saw beyond the state of the place as it was and could instantly see what it would look like once it was finished. Her enthusiasm was infectious, and I was sold on her vision. She'd turned her own place in the centre of Edinburgh, a former backpacker's hostel, into a beautiful three-bedroom flat and I trusted her abilities and her creativity.

Armed with the confidence and excitement to be working together, we managed to buy the property for well under valuation, partly due to the time of year and partly because so few people would have wanted to take on such a project.

Located just a five-minute drive from the first tee of The Old Course, we got the keys at the start of February 2023 and set to work creating 'The House of Golf.'

A self-contained one bedroomed unit for me to live in on one side and a four bedroomed unit for short stay lets on the other.

SURVIVING 'PAINTGATE'

Kerry already had a few renovations under her belt. Nicknamed 'The Painter' by her friends and family, she was a dab hand with a paintbrush and a power tool. I, on the other hand, had never been much of a Do-It-Yourself person or a Doer Upper. If Kerry had known just how wet behind the ears or useless I was, I doubt she'd have got involved.

I was introduced to tools I'd never used before - a wallpaper stripper, a sledgehammer, a trench shovel, a thwacker, a wheelbarrow and my nemesis, the paint brush and roller! The paintbrush and roller nearly ended our beautiful relationship. I just couldn't get the hang of painting and promptly threw all my tools out of the pram, figuratively speaking of course!

The result? Some words and sulking, all entirely from me, I'm embarrassed to say. Kerry ended up painting the whole house inside and out, walls, ceilings, woodwork, gutters, windows and flashings.

In fact, the whole kaboodle, even balancing on one leg up a ladder, paint can in one hand, paint brush in the other whilst I held the ladder very tightly for her! She was the creative genius, and I was the labourer ... provided the labouring didn't involve painting!

Electrical, heating, joinery and plumbing services were all provided by friends of Kerry and, by the end of April, I was able to move out of my rented property in Leuchars and into the building site in St Andrews.

Two months later, the house was nearly complete, and I applied to the Council for my short term stay licence. 'The House of Golf' opened for business at the start of September 2023.

Kerry had created a one bedroom unit for me to live in at the back of the property, allowing me to live in St Andrews, be based within a five-minute drive of the first tee of the Old Course and the beloved practice facilities at the Academy AND get my residents links ticket, which entitled me to play on the seven links courses for only a few hundred pounds a year! Golfing heaven.

I was a lucky guy. Thank you, Kerry, and thank you, Tinder Gods. If I hadn't moved to St Andrews, then we wouldn't have met.

Thankfully, we survived 'PaintGate'... just! ... and continued our love affair. We just don't mention painting!

WELCOMING THE WORLD

I'm very proud as I walk around the house looking at the lovely space Kerry has created and realising how lucky I am. My golfing photos and memorabilia are displayed proudly for all guests to enjoy. My signed Masters flag, images of Seve and St Andrews, the framed picture Big Andy had given me at The Olympic Club of 'Arnie's farewell to St Andrews' and so many more.

I welcomed guests from the start of September. The spacious kitchen/diner, the four double bedrooms, two bathrooms and the driveway with parking for four cars had all become a reality and the five star reviews from guests over time reflected that they loved it too.

We've had golfers, family get-togethers and wedding guests, with all nationalities visiting. I've been privileged to welcome LPGA player Morgane Metraux to the house for the 2024 British Womens Open and Hugo Dobson to caddy for Tyrell Hatton on his way to winning the 2024 Dunhill Links Championship. As I write this, a DP World Tour winner has just booked the house for this year's Dunhill Championship in October 2025. Here's hoping some of last year's magic rubs off on them too!

I look forward to welcoming a player and their team to The House of Golf for the 155th Open when it returns to St Andrews in 2027. Perhaps I can even emulate my friend, Max, who rented his house to eventual winner Louis Oosthuizen in 2010 when Louis slept with the Claret Jug in Max's bed on the Sunday night he won!

More details of The House of Golf can be found at: www.thehouseofgolf.co.uk

Heart IV: The Magic Of Golf

NEXT UP ... PROJECT GOLF

With the house finally completed in late 2023, Kerry was then able to turn her attention to her next 'project', which was to get a handicap. Until that point, she'd been pottering along, content to swing a club and take a few group lessons from time to time. She'd had little time to do much else with the house refurbishment but was aiming to play and get into this game we all love in a big way. The magic of golf was about to grip her.

However, January 2024 started with some harsh words from me. We'd provisionally booked a golfing holiday to Portugal for April, but I didn't think Kerry's game was anywhere near good enough for this. She seemed distracted anytime we went out to play on the links in St Andrews and I didn't think she was progressing enough to justify either of us spending a few thousand pounds to play three games of golf on some of the manicured courses around Vilamoura. I pointed out that we could have three games in a week in St Andrews for a fraction of the price.

Kerry disclosed that she just wasn't happy with the way her game was trending either and had been trying to source a female coach to help her take her game forward. She was a member of several online female golfing groups, constantly seeking tips and encouraging words from other like-minded women, and it was here that she was recommended to find a female coach which she did: Chloe Thackeray, a female professional coach based at Swanston Golf Club in Edinburgh.

Kerry went for a half hour 'getting to know you' meeting with Chloe to see how they got on with each other. They bonded instantly and laughter has accompanied learning ever since their first get-together.

What followed has been nothing short of sensational, as Kerry got her handicap, we golfed in Portugal and played our first mixed open tournaments in 2025, culminating in a second-place finish in our second tournament at Carnoustie Golf Links no less!

Kerry's enthusiasm for the game is infectious, and her work ethic is second to none. She'll finish work and then head straight to the driving range or out for nine holes of golf herself, doing her homework from Chloe.

Chloe shows her a movement with her swing in one of their regular lessons and Kerry will go back home and, for the next five days after her lesson, she'll practice that movement repeatedly, sometimes a hundred times a day, in the mirror until she cracks the move. As a former professional dancer, that's how she was taught dance moves, by doing them in a dance studio in front of multiple mirrors. Kerry thought it just made sense to do the same thing with her golf swing. It was just about transferring skills from one discipline to another, and it worked.

NERVES ABOUND

I've watched Kerry blossom technically as a golfer, but she still suffered from first tee nerves. This would frequently lead to her missing out the drive from the first tee shot to avoid playing in front of the clubhouse and the waiting golfers or golfers finishing their round on the 18th green.

This was going to be a problem long term and Kerry knew it. Rather than shy away from it, though, she faced it head on, 'put on her big girl pants' and joined the newly formed Monday Seniors Section at her golf club, which was made up of twenty-three male senior golfers and Kerry. Wow, she had balls ... or, in fact, was the only one who didn't have them!

I couldn't believe that she was pushing herself to do this, but her simple answer was that if she didn't, then how could we go away on golfing trips or play in mixed tournaments if she didn't get over her fear and what better way to do it than by doing this. What a girl. That was love!

How she did it in those first few weeks, I don't know. She was shaking and would feel ill at the thought of going on a Monday, but she pushed herself to go and to keep going, hitting fifty balls as a warmup before heading in for a much-needed hit of caffeine.

She did it, though, and she's just got better and better, really looking forward now to her Monday games.

What she did took some courage. I'm not sure I could've done what she did and I admire her tremendously for it. I'm so proud of her work ethic, her mentality and her attitude. She is truly a one-off. Kerry pushes herself into uncomfortable situations, even if they make her feel even more anxious in the short term. She's worked out that the long-term benefits for her golf game, and our golf games and mixed opens will make it all worthwhile.

As the legendary soccer coach Jose Mourinho once said, "The most important quality a player can have is not skill but mentality." Kerry has that mentality and doesn't know just how good she is, but her coach Chloe and I do. Every time I play with Kerry, I always notice a massive improvement between games.

How good can Kerry be? Only time will tell!

THE JOY OF GOLF

I finally knew that I was second best to golf the week that we'd agreed that Kerry would travel up from Edinburgh to St Andrews for a night together.

Within twelve hours of arranging our rendezvous though, Kerry had texted to say she'd just been asked to play golf with one of her friends and could we put our own meeting off! I couldn't really say anything as I'd done the same before! Our love for the game equalled our love for each other.

Heart V: The Magic of Learning

SOMETIMES IT'S HARD TO BE A WOMAN!

I've learned a lot from Kerry over the time we've been together. I've learned some DIY, I've learned not to speak about painting, but I've also learned that sometimes it can be hard to be a woman golfer, and I'd never really appreciated that before.

DRIVING RANGES AND 'MANSPLAINING'

A lot of women golfers have to put up with being bothered at Driving Ranges and with 'Mansplaining'. Quite often the two can happen together.

A woman at a driving range is normally in the minority and it can be a novelty for men to see them there on their own. Some men take this as a cue to start speaking, perhaps seeing the driving range as a dating range? Others seem to enjoy offering their own unsolicited opinions and advice on what she should or shouldn't be doing.

I didn't know any of this until I heard the stories, saw the evidence myself and watched some of the videos from Womens Golf Networks. One such cringeworthy video on TikTok went viral and involved professional golfer Georgia Ball with an anonymous guy, who was caught on video mansplaining to her what she was doing wrong, because he'd "been golfing for 20 years."(Just type in 'Georgia Ball Mansplaining' into Google and become one of the 15.4 Million viewers as of 16th July 2025.)

Unless a woman approaches you at a driving range, you leave them alone don't you, knowing how intimidating a place it can be for them? I'm not sure that men realise just how creepy it can come across to women. Chloe's advice for Kerry is to put headphones on and listen to, or pretend to listen to, music. That's how bad it can be for women.

I witnessed an example of this 'creepiness' myself when we were playing on a beautiful golf course in Northumberland on an unseasonably warm day in November. We passed three guys, and one commented on the weather and then said to Kerry, "You should be in a bikini." Predictably, there was no mention made to me that I should be wearing my speedos!

Kerry is thick skinned, but she admitted to me afterwards that comments like that coming from a group of male strangers when she's on her own in the middle of nowhere on the fourteenth hole of a golf course would make her feel more than a little uncomfortable. She might not even continue with her round if it meant that the holes she was going to play were a little isolated from the rest of the course! That was sad and it certainly made me think about how I engage with women golfers on their own. I speak to them now as a golfer, not as a man to a woman, and only in the same way as I'd interact with a male golfer.

MEN ARE FROM MARS AND WOMEN ARE FROM VENUS

It appears to me that women golf coaches seem to be a great fit for women golfers, whatever stage of the game they're at. Whether they're beginners, mid or low handicaps, women just get women.

Men don't have boobs and have no perception of what it's like to have to hold the club and swing a club, taking account of those two lumps sticking out in front of them. 'Moobs' don't count! To quote Kerry, "They don't half get in the way!"

Men don't get periods. Once a month women get mild cramps if they're lucky and worse if they're not. Some women suffer from brain fog and processing goes out the window. It's all a bit overwhelming and trying to swing a golf club when your body has changed isn't much fun. I've witnessed the impact it's had on Kerry when one day she has been swinging and playing well and the next she is struggling to swing or golf at all. The only difference is that her period has arrived. Chloe has some fixes for this which have helped, but the couple of days before are just as challenging, with emotions running high and anxiety sometimes running even higher. Just teeing off on the first hole can be a struggle again.

Men take toilets, or the lack of them, on the golf course for granted. There are bushes or trees dotted around the courses, so there's no problem most of the time. For women golfers, toilets aren't just for relieving themselves. They've got to cope with two to seven days out of every month dealing with tampons and pads with sometimes hourly to four hourly changes. Just one toilet around the halfway mark is all that's needed but you'd be surprised at how many courses we've been to where there aren't any on-course toilets. I made the mistake one time of saying to Kerry, "Can't you just go behind a bush?" without fully realising what was involved in a change. Now I always ask at the starters hut where the toilets are located on any course we're playing.

Men don't have to go through multiple swing changes during their lives. Chloe has talked to Kerry about women having to change their entire swing to incorporate the difference in movement that the changes in hormones make through pregnancy, again after pregnancy, through perimenopause and then finally after the menopause. Four swing changes ... I know men who can't cope with one swing change, me included! Well done, girls!

I've certainly acquired a new-found admiration for women golfers thanks to meeting Kerry and Chloe. Guys are just guys all the time! We're grumpy, we like a moan and we're always tinkering with our swings, not because we have to, but because we feel the need to.

Hector The Tinkerer, take note!

Heart VI: The Magic Of Golfing Together

KEVIN AND KERRY GO LARGE ...

On the golf course, I like to think that I stay silent until spoken to by Kerry and she's confirmed that. When Kerry does ask me something about her swing, I just say to her, "Ask Chloe, she's the professional." Even though I'm a low handicap golfer, I'm not trained to look at someone else's swing and offer advice. Chloe joked with Kerry that she liked me before she'd even met me, because I didn't try and coach Kerry. This approach has also helped us since we've started playing seriously together.

PRESSURE IN PORTUGAL

We made it to Portugal in April 2024 playing three games on the Dom Pedro courses near Vilamoura, spending three days at the beach and enjoying some fantastic meals in the marina every evening, all due to Kerry's hard work with Chloe in getting her game into shape.

Ex-pat Tristan was paired with us on day one and his calm nature helped Kerry acclimatise to playing with a stranger for the first ever time. Kerry then overcame her nerves on the second day when we were paired with a couple from Finland and ended up outdriving them both on the first tee. She really seemed to thrive under pressure and be able to focus intensely. I was bursting with pride.

PARS AT PITLOCHRY

We finally consummated our competition golfing relationship in 2025, more than a thousand days after we met. We played in our first mixed open together, a greensomes tournament at the picturesque Pitlochry Golf Club where the first four holes require an oxygen tank attached to your trolley. Despite this, we parred the first and the eighteenth holes and made some new golfing friends in our partners, Hazel and Tom.

CARNIVAL AT CARNOUSTIE

Foursomes was up next at The Burnside Course at Carnoustie, which had been graced by none other than Ben Hogan during qualifying for the 1953 Open at Carnoustie, which he subsequently won. Incredibly, we finished second at our only second ever tournament and in a forty mile an hour wind and won £70 worth of vouchers. We were off and running.

DISASTER AT DORNOCH

We thought we'd been fortunate to come out in the ballot for Dornoch for their Captain's Mixed Open Foursomes in June. In hindsight, we were unfortunate.

The starter apologised as he handed us the cards. He told us that the heavy overnight rain had washed away a lot of the sand from the bunkers and that the course wasn't what it should be.

For anyone who has played Dornoch, the upturned saucer greens lend themselves to roll offs into the many bunkers surrounding them, so we were likely to be visiting a great number of the hundred or so bunkers strategically placed around the course.

I wasn't wrong. I think we found one every second hole and the rain had indeed washed the sand away, to leave a shot from sodden earth awaiting either Kerry or me. In between downpours, we were putting on and taking off our waterproofs and searching for wet weather gloves at the bottom of our bags. From the glory of coming second at Carnoustie, we came last at Dornoch!

The positive to come out of it, though, was that we never had a cross word between us, were encouraging to each other and we loved sharing the golf course and the views together.

DAZZLING AT DUFF HOUSE ROYAL

I spent my early teenage years living in Banff above a pub, The Castle Bar, which my mum and dad had bought to run together.

The bright spot of my couple of years there was being a junior member at the marvellous Duff House Royal Golf Club which had been redesigned by Alister Mackenzie in 1923. This was before Mackenzie designed three of the world's best courses, Royal Melbourne in Australia (1926), Cypress Point (1928) and then his last, and arguably the most famous, at Augusta National, home of The Masters, in 1933, one year before his premature death in 1934.

I was desperate to take Kerry to the glorious playground where I used to play twice a day as a thirteen-year-old, so I signed us up to play the mixed open there at the end of July 2025. I wanted her to enjoy the setting, the course and the two-tier greens which were the precursor to those that Mackenzie created at Augusta.

We stayed at my Mum's house the night before and my Mum reminded me, in a private moment, that her father had made her play off the first tee situated right in front of the very large floor to ceiling windows of the clubhouse. She shared with me how she was always terrified having to do this and how the experience had nearly put her off playing golf forever.

I pleaded with her that on no account should she let Kerry know about this terrifying first shot as it would only fill Kerry with dread, she'd be a complete bag of nerves and might even worry herself all night about that first shot.

We did manage to keep the ordeal from Kerry and set off on the Sunday morning of the tournament full of optimism.

As we sat down in the clubhouse well ahead of our tee time, I could tell Kerry was nervous because she couldn't eat anything, She was lost in the screen of her phone when she was suddenly torn from it by the announcement over the tannoy calling the next two couples to the tee.

"What was that?" she said.

"The next couples being announced on the tee," I replied quietly, praying she wouldn't take it in.

"What?" she spat out, all colour having drained from her face. "Are you joking? Where do they tee off from?" she asked.

Reluctantly, I had to point to the first tee right in front of the large clubhouse windows.

"There," I said, head down whispering the word, "but it's ok, the ladies tee off from down there," pointing at the ladies' tee which was situated down the hill and a little less in the eyes of the clubhouse.

I looked up to see what Kerry's reaction was to my calming words, but she'd disappeared already. The toilet was calling.

Kerry needn't have worried, though. When the time came for us to be announced on the tee and meet our partners, she thrived under pressure again and smashed her drive right down the middle of the fairway.

Even better was to follow from her as we were finishing our round on the eighteenth hole. I'd pulled the second shot, which had come to rest left of the green right in front of the clubhouse again. I couldn't believe where I'd left it for Kerry to play the next shot from, but with a bit of mind games from me and some dazzling chipping magic from Kerry, she calmly negotiated the bunker and the sloping green to leave the ball defying gravity, holding on for dear life on the top tier of the Mackenzie green.

Not only had I found a golfing goddess, but I'd found a golfing gladiator too!

The Magic Of Golfing Together!

Heart VII: Seeing Magic

As I reflect on the love that I found on the links, it would be remiss of me not to mention the other forms of love on the links I've also come across in my time in St Andrews ...

MAGIC MULTIPLIED

I've seen magic close up on the links on several occasions when I've golfed on The Old Course, playing with visitors, guests and golfers from the singles queue. The look of wonderment on their faces is quite magical as they tee off in front of the R and A Clubhouse, make a par on the first hole, pose on the Swilcan

Bridge and walk down the eighteenth fairway waving to the imaginary crowds.

Putting out on the 18th green moves many to tears and you can multiply the magic by a hundred if they're doing it with their parent or their child, and by a thousand if there's a grandparent in the group too.

LOVE ACTUALLY

If you want to see magic for yourself, then just stand alongside the 18th Green of The Old Course when you arrive in town and share the moments as golfers play into and putt out there. Standing there watching golfers embrace each other always reminds me of the end of the movie '*Love Actually*' where the film captures the love and excitement of people being greeted by loved ones as they walk through the airport arrivals gate. It's truly magical.

THE GIFT OF MAGIC

I recently caddied at The Castle Course for a single golfer from El Paso in the United States, whose wife had just bought him a gift of a round of golf at St Andrews for his birthday.

They'd made the detour here from their main family vacation at Disneyland Paris, as they 'were close by anyway' and it was truly magical watching the golfer, his wife and his two young kids walk, all dressed in matching royal blue hoodies bought a little over an hour before from The Open Shop, walk round the course with their dad as his dream came true on a gloriously calm summers evening in July. The joy on their faces was matched only by the joy on mine as I witnessed love on the links at close quarters.

Heart VIII: The Magic Of Bobby Jones

BOBBY JONES

Bobby Jones came to play the Old Course in the 1921 Open. Playing the par three 11th hole, his tee shot landed in the large bunker to the left of the green and he never came out. Quite literally he could not get out. He picked up his ball and walked in from there, vowing never to return to St Andrews.

He mellowed, though, and came back and won the 1927 Open on The Old Course and, when he was granted the Freedom of the Town in 1953, the great man - who was a lawyer by profession and only ever an amateur golfer - said in his acceptance speech, "I could take out of my life everything except my experiences at St Andrews and I would still have a rich, full life."

Bobby Jones had learned to love The Old Course and The Old Course loved him too, with the 10th hole being re-named after the seven-time major champion following his death in 1971.

Also, in a strange twist of fate, the first letters of the six golf courses in the town itself spell out B JONES... Balgove, Jubilee, Old, New, Eden, Strathtyrum-incredible!

THE BOBBY JONES CUP

His remarkable legacy lives on in many ways. The Robert T. Jones scholarship programme is an exchange programme between Emory University in Atlanta, Georgia, where Jones studied, and St Andrews University. It supports four final year undergraduate students from St Andrews 'for one year of study and life changing experiences' (Source: St Andrews University) and previous scholars have attended The Masters at Augusta. Legend has it that some have even been able to play the legendary course, which was the brainchild of Jones himself.

Bobby Jones is also a former honorary member of The New Golf Club and every year a group of twelve of our members play a team from Ireland for The Bobby Jones Cup, one year in St Andrews and the following year in Ireland. Lifelong friendships have been forged from the matches which are always played very sportingly.

I'll have been fortunate enough to play in four editions by September 2025, two at home over the Jubilee and New courses and two in Ireland, taking in The K Club's North and South courses in 2023 and Headfort and Killeen Castle in 2025. I'll also have the great honour of captaining The New Club's team in 2025 as we try to bring the Cup back over the Irish Sea with us for only the second time.

In 2024, The New Club won in Scotland, but only by 9 ½ to 8 ½ points and we had 'the luck of the Irish' on our side when we were the beneficiaries of the first two holes-in-one in the history of the Cup to overcome their plucky side!

There was a magnificent act of sportsmanship, though, shown by their Captain Diarmuid that Sunday afternoon.

Diarmuid's brother, Caoimhan, had instigated the Cup back in 2007, and Diarmuid had taken over the running of it from him after COVID. Diarmuid's enthusiasm for the match and for building friendships between the teams was infectious, as was his constant banter and reminders to us of his Irish team's winning run. He was passionate about The Bobby Jones Cup and was desperate to win it every year.

His opposing captain for 2024 was Locky, whose wife Isla was undergoing treatment for cancer at the time. On Sunday Singles Day, Locky was playing Diarmuid in the traditional Captain's Match, when he received a call on the fifth hole from Isla saying that she'd had a relapse and could he come quickly. Locky departed quickly, but not before Diarmuid had immediately made it clear that their match would be declared a half and not a win for the Irish team because Locky couldn't finish the match. Sportsmanship at its best.

That half point made all the difference to the final close result, with a drawn match at 9 vs. 9, meaning the Irish team would have retained the Cup and taken it back home with them. Diarmuid graciously said that he would have done the same again as he handed the trophy over to Locky, who'd come back after Isla had stabilised and insisted Locky return to the presentation meal.

The Magic of Bobby Jones and his Cup. I'm sure he would have loved it!

Heart IX: The Magic Of Friendship

Although I may not go on cinema dates with my friends from the links, I definitely look forward to our play dates together.

Whether it's Wham! Matches, Tuesday Golf Matches or games with the Monday or Wednesday Fellowship groups, there's never a dull moment. Golf also allowed me to reunite with University pals (Aberdeen Uni Casuals) and my football teammates (Kinross Legends) after many years apart . Golf with all of these groups is as close to the dressing room banter I used to enjoy when I played football, before a bad knee injury and a distinct lack of talent ended my undistinguished amateur career at the age of just thirty-five.

Friends willing your ball to stay out of the hole in close matches, ribbing you when you top a tee shot, keeping you going when you aren't having a good day or just someone to talk to about life matters.

During COVID in particular, when we were restricted in Scotland to just playing in two balls, these games developed relationships and cemented friendships with the banter and competitiveness of the games helping a lot of people get through some dark times. A birdie, birdie finish by me on the Jubilee course which allowed me to beat Iain, a Fellowship stalwart, by one hole was definitely a highlight from that time… for me anyway if not for Iain! He still mentions that 'smash and grab' in dispatches years later…sorry Iain!

'Holiday Ronnie' became a great friend, with his wife Linda, a former HR professional, providing great support for me with an employer issue I was to have further down the line. Others would always have a cheeky quip in the Clubhouse to keep everyone's spirits up and these interactions saved my sanity during some long, lonely days. Some would sometimes take it just too far. Jimmy C, a lifelong Glasgow Rangers fan, knew I was an Aberdeen fan and turned up one morning wearing a winter bonnet stuffed with the headlines from that morning's local sports newspaper of *Darvel 1, Drivel 0*, in reference to Aberdeen Football Club's Scottish Cup exit the night before to the part time team. Ten out of ten for creativity, though, JC. Interactions like that are the oxygen for banter and friendship.

I'm still carefully plotting my retribution!

Heart X: For The Love Of The Game

Love is a many splendored thing and comes in many forms. Whether it's playing with your other half, your parents, your children, your grandparents, your grandkids, your friends or your teammates, this game of golf we love just keeps on delivering.

It's said that golf mirrors life and if that's true then we should be mostly surrounded by great people.

Let's toast those people who introduced us to the game, those who support us and those we play with and against …

"To Golf and To Finding Love on The Links … in whatever form that takes!"

THE POSITIVE GOLFER
Part II

CHAPTER 12: LOST MY JOB, FOUND MY CHIPPING

YOU'RE FIRED!

On the 17th of December 2024, just four days before the festive holidays, I received an email from my employer terminating my employment with immediate effect. I'd been fired!

Do not pass Go. Do not collect your Salary. Go straight to Mental Hell.

It was a debilitating feeling. One minute I was helping clients with the biggest decisions of their lives, buying or selling their homes, the next I was left wondering if I'd be able to afford to keep my own home!

Despite having a signed contract with a three-month termination clause in it, my December salary and the three months' notice payment both went unpaid. There are employment laws in place in the UK to protect employees from this type of behaviour, but it would take time to get proper recourse. A long time! More on that later.

That Christmas period was not a merry one. I was there in body but not really in mind. I was constantly worrying about what I needed to do next to try and get the monies due to me.

I 'celebrated' it in Ellon at my Mum's house and then travelled to Edinburgh to spend my birthday with Kerry and our mums. Traditionally, Kerry and I would go to a show at The Playhouse Theatre in Edinburgh with our mums. That year it was 'Joseph and the Amazing Technicolour Dreamcoat'.

After sitting through the show, Joseph got it in the neck from me. Not face to face, but from me as a critic to Kerry and her mum. Looking back, I don't think the show was really that bad - audiences around the world have flocked to see it, after all -- but I was tense and on edge and my mind was elsewhere. In fact, I could have done with borrowing Joseph's amazing coat after the show to see what the future held for me.

On reflection, my workplace had been taking its toll on me well before December. What was supposed to be a three or four day a week job had become much more than that. I had been signed off by my doctor at the start of September 2024 for four weeks with work related stress. This was the first time in my life I'd ever had to take any time off work.

Never a slacker, I was back at work within three weeks, refreshed and rejuvenated, with assurances from my employer that things had changed.

They hadn't ... in fact, they just got worse.

Anytime I travelled to Edinburgh to see Kerry, I would offload my issues with the management of the company on her, we rarely golfed together anymore, and our previously strong relationship showed real signs of cracking. Kerry shared with me later that she wondered whether we would survive that time. How sad that a workplace could have the potential to break our bond.

I was deeply despondent, stressed, and had no work-life balance;

my golf, my health and my mental state were all deteriorating rapidly.

There was no way, though, I could have predicted just how much my employer's decision would positively impact on my happiness and on my golf game in 2025.

FOUND MY CHIPPING

Thankfully in the short term I had 'The House of Golf' and then caddying to supplement my income, so I was able to get back onto the golf course regularly again in early 2025.

I was even able to regard my employer's early Christmas 'present' as a godsend. I had my freedom, was back in control of my life, had a calmness about me and I was happy! With no drama or rollercoaster of emotions caused by my former employer, a stress-free Kevin was in a much better place again.

I resumed my competitive games with Hector The Tinkerer and Big Ian. Colin The Metronome was unfortunately out of action due to a knee replacement operation, but three handicap Keith stepped in as an able substitute for our regular weekly game and the Tuesday golf WhatsApp group was born!

In late January, Hector, ever the tinkerer, had received some chipping lessons and he wanted to pass on the benefit of these to me during a match on the Old Course. He'd tried to help before in the past and I'd always switched off, resigned to the fact that my chipping would always be poor due to my chipping yips. However, this time something seemed to click in my head; maybe I was now in a better state of mind?

Whatever it was, I went to the range to practice Hector's new technique. It seemed to work consistently. I started chipping to thirty yards away, to twenty yards, ten yards and then five yards. They all seemed to work. Wonders would never cease! However, the proof would be out on the course. There had been so many false dawns before. Great hopes after great practice, only for them all to be dashed with the very first chip on the course. My confidence destroyed and back to square one.

Not this time though. It seemed to be different. This was working!!

We had a rematch the following week and my chipping was stellar, even drawing praise from Hector, which was a first for me. Something was stirring. I was now looking forward to chipping. It was magic and the race to scratch and beyond was back on!

UPGRADING MY MINDSET

Around the same time as my chipping epiphany, I bought a book called *'The Expectation Effect'* by David Robson, which had been recommended to me by Tuesday Keith. Although not a golf-specific book, it discusses the power of the mind as a prediction machine and gives numerous examples of affirmative thinking and autosuggestion.

Having read just a few chapters of it, I decided to introduce some of its ideas on and off the golf course.

Every morning, I said to myself ten times in the mirror, "I'm a plus handicap player."

On the golf course as I surveyed my shot, I said to myself, "What would a plus handicap player do here?"

Right before playing my shot, I recited to myself, "I'm a plus handicap player."

It started to work wonders immediately and on Valentines Day, no less.

Kerry and I had decided to spend the day playing golf together at Kings Acre where she was a member. I'd woken up and spent a few minutes looking in the bathroom mirror chanting to myself, "I am a plus handicap player." Kerry walked past the closed door and asked if everything was ok? I hoped it would be.

Chipping on the first hole to a slightly elevated green I said to myself, "What would a plus handicap player do here?" My answer was, "They would chip it in."

I stood over the uphill chip with the pin lurking just five yards over the brow of the hill and said to myself, "I am a plus handicap player." I took the wedge back and connected beautifully. It went up in the air, bounced, rolled and dropped in the hole for a birdie three with The Golfing Gods and Kerry being my witnesses. The Prediction Machine was at work, and I wondered where it could take me.

From Valentines Day through to the 12th of March, a total of twenty-seven days, I played nineteen times with this new upgraded mindset but only achieved a handicap cut of 0.1 from 3.2 to 3.1.Those rounds contained nothing spectacular and included a very poor round in the Monday Fellowship of twenty-six Stableford points.

Then came the most amazing twelve-day period which I can only put down to my upgraded mindset having bedded in.

THREE TO SCRATCH IN TWELVE DAYS!

My Scores ...
- 13th March Thistle Medal Jubilee Bronze: Score 68 /Par 69, 3.1 cut to 2.4
- 15th March NGC Stableford New Course: Score 38 points, 2.4 cut to 2.1
- 20th March NGC Medal New Course: Score 69/Par 71, 2.1 cut to 1.2
- 25th March General Play Old Course: Score 68/Par 72 , 1.2 cut to 0.2

I FINALLY GET TO SCRATCH

I treated that day like a medal. I went to the driving range first and hit sixty balls. I hit my sixty first ball off the first tee of the Old

Course, where I was playing with Big Ian and Tuesday Keith. I was in good form, and I'd decided to put in a General Play Score. What a decision that turned out to be!

I knew I was onto a good thing when I was three under par at the turn, into a two-club wind which was unusual for the front nine of the Old Course. I kept reminding myself to focus on the process and not the outcome and kept going through my routine.

I left two putts short on the tenth and eleventh greens for birdies and was caught between clubs on the thirteenth where I ended up with a bogey. A birdie followed on the par five fourteenth and that was followed by an outrageous birdie on the eighteenth green where I received a rapturous round of applause from the watching throngs who were gathered round the green on that beautiful sunny day. The Golfing Gods had delivered an audience for me as I got to scratch.

A HANDSHAKE FROM HEAVEN

The next day, my handicap was updated on the New Golf Club's list of handicaps online. I was a scratch golfer. The date was 26th March 2025. It was the anniversary of my Dad's passing thirty-one years before!

I'd reminded my mum and brother of the anniversary the night before and my mum had texted back to say, "He would have been very proud of your golfing achievement and perhaps he'd have shaken your hand as you came off the 18th green."

My first touchpoint with St Andrews was with my Dad in 1984 for Seve's Open at The Old Course. Seve made a twelve foot right to left birdie putt on the 18th green on the Sunday to claim the Claret Jug. Incredibly, I'd ended up raking in a twelve foot right to left birdie putt on the 18th green to be listed as a scratch golfer on the anniversary of my Dad's death!

There had been no fist pump from me, but I did acknowledge

the applause from all sides of the green from the fifty or so people who were gathered there and received warm handshakes from my playing partners, Big Ian and Tuesday Keith, and perhaps that handshake from heaven from my Dad. What a moment and what a place to do it ... right there on The Old Course.

From the lowest of lows at the start of the year, I was now in a state of well-being again. The Magic of Golf and The Magic in St Andrews had delivered their own version of therapy to heal my wounded mind.

The Positive Golfer was back!

MY GOLD MEDAL GOAL

Having made it to scratch, my competitive nature now wanted more.

One of my most cherished goals was to play the Old Course on a Sunday. It was a big deal because the Old Course is normally closed on a Sunday to let the people of the town enjoy it as a public park. Dogs roam across the fabled links, small children play in bunkers and families picnic on the 18th fairway.

In a non-Open year there are only four Sundays when the Old Course is available to play on: The Dunhill Links for professional golfers, The St Rule Trophy for female amateurs, the Links Trophy for male amateurs ... and The Gold Medal.

The Gold Medal is played over The Old Course on a Sunday in the middle of May. Entry is open to all St Andrews golfers with a handicap of less than three, but only the top sixty lowest handicap players get to tee it up on the first hole. Last year's handicap cut off plus one, meaning that anyone at plus 0.9 and below was placed on the reserve list. It was unlikely to change much that year, so I knew what I needed to do. It was a tall order as I only had two medal rounds to do it, but with my new upgraded mindset and chipping technique, I was ready for the challenge.

GOING FOR GOLD

My Round One: Thursday 3rd April. Monthly Medal (Eden Course), Handicap 0.2.

I woke up early, nervous for my date with destiny. As I walked through the driving range to do my final prep, I saw a message on one of the walls of the teaching booths saying, 'Write Your Own History'. I was yearning to do just that.

Playing well, I was one over par and about to play the fifteenth hole. The closing four holes were all into the wind so this would be a challenge to try and finish level par for them. Finishing level par for them would mean a gross 71, my handicap would be cut from 0.2 to +0.2 and I would be a plus handicap player. I would be within touching distance of playing The Old Course on a Sunday. I had this.

Bugger! Three putt bogey on fifteen! Where had that come from?

I parred the par five sixteenth and negotiated the difficult drive into the wind at the seventeenth, staying well clear of the out of bounds up the right side and landing ten feet short of the first fairway bunker. That was the hard part done ... or so I thought. I should have let my brain slumber!

I hit my three wood well into the wind but the ball cut low and bounced to the back of the green, settling sixty feet from the pin. I had a wicked downhill putt which broke right to left and there was also the bunker on the right which was catching my eyeline.

I had this. Two putts and a par down the last and I would be cut to 0.0 exactly and I still had one round to shoot a gross 65 and get to plus one.

Just eat the elephant in small chunks, Kev.

DAMN THAT ELEPHANT!

If I could have got in a time machine and taken that sixty-foot putt again, I would have paid quite a lot of money for that time machine.

Maybe not quite as much as I paid for my Masters Tickets back in 2003, but certainly a tidy sum. I didn't want to buy the time machine; I just wanted to rent it for two minutes at most!

That's how long it took for me to sclaff the putt forty feet, not even making it down the hill.

"I could still three putt from where I ended up," I said to myself.

Where had that negative thought come from? Where was the positive golfer? Where had the sclaff putt come from? I could only think that The Negative Golfing Gods had got wind of my opportunity and were throwing everything they could at me to try and mess with my big moment.

I putted nicely up to the hole, leaving a nine-inch putt for bogey. I went through my routine just as I'd been doing all day, lined it up, looked at the hole, back at the ball and rolled the putt. It slammed left on me and missed ... I had four putted!

I was reeling. I was now four over par and my score would be a non-counter. Wow, all that hard work undone in two crazy minutes with two crazy putts!

No one said it would be easy. Next time I would do better, I vowed.

ALWAYS RESPECT THE GOLFING GODS

I woke up still thinking about things, but I was more contemplative now.

My upgraded mindset had been tested, and it hadn't passed the test at the crucial moment when a slumbering brain and a rock-solid routine was required. Level par, though, in Round Two on Saturday 12th April would get me to plus 0.3, with anything better being a bonus.

I wondered what The Golfing Gods had in store for me. Maybe a certain Golfing God called Scratch had been mulling over the fact that I'd previously been desperate to get into their team, striving to go from ten to scratch in ten months, and that I'd narrowly missed out.

Maybe Scratch was miffed that I wasn't celebrating more, having finally made it into their team and even more miffed that I wanted to leave their team so quickly for Plus's team.

Maybe Scratch had sent one of their deputies to dance around on the 17th green the day before waving their hands and making mincemeat of my brain?

I hoped I hadn't made an enemy of The Scratch God on the Links the day before but only time would tell!

CHAPTER 13: INTRODUCING THE GOLFING GODS

A TUG OF WAR.

Where The Golfing Gods hang out in St Andrews, a tug of war was developing between two of them. At least, in my head it was!

Scratch and Plus were debating who wanted or didn't want me.

"I don't want him, you have him," said Scratch. "He's only been in my team for just over a week and he wants out already. He's an ungrateful so and so!"

"Well, I don't want him," said Plus. "He was in the Under Five team at 3.1 handicap less than a month ago. It's too soon for him to join my team. He's not ready yet."

Scratch interjected, "I already messed with his head on Thursday when it looked like he was going to leave my team. He'd pieced together this great round in tricky conditions with a two-club wind on The Eden Course. He was standing on the 15th one over par and if he'd finished level par to the finish he'd have joined your lot. So, Wind and I tricked up the course and changed the prevailing wind direction, so that the last four holes were into the wind and provided the toughest test that the Eden can deliver. We wanted to see what he was made of."

"Why was I not aware of this?" said Plus.

"Because Wind and I didn't think you needed to know. He wasn't in your team yet and he'd only been a member of mine for less than a week. You'd said that you only wanted to be kept informed of prospective plus players. This guy flew under my radar. He came down from three to scratch in twelve days."

"Twelve Days?! How is that even possible?" said Plus.

"The new handicap system has made it possible, Plus. We discussed this at the time when the powers that be on earth were putting it together. It's possible, just not probable," sighed Scratch.

"Well, what's he doing differently? Has he been taking lessons over the winter?"

"No."

"Has he been playing more?"

"Yes … he lost his job, and he's had time on his hands, and he's used it well. The last count shows that he's played sixty days since the start of the year."

"But it's only the 6th of April. There's only been ninety-five days of this year so far."

" … And he didn't start playing this year until 15th January because of the Cold Snap we sent to St Andrews."

"So that's sixty out of eighty days, then! Seventy-five per cent of the time, three times every four days, almost six times a week?"

"Yes, that's right," said Scratch.

"He needs to get a job!"

"We've arranged that, Plus. He's got an interview next Tuesday."

"Ok, well, at least that's something."

"But in the meantime, he's due to play another seven times before then, the last of which is in a medal when he could get down to plus and into your team."

"I see ... but he's played a lot before, hasn't he? I checked the records this morning."

"Yes, he came down from 10 to 1.5 in ten months and was within two weeks of getting to scratch and into my team in the middle of May 2021, but he got in the way of himself and started looking at the outcome rather than just focusing on the process. He was on my radar then, but he didn't have what it takes back then. He has a history of sailing close but crashing and burning!"

"Bit harsh, Scratch, but I can see why you didn't alert me then. But he's made it into your team now so he must be doing something right?"

"Well, he has been reading 'The Expectation Effect' over the last month or so."

"That's not a golf book though, is it?"

"No, but it's a mind book and he appears to have taken what's been written and tweaked it to his own golf game. He calls himself The Positive Golfer too!" said Scratch.

"It's about game improvement in the end, though, Scratch. That's why we invented the game remember. And this guy wants to improve, doesn't he?"

"Yes, I suppose he does, Plus," Scratch grudgingly replied.

"Is he ready to join my elite team then?" asked Plus.

"I'm not sure, Plus."

"Well, let's wait and see. But I like the sound of him more and more. When's this medal?"

"Next Saturday. We've already put Brian The Putt Reader with him. That'll test him!"

"Ok, Scratch, organise a Watch Party. Get everyone together and let's see what The Positive Golfer can do."

"But it's The Masters next weekend, Plus."

"Not until the afternoon, Scratch. Kevin and Brian are teeing off at 08:48. That's plenty of time before The Masters comes on."

"Yes of course it is, Plus. I wasn't thinking. We can watch them on the Eden and then watch The Masters later."

"Ok, so that's sorted, then, Scratch. Watch Party for next Saturday morning. Usual Place. See you then."

And with that they were gone from my head as quickly as they'd arrived in it.

FRIDAY 11TH APRIL 2025, MORNING

"Have you got that Watch Party organised ok for The Eden tomorrow, Scratch?" said Plus as they passed each other.

"Yes, Plus, it's an all-dayer with the third round of The Masters right after it. All the troops are excited. It's been a while since we've had an all-dayer. By the way, what did 'The Triumvirate' do to Rory McIlroy yesterday? He was going along so well, I thought this was going to be his year!"

"It might still be, Scratch. They just wanted to see if he really is ready to make the step up now to take his place in golfing immortality as a Career Grand Slam golfer."

The Career Grand Slam is where a golfer has won all four majors, the US Open, The Open, The US PGA and The Masters - Rory was one short going into 2025, having not yet won The Masters."

Plus continued, "Unfocused did a great job on the 15th and 17th holes to test Rory, and as we know you need Patience around Augusta. In fact, Kevin will need Patience tomorrow on The Eden too if he wants to achieve his goal, so tomorrow should be a good watch."

"Not quite the same is it, though?" piped in Slice, who was passing and had overheard their conversation. "Rory getting the

Career Grand Slam and Kevin getting to plus handicap?"

"It is, Slice. They're both striving to achieve their Golfing Goals, which is always great theatre to watch. Different levels, yes, but same outcome. This weekend Kevin and Rory and so many other golfers will be joined by that same desire. Anyway, haven't you got someone's swing to be playing with, Slice?"

"That's if Rory gets through today," Scratch popped in.

"We'll see what he's made of then, won't we. It should be a fun day today. Make best friends with Pressure and Patience and what will be will be ... and by the way I already know what happens this weekend. You're going to love it!" Plus replied.

EVENING

Plus passed by Scratch ...

"We sent Lady Luck out to Rory on the 12th and 13th holes today, Scar Tissue was following him on the 15th and 17th, but Focus was with him all the way round."

(Rory carded a second round 66 after his first round 72.)

"It was some round. I can't wait for this weekend. See you at the Eden Watch Party tomorrow morning – 8:48 tee off," Scratch replied.

"Remember I know what happens," said Plus, with a knowing wink.

SATURDAY 12TH APRIL 2025

My Round Two: Monthly Medal (Eden Course), Handicap 0.2

I'd reached the turn in one under par and got up and down on the eleventh with some stellar chipping for a par. Plus handicap was on. I'd played good golf in no wind and was just seven holes away from achieving my goal.

However, some dodgy chipping, a three putt and some poor

course management followed, leaving me four over par after seventeen holes and my plus handicap dream in tatters. Not even an outrageous birdie on the 18th helped salvage my gold medal goal. It was over for another year. I was staying in Scratch's team for a little while longer ... It wasn't a bad place to be.

MY ROUND THROUGH THE EYES OF THE GOLFING GODS

"He's joining your team, isn't he?" said Scratch to Plus, just after my chip from behind the 11th hole. "That was a great recovery and one befitting a plus player."

Plus said nothing.

"Oh!" said Scratch as Duff, Distracted and Unfocused made their way back to the Watch Party from the 12th Hole where they'd all toyed with me.

"Good work, guys," said Plus. "I wanted to see if he could deal with you, and he didn't. I'm not sure he's ready yet."

Careless was sent on next at the 14th and then again at the 16th. It was a double blow and Scratch looked round to see a wry smile come across Plus's face.

"He's not ready yet. Two mental errors cost him when he should have stepped away and reassessed the situation. That's what players in my team do," said Plus, "but I think he has it in him to learn and come back better. He's not a bad person to have in your team for a little longer, Scratch, and I think he'll respect you too. Hey, we can't blame him for having a goal and trying to get there quickly, can we? He's going to have to serve his apprenticeship with you. It just remains to be seen for how long."

At that, they both sat bolt upright as my birdie bomb dropped in on the 18th green.

"Maybe not for that long after that finish," said Scratch. "I'm beginning to like the guy! Now for Rory's Watch Party. Let's see if he's ready to grab his Golfing Goal this weekend.'

Plus's wry smile appeared again. "One dream down this weekend, one to go, Scratch"

COME ON RORY!

I settled down at The House of Golf for my Saturday evening's viewing of The Masters just in time to see one of my previous house guests in Scottie Scheffler's group. Hugo Dobson was caddying for Scheffler's partner, Tyrell Hatton.

Would the Magic in St Andrews which Hugo and Tyrell had enjoyed six months before at the Dunhill Links Championship travel across the pond? What a story that would be! I suddenly had someone else to cheer for this evening.

What another fantastic round from Rory in that third round! His electrifying history-making start of six threes was exhilarating for everyone watching, but I'm sure it had all his doubters wondering when he was going to implode. His 'wobble' came in the middle of the round - if you can call a bogey, par, bogey on holes 8, 9 and 10 a wobble - after three birdies and an eagle. Two Negatives thrown in against five Positives. That wasn't even balancing the books. Rory grabbed four more Positives on the back 9 with two birdies and another eagle.

To lead at the end of the third round, albeit just by two shots from Bryson, after Bryson's own birdie bomb at the eighteenth, would have been a place Rory would have loved to be at the start of the week. I was sure he would have a date with a certain Bob Rotella the next morning to check his mindset and get him ready for the rollercoaster of Masters Sunday.

Was Rory ready to become a Grand Slam Career Winner? To become only the sixth person in history at the age of thirty-five and eleven long years after winning his last major. With seemingly the whole world aware of the significance of what a win meant, I hoped so, but it was in the lap of The Golfing Gods now.

RORY'S DATE WITH DESTINY
SUNDAY 13TH APRIL 2025

Rory's great pal Tiger Woods had won his first Masters on this same date back in 1997, winning by twelve shots. Rory was nearly six years old at the time. Bryson DeChambeau was three and a half years old.

Everything was set as I sat down to watch. All signs led back to Rory winning. It was written in the stars. Or was it?!

THE GOLFING GODS PLAY THEIR JOKERS ON RORY

The Positive and the Negative Golfing Gods were all watching too, ready to play their jokers during the final round. I noted them down as I watched, with the negative ones in italics and the positive ones in bold. It made for interesting reading…

Hole 1. *Double Bogey 6*	Hole 2. **Par 5**	Hole 3. **Birdie 3**
Adrenaline	*Adrenaline*	*Pressure*
Pressure	*Pressure*	*Nerves*
Nerves	*Nerves*	**One-Putt**
Bunker	*Bunker*	**Birdie**
Hesitation	*Unlucky*	
Uncertainty	*Fat-shot*	
Double Bogey	**Reset**	
Three-Putt	**Focus**	
	Two-Putt	

Hole 4. **Birdie 2**	Hole 5. **Par 4**	Hole 6. **Par 3**
Pressure	*Pressure*	*Pressure*
Nerves	*Nerves*	*Nerves*
One-Putt	*Slice*	**Courage**
Birdie	*Trees*	
	Up & Down	
	One-Putt	

Hole 7. **Par 4**	Hole 8. **Par 5**	Hole 9. **Birdie 3**
Pressure	*Pressure*	*Pressure*
Nerves	*Nerves*	*Nerves*
Hook	*Mishit*	**One-Putt**
Trees	*Slice*	**Birdie**
Confidence	*Bunker*	
Magic		
Genius		

Hole 10. **Birdie 3**	Hole 11. *Bogey-5*	Hole 12. **Par-3**
Scar Tissue	*Pressure*	*Adrenaline*
Adrenaline	*Nerves*	*Pressure*
Pressure	*Gung-Ho*	*Nerves*
Nerves	*Mishit*	**Focus**
Focus	*Bogey*	**Concentration**
Concentration		
Lucky		
One-Putt		
Birdie		

Hole 13 *Double Bogey 7*	Hole 14. *Bogey-5*	**Hole 15. Birdie-4**
Nerves	Nausea	Scar Tissue
Pressure	Adrenaline	Severe Pressure
Lapse in Concentration	Nerves	Nerves
Lack of Focus	Severe Pressure	**Re-Focus**
Distracted	Slice	**Magical**
Duff	Clumsy	**Carpe Diem**
Double Bogey	Bogey	**Shot of a Lifetime**
		Tentative
		Birdie
Hole 16. **Par-3**	Hole 17. **Birdie-3**	Hole 18. *Bogey-5*
Adrenaline	Scar Tissue	Adrenaline
Nerves	Adrenaline	Nerves
Severe Pressure	Nerves	Severe Pressure
Courage	Severe Pressure	Delay
Carpe Diem	**Courage**	Fear
	Carpe Diem	Lapse in Concentration
	Shot of a Lifetime	Bunker
	One-Putt	Tentative
	Birdie	
1st Play Off Hole.	**1st Play Off Hole**	Birdie-3
Negatives	**Positives**	
Nausea	**Reset**	**Destiny**
Fear	**Courage**	**Trumps**
Self-Loathing	**Shot of a Lifetime**	**Everything.**
Adrenaline	**Carpe Diem**	
Nerves	**One-Putt**	
Severe Pressure	**Birdie**	

What unfolded that evening was true golfing theatre, the likes of which I'd never witnessed before in all my years of watching The Masters.

Rory was like a boxer on the ropes who just kept coming back for more. Every time I thought he was down and out, Rory got back up as the count to ten reached seven and he kept throwing punches.

I felt sick to my stomach at the 13th hole when Rory dumped his ball into Rae's Creek. I gasped in awe at his second shot at 15. Rory had got back off the floor again and looked a certainty to knock out the field, once and for all.

Immortality beckoned from inside the Butler Cabin, but Rory was caught by a sucker punch at the 18th green. I held my breath as he tried to make the putt that would have him slipping on The Green Jacket for the first time and becoming a Grand Slam Winner. The Golfing Gods had other ideas, though.

Rory had once again seemingly grabbed defeat from the jaws of victory. It would only be made a little easier for me to take because it was going to be the affable Englishman, Justin Rose, who was going to win The Masters for the first time, having been denied in a play-off before by Sergio Garcia in 2017.

If Rory was to capture both the Green Jacket and The Grand Slam he would have to show true fighting spirit. 'The Triumvirate' wanted to see what Rory was made of. He'd been working out physically for a long time now but maybe they wanted to see if he had been working out mentally too.

DIAMONDS ARE FOREVER

Rory looked a broken man, shoulders slumped as he made his way off the 18th green to the golf cart to take him back to the 18th tee for his showdown with Rose, his friend and Ryder Cup team teammate.

It took some wise words on the golf cart from another friend, his much-maligned caddie Harry Diamond, to jolt Rory from his despair.

"Well, pal, we would have taken this opportunity at the start of the tournament," said Harry, with Rory crediting Harry's words helping him to reframe the situation and put matters into perspective brilliantly. It was the positive reset Rory required from someone who had been with him all his golfing life.

The golfing world watched as Rory summoned up the inner strength to dig deep and play his second shot after Justin's ball had disappeared over the brow of the green landing, for all Rory knew, very close to the hole.

Undeterred, Rory played the shot of his life and his ball landed on the green and rolled closer to the hole than Rose's ball.

Justin was to putt first. It was a classic match play situation with a Green Jacket on the line for Justin and golfing immortality on the line for Rory. If Justin holed it, surely Rory couldn't miss his? Justin prowled round the hole, sizing his ten-foot putt from every angle. Rory couldn't look up, lost in his thoughts.

Finally, Justin was ready to putt. He tucked his left sleeve into his left armpit. He squared his shoulders, and he rolled the putt at a fantastic pace. His naughty golf ball had a quick look left at the hole but decided not to grant Justin his dreams yet… rolling less than a foot past the cup. Justin put his right hand over his mouth, mouthing something at the hole or his ball or both.

Now it was Rory's turn - from two feet - he couldn't miss, could he?

He lined up. I held my breath; The World held its breath; The Golfing Gods at their Watch Party held their breath. Only Plus was breathing normally.

Rory holed his putt and fell to his knees sobbing uncontrollably. Everything Had Led To This.

Rory got up from his knees just as Harry was replacing the flag in the hole. They embraced for what seemed to be an eternity; all the emotions, all the scar tissue and all their friendship were woven into that moment. A still emotional Rory embraced a crushed but equally delighted Justin Rose.

The crowd around the 18th green chanted, "Rory, Rory, Rory!"

The Golfing Gods at the Watch Party chanted, "Rory, Rory, Rory!"

Scratch turned to see Plus chanting, "Rory, Rory, Rory!"

Plus looked at Scratch, wiping a tear from his eye, "I told you you'd love it."

At his press conference after the presentation, Rory, wearing his Green Jacket shared his inner thoughts …

"I started to wonder if I was ever going to win it. I was really nervous going out and the double bogey settled me!"

A double bogey which was sent to test him had settled him! Wow! He had four double bogeys in the tournament and was the first Masters Champion to do that. He'd just never given up in the pursuit of his dream.

What a great champion!

WHAM! BAM! … OUR SUPERHERO BEATS THE DOUBTERS

"That's what Great Champions don't do," said golf analyst Paul McGinley on Sky Sports Golf's coverage on the Thursday evening, referring to Rory's double bogey at the fifteenth hole on Day One. I'm sure he wasn't the only one whose comments have been captured for posterity and may even have been used by Rory as brain fodder to push him on that weekend.

Great Champions recover from moments like that, and the one which followed two holes later at the 17th when Rory took another double bogey. Great Champions forget and reset. Great Champions have great mental strength. Great Champions write their own history.

Rory McIlroy was a Great Champion, and I couldn't wait to come face to face with him one day for him to sign my Masters flag.

As I went to bed exhausted, I wondered when that day might come and what number signature he would be.

CHAPTER 14: IN PURSUIT OF RORY

HAPPY BIRTHDAY FUTURE KEV.

Kerry had given me an envelope for my 56th birthday in December 2024. Inside the envelope was an itinerary for July 2025 for Future Kev to enjoy with Future Kerry.

Wednesday 9th: a day trip to the Scottish Open Pro-Am and a stay at a beautiful apartment in Berwick- upon- Tweed in a house with a big copper bath in the bedroom.

Thursday: Play Goswick Golf Course together

Friday: Play Eyemouth Golf Course together

I wasn't to know when I opened my envelope, that Kerry's present to me would give Future Kev a chance of securing Signature Nineteen on my Masters flag.

THE SCOTTISH OPEN

I'd packed my Masters flag ahead of our trip and we set off from Kerry's place for The Renaissance Club. An hour later, we were having our tickets scanned and getting ready to watch some golf.

The only Masters Champion who was playing that year and who

hadn't signed my flag was the most recent one.

Rory was teeing off on the first hole at 8am, but as luck would have it he was the only player who was playing all eighteen holes of the pro-am and he was due to start the back nine at 10:25. We asked a steward if Rory was still on the course and he confirmed that he was somewhere around the twelfth hole.

Kerry, as ever a willing and enthusiastic participant, was happy to head out that way to see if we could join his group and get his signature on my flag. We walked the length of the eighteenth hole, round the back of the seventeenth, and headed towards the sixteenth green. Aaron Rai was just finishing putting there and, as he came off the green, he stopped to sign some flags at the walkway to the seventeenth tee. This would be the perfect spot to see Rory and try and get my flag signed.

WAITING FOR RORY

We could sense Rory was coming over the hill on the sixteenth before we saw him. A ball landed further down the fairway than any had landed before. That must be Rory's ball. The crowds coming over the hill were different too, more people, more buzz.

Rory looked immaculate in grey trousers and matching grey jumper. People joined us at the corner of the ropes where we'd been standing for a good forty minutes now. We had our own little spot either side of the long metal rope peg, so we had both sides of the rope covered. Kerry was good at this.

Adults and children alike got out yellow Masters flags ready for Rory to sign -pristine new 2025 Masters flags, unsigned so far. I was almost reluctant to take my heavily signed 2001 flag from its hiding place in my rucksack, withdrawing it from its protective sheath and testing my thick black sharpie. It was working. Everything was ready, everything had led to this!

Rory hit an exquisite chip onto the green from fifty yards.

We were ready, but were interrupted by Rory's legendary security man, nicknamed "The Ginger Ninja' on social media. Everywhere Rory went, GN was always just a few steps away, backpack on, and here on sixteen GN walked ahead of Rory as he was getting ready to make his birdie putt and stopped to wait for him.

He could see the throng of Masters flags waiting to be signed, and to his credit he announced that Rory had been asked to move things along by the tournament organisers and wouldn't be stopping to sign anything here. Rory had to make up the time and move on to the 17th hole, but he would be signing everything he could at the end.

I asked GN to clarify if that meant 'everyone', and he replied that was Rory's intention, although he wasn't sure how Rory would be able to make good on that promise if everyone converged behind the 18th green.

I knew what I wanted to do and where I wanted to go, but we hadn't really seen much golf or much else of the course and we'd been standing at this one spot for quite some time by then. I looked at Kerry.

"We need to be only one place now!" she exclaimed. "Let's get to the eighteenth green and get that nineteenth signature on your flag!"

I was one lucky guy!

****

SIGNATURES 17 AND 18

These had both been secured back in 2022.

Ian Woosnam, the 1991 Masters Champion, was Signature 17 at the British Seniors Open at Gleneagles and Danny Willett, who capitalised on Jordan Spieth's capitulation at Amen Corner at the 2016 Masters, added the 18th signature to my flag at the Alfred

Dunhill Links Championship in St Andrews on an October Sunday afternoon beside the 14th tee snack bar where I was marshalling.

The Dunhill is the DP World Tour's wonderful version of the pro-cel-am tournament which is held at Pebble Beach each year. Stars of stage, screen and sport descend onto the fairways and watering holes of St Andrews for a week of fun for them and a week of celeb spotting and selfies for fans. Hector The Tinkerer is in his element!

In 2025, the tournament will be graced with major champions Brooks Koepka, Cam Smith, Louis Oosthuizen, Martin Kaymer, Padraig Harrington and Matt Fitzpatrick along with European Ryder Cup stars Tyrell Hatton, Tommy Fleetwood and Scotland's own Bob MacIntyre.

Past Masters Champions Dustin Johnson, Patrick Reed and Danny Willet will be there along with Gerry Lester Watson Jr, otherwise known as Bubba Watson, a two-time Masters champion in 2012 and 2014. Bubba doesn't come across to these shores very often so his signature would be a nice one to get on my Masters flag.

So would Rory's, though!

The opportunity has arisen before when I was at that 14th tee at the 2022 Dunhill. Rory was playing with his Dad, Gerry, and they were stood just two yards away from me for ten minutes as they waited for the group ahead to play their second shots. My Masters flag remained firmly in my rucksack, though, with Future Kev giving me no heads up whatsoever of what was to happen at Augusta in April 2025.

No Masters win, no signing of the Masters flag … those were the rules, and they had to be followed, regardless of the fact that I truly believed Rory would win it and sign my flag someday.

Hopefully, that day was today.

****

FACE TO FACE WITH RORY

We had to manoeuvre our way back along 17 and down 18 again. Beside the 18th green was a walkway where players from the 5th green would head to the Stadium 6th hole and players from the 18th green would come off and head to the clubhouse for lunch.

Ropes kept the players and spectators apart and there was already a good number of kids there and adults pushing kids forward, waiting for players to sign. We had hurried down to beat the McIlroy Melee and I made my way to stand behind a small child and a young girl both grasping Scottish Open flags to be signed. The Masters flag brigade hadn't arrived yet. We had beaten that crowd.

Kerry stood back. I didn't dare move from my spot. We weren't reunited for over thirty minutes.

Two groups came in before Rory's group came into view for Kerry. My view was only of six security marshals and around a hundred adults and kids on the opposite side of the rope with a similar number now surrounding me. I couldn't see the green and could only sense McIlroy mania as the crowd noise went up a few decibels and I could start to hear the screams of "Rory, Rory!" coming closer.

Would The Ginger Ninja's prediction stand good? Would Rory sign everything for everyone? There were so many people there, all with something to be signed: putter covers, Masters flags, Masters tickets, hats and golf balls.

Rory started signing at one end of the rope. I was standing at the other end. He had a lot of people to get through before he got to me and at any moment he could just swivel around and start signing on the other side so neither side felt left out. Would I miss out? Would I have to return to Kerry and announce that my flag was still Rory-less?

I was the Positive Golfer. Be Positive, Stay Positive.

I could hear Rory further down the line saying to someone with a flag, "Do you want me to sign anywhere on here?"

Wow, he cared. There must have been other signatures and Rory was aware that to sign in the wrong place might have been a disaster for the person to whom the flag belonged. That was class!

He was not just signing the stuff for the people in the front row but for the people behind them, and those behind them too, accepting and passing back flags and hats. He was alert too, though. One man had handed a Masters flag to Rory with one hand, Rory had signed it and then the same man handed a Masters ticket to Rory through the crowd with his other hand. He knew what he was doing, or so he thought. Rory was onto him, though.

"I've already signed a flag for you," said Rory politely but firmly, leaving the guy in no doubt that he wasn't going to suffer liberty takers.

"But Rory, I was there. You know I travel," whined the guy.

Rory moved on, just managing to bite his tongue. He was getting closer. Just three signatures away now. Would this be the moment he would swivel to the other side of the crowd, though?

And there he was. Right in front of me. The 2025 Masters Champion. Only the sixth man to win the Career Grand Slam. A generational talent.

He signed a Scottish Open flag for the young girl in front of me and then he took my flag. I saw him pause as he checked out the signatures and looked at the year '2001' in the middle of the flag.

"Billy Casper gave me the flag," I said.

"Best I leave his signature alone in the middle, then," said Rory.

"Thanks," I said, adding, "well done on the win."

Rory smiled and moved on. He still had another hundred odd signatures to do and would be there for at least another twenty minutes I reckoned. I think he was true to his word and signed everything – well, almost everything. There is a Masters ticket still unsigned somewhere!

Signature Nineteen on the flag. A priceless birthday present from Kerry. Who would have known when Past Kev opened that envelope back in December in the depths of despair that Rory would win The Masters three months later and the present could easily have read: 'Happy Birthday, Kev. Rory McIlroy will sign your Masters flag at The Scottish Open in July!'

The stars had aligned!

I rejoined Kerry and we rejoiced together as she'd witnessed Rory sign my flag. The happiness on her face matched the joy on mine as we shared this magical moment together.

Thanks, Kerry and thanks, Rory.

THE MAGIC IN ST ANDREWS
Part III

CHAPTER 15: PLAYING THE OLD COURSE

DREAMERS DREAM

On any summer's evening in St Andrews, if you take a stroll or a drive down by the 18th Green of The Old Course, you'll see multiple groups milling about.

People standing gazing at The Swilcan Bridge from the white fence alongside the eighteenth tee, taking photographs, some not sure whether they can go on to the course while golfers are playing, others just barging forward.

On the rooftop terrace of Rusacks Hotel, diners come out to watch the last of the golfers play their shots into the green. If the shot is good, they get a cheer and a clap, if not they get some friendly abuse.

Behind the green, at the steps leading to the R and A Clubhouse are a group of four young guys all sitting on the steps. They appear to be having a semi-religious experience. One of the guys gets up, walks down the steps and touches the grass. He can't believe he's here ... at The Old Course. He's moved to tears. He swings an imaginary pitching wedge to the pin which is located at the front of the green. In his mind he's just managed to get 'up and down in two' from there. Cheers echo in his head from the Rusacks and the gathered crowds.

Dreams of playing The Old Course are everywhere you look, but will these dreams become a reality over the next few days?

FOUR STEPS TO GOLFING HEAVEN

Unless you are the holder of a treasured Links Ticket, there are four ways to play The Old Course:-

1. You can secure a Guaranteed Tee Time with a tour operator accredited by The St Andrews Links Trust. This gives you a tee time on a given day at a given time and can normally be booked up to twelve months ahead. This is almost certainly the most expensive way to play The Old Course, as the tour operator will normally book your whole trip including accommodation, other courses and transport and you get one figure at the end for your whole trip. Normally nothing is broken down, but if money is no object and you want to know you'll definitely be playing it, then this is the way to go.
2. You can enter The Ballot yourself if there are two or more of you, from 5pm three days ahead, up to 2pm two days ahead of the day you want to play. The ballot results are then published online at 5pm UK time and you'll also be emailed to advise you if you've been successful or not.
3. You can enter The Singles Daily Draw if you're unsuccessful in the Ballot and you're still looking to play in two days' time or you're just a single golfer. The catch, though, is that you have got to be physically in St Andrews between 9am and 5pm the day before you want to play.

Head to either The Links Clubhouse or The Starters Pavillion by the first tee where you're asked to enter your details on an iPad there together with anyone else in your party who wants to play, and the iPad captures a real time photo of you. The Singles Daily Draw is then made after 5pm, and you're informed by email whether you've been successful or not, what position you are in the Draw if you are successful and you're allocated a number and instructions on what time to turn up at The Starters Pavillion.

You may be joining a two ball with someone else from the singles queue or a three ball who've been fortunate enough to come out in the ballot two days before. Lifelong friendships have been formed this way and is an excellent alternative to the previous longstanding tradition of having to queue up outside The Starters Pavillion, from as early as 11pm the night before to have a chance of playing the next day.

4. You can Befriend A Local Links Ticketholder. However, even with that treasured Golden Ticket, they've still got to ballot for a tee time two days ahead with everyone else. They do have certain priority times from 8-9am every day, every second time from 12 noon on a Thursday and every second tee time on a Saturday so statistically they have a slightly higher chance of coming out in the ballot. They can only sign on bona fide guests and those tee times cannot be used for commercial or personal gain.

My Tips:

Pre-Submission

1. Caddy Services: When you're submitting your application, there is an option for caddy services and although I'm not privy to the workings of the ballot draw, I suspect that submissions with a request for caddies may be looked on more favourably than ones which don't. The Links Trust does, after all, want to keep the wheel spinning and caddies working.
2. Dark Times: When you make your ballot application you'll be asked if you want to play in a 'dark time'. Playing in these times mean that you're unlikely to get all the way round the course, not play the iconic 17th and 18th or be playing them in the dark which somewhat defeats the purpose. I wouldn't recommend ticking that box if you're looking to play it for the first time. Leave those 'dark times' to the local students who are just looking for a quick hit later in the day. Also, the Halfway House at the ninth hole has stopped serving food and drink as golfers from those dark times pass through.

Post-Submission

1. If Successful: Turn up at the Starters Pavillion at least thirty minutes before your tee time to settle green fees, grab some food, hit some putts and meet your caddy. There is no driving range near the first hole, so any warming up should be done in the hour or so before that at The Academy, where a shuttle bus runs between there and the Starters Pavillion https://standrews.com/page/shuttle_bus
2. Don't Be Late: The starters do not have any discretion to let anyone who is late onto a fully booked course and that goes for any of the courses on the Links.

3. Handicap Certificate: Please respect that the maximum for men and ladies is 36. You will be asked for a valid handicap certificate at The Starters Pavillion by Gavin, Paul, Marion, Derek or Bruce so make sure you have a valid handicap certificate with you. Extreme disappointment never looks good. Everyone wants you to enjoy, not endure your round here, so that you go back home and tell everyone about your wonderful experience on The Old Course and in St Andrews.
4. Playing The Old Course before you're ready to do so, isn't good for anyone!
5. Caddy Fees: The caddies are self-employed and pay a fee to the Links Trust to gain access to the course. Settlement of caddy fees by a player is directly with the caddy at the end of the round, normally behind the 18th Green at the steps leading up to the R and A Clubhouse.

Your knowledgeable caddy will have given you lines, read putts for you, regale you with stories of The Old Course and St Andrews and may have taken photographs of you and your party around the course. You'll probably have shot anywhere between five and ten shots lower than if you hadn't taken a caddy. Their help will add to the special memories made in this magical place and hopefully your payment to them will reflect what they've done for you.

In 2025, the caddy fee is £75 with the recommended minimum gratuity being £35, so a minimum of £110 is the starting point. Of course, paying more than that will be reflective of the service they've given you, the fun you have had and the memories they have helped create on the course for you.

Generosity is very much appreciated and remembered for a long time by the caddies … and of course by The Golfing Gods too.

KEVIN DAVIDSON

YOU NEVER FORGET YOUR FIRST TIME

You may have played The Old Course on a simulator or a video game and think you know it well. However, when you play it for real, it bears no resemblance to those experiences. History and Ghosts of Legends surround it and nothing can replicate the wind at your back or in your face, as you try and tee it up for the first time on the first tee, with your knees knocking and your hands trembling.

I've been fortunate enough to play the Old Course on countless occasions for real, and I still enjoy it as much as I did the first time. It's a true privilege I never take for granted and why, where possible, I try to take one or two people off the singles queue every time I play. I love watching their wide-eyed wonder as they get their photograph taken in front of the R and A Clubhouse, silently praying that their nerves won't stop them hitting a good drive up the first, that tee shot they've dreamt about for days, months or even years before. ("Aim at the small gorse bush to the right of the Swilcan Bridge") Surely the biggest anti-climax in golf is going out of bounds on either side of the wide first fairway with your tee shot or landing in the Swilcan Burn as you play into the first green!

I film them on their own phone at the seventeenth tee as they call out a letter to fire their drive over the green sheds on which the words Old Course Hotel sit to the right of Scotland's lion rampant. Sometimes they hit so far left of the 'O' of Old that I swear I've seen the Lion Rampant duck and I've got to ask them if they really picked the 'R' of Rusacks, the hotel halfway down the 18th fairway!

After the drive off the eighteenth tee ("Aim at the Clock on the Clubhouse"), it's on to the obligatory photograph which will adorn their office desk or wall for ever more- them standing triumphantly, regardless of their score, on the Swilcan Bridge.

As an aside, The Swilcan Bridge provided Kerry and me with our own lifetime photograph, which is still the screensaver on my phone. This was well after our first date in St Andrews, though, when Kerry misheard me when I mentioned 'The Swilcan Bridge'. She thought I 'd called it 'The Smoking Bridge' and later admitted to me that she thought that smoking was banned on the course, that the only place you could smoke was on the Bridge; that's what people did and that's why they were standing there.

After I'd updated her of its correct name sometime later, we headed there for our own cherished moment on the Bridge. There wasn't a cigarette in sight! We do still refer to it light heartedly as 'The Smoking Bridge' though, every time Kerry comes to town!

THE 18TH

That walk down the eighteenth fairway after the Swilcan Bridge is the one everyone looks forward to and one no one ever forgets.

Whether you're playing into the cavernous green, in front of ten or a hundred people, with another forty on the balcony of Rusacks Hotel, you walk in the footsteps of thousands who've made that journey before you, including all the Golfing Game's Greats.

For five minutes though, you are centre of attention on the 18th hole. Crowds gather at the side and at the back of the 18th Green just to be near to The Old Course. Some may have times in the next couple of days, others can only dream. They are all united by their love of golf.

They're all now watching you, some betting on how many in your group will three putt the undulating mass called the 18th Green. Fifty per cent is a fair number and those who two putt deserve the round of muted applause from the educated few who know how hard that green is.

The loudest cheers are always reserved for the occasional snaking thirty-foot putt which drops into the hole, or the great second shot to six feet resulting in a chance to make a birdie on 18 on the Old Course. That fabled birdie, if it's made, will probably quite rightly be recounted every time that golfer ever opens their mouth again, such is the enormity of that moment.

Whatever the score, it's the end of a never to be forgotten day for many and they acknowledge the crowd, imagining they are 'The Champion Golfer of the Year', take one last look around at the amphitheatre of famous buildings, before heading up the steps, past the crowds to tot up their scorecard. This is of course entirely secondary to the exhilarating experience of just having played the oldest, most famous and iconic golf course in the world.

TAKE A CADDY

Now, I may sound like a seasoned pro, but it's all a far cry from my own first time when I nervously walked onto the first tee of The Old Course to play in the New Golf Club's Spring Meeting on Saturday 4th May 2019.

I figured you only play The Old Course for the first time once and I wanted to do it right and navigate it properly. Normally caddies are requested the day before at the latest, but I'd only arrived at my shrewd decision twenty minutes before I was due to tee off!

The starter made a quick call and told me that my caddy would be there as quickly as possible but would catch me up on the first hole if he wasn't there at the start. On the first tee there was no one to tell me to aim at the small bush to the right of the Swilcan Bridge and I felt that a driver might take me into the burn. Indecision had already gripped me and twinned knottingly with those first tee nerves, I embarrassingly and life-lastingly topped the ball twenty yards off the tee. I've since had everlasting empathy with all Old Course first timers after that.

I played my second shot before my caddy arrived and as he hurried up the first fairway to where my ball had landed around 140 yards short of the green, he took my bag and asked me what club I hit 150 yards for my second shot. Sheepishly I told him it was actually my third shot and that I hit my seven iron 150 yards.

He didn't look surprised. He'd seen it all before!

My nerves were not calmed when I asked him if he played golf and he replied casually that he used to play on the European Tour in the 1970s and introduced himself as Bill McColl. I'd heard of Bill and when I googled him after the round, I discovered he'd played for fourteen years on the Tour, played in seven majors and finished tied twenty third in The Open at Muirfield in 1980! Bloody hell and now he was caddying for this duffer!

Bill sadly passed away on the 10th of July 2023, after suffering a heart attack in his car on Gibson Place situated on the other side of the 18th fairway of The Old Course. The course was brought to a standstill for an hour and a half as an air ambulance landed on the 18th fairway to try and save him.

The Old Course was brought to a standstill again nearly a month later as his funeral cortege made its way across Grannie Clark's Wynd followed by friends, locals and caddies alike, keen to pay their last respects to Bill.

I cherish the photo we got taken together on The Swilcan Bridge. Rest in Peace Bill.

STEER CLEAR OF THE BUNKERS

Bill's main advice that day has stuck with me ever since and I've passed it on to all first timers I play with …

"If you get in a bunker, just get out. However, you do it, just get out!"

Sometimes you've got to play out sideways. Others you play out backwards. Most of the time you just knock it forward five yards, take your medicine and accept your dropped shot. A good Old Course caddy will guide you round the course and away from the bunkers.

For those who choose not to take a caddy for the first time they play it, then beware the bunkers. I've seen one poor lady take ten shots to get out of one of those beasts.

STEER CLEAR OF NEGATIVE GOLFERS

For anyone who says The Old Course is easy, they haven't played it in a two to three club twenty-five miles an hour wind, blowing with you on the front nine and against you coming back in.

For anyone who says they don't know what all the fuss is about, either they don't get golf history or they're so devoid of emotion that they'd probably describe the raw beauty of The Grand Canyon or the ear shattering noise of Niagara Falls as "Not being sure what all the fuss is about"

This is history. This golf course has been around in some shape or form for nearly five hundred years since 1552. It has seen off twenty-two monarchs, fifty-eight prime ministers and has crowned and lauded thirty champion golfers of the year. One monarch who was rumoured to have commissioned and played the course was Mary Queen of Scots, who is credited with being the first ever female golfer. This is a special place!

Eighteen-time major winner and considered by many to be the greatest golfer of all time Jack Nicklaus once said that "A golfer must play St. Andrews at least a dozen times before they can expect to understand its subtleties." (Source: Sports Illustrated 1970)

The course changes from one day to the next with the changes in the wind. One day might be calm and you shoot a good score, the next day the wind might be blowing hard and you're lucky to finish with any score instead of having letters after your name. (NR for No Return)

To most golfers The Old Course is the Eighth Wonder of the World. For those for whom it's not, they're more likely to have been touched by The Negative Golfer, their life in general is negative and they will typically spoil golf rounds for others with their pessimism, their bad attitude, their club thumping and their occasional tantrums and outbursts.

Steer clear of Negative Golfers. They can seriously affect your golf game!

WHAT'S IN A NAME?

There are one hundred and twelve bunkers on The Old Course with each bunker having a name and each one having a story behind it. The experienced caddies will enjoy sharing these stories with you.

'Shell' on the 7th, 'Bobby Jones' and 'Strath' on the 11th, 'Hell' on the 14th and the 'Road Hole Bunker' on the 17th are the ones you should really avoid, to keep a good score going. I've come to grief in each of them at some time in the past, sometimes taking five shots to get out of at least two of them. I have different names for them!

As is also the norm at most golf courses, every hole has a name too, but it strikes me that some of the names of the holes on The Old Course could do with updating. Cartgate Out (3) and Cartgate In (15), Hole o Cross Out (5) and Hole o Cross In (13), Heathery Out (6) and Heathery In (12) and High Out (7) and High In (11) could benefit from a rename.

Leaving the names 'Cartgate', 'Hole o Cross', 'Heather' and 'High' in place, then there are four holes to rename and with the tenth hole being renamed 'Bobby Jones' in the early 1970s, there is fairly recent precedent for it being done.

'Bugger' immediately springs to mind for the eleventh hole. It must have been uttered so many times as a golf ball lands short of the green in 'Strath' bunker or goes long beyond the green when a seemingly great tee shot has been hit.

'WTF' for the twelfth hole. Standing for 'What's the Fuss', once you've played it, you'll know what the fuss is about.

So that leaves two more holes to be renamed. Noone has ever won the Open at St Andrews three times. Five people have won it twice. Bob Martin in 1876 and 1885, JH Taylor in 1895 and 1905, James Braid in 1905 and 1910, Jack Nicklaus in 1970 and 1978 and Tiger Woods in 2000 and 2005. There's probably a very good reason that no one has ever won it three times here as it would mean that a player would likely have to remain at the top of their game for fifteen years, with the Open normally returning here only every five years.

Jack Nicklaus in his pomp must have been a shoo- in to have made it three, but in 1964 he was beaten by ex-marine, 'Champagne' Tony Lema by five strokes. After his wins in 2000 and 2005 Tiger Woods was tied 23rd in 2010 and he missed the cut in 2015 and in 2022 at the 150th Open.

So, can anyone grab a piece of golfing history and have their name on an Old Course Hole like Tom Morris at the 18th and Bobby Jones at the 10th?

I would make the case that Tiger and Jack shouldn't have to wait until they pass before they are bestowed this honour and what better time to do it than when The Open returns to St Andrews in 2027?

To be fair, I wouldn't put it past Tiger to get himself fit enough to win it for a third time, but whatever happens what a spectacle it would be, for it to take place while both these great golfers are still alive and able to enjoy it, hopefully together.

Over to the powers that be!

A RACE AGAINST DARKNESS WITH THE TEN MILLION DOLLAR MAN

When you live in St Andrews, sometimes you can have nothing planned for the weekend ahead and suddenly you receive a text on a Thursday evening, asking you to join a game and it turns into one of your most memorable weekends in the town.

That's exactly what happened when I received a text at the start of May 2025 from a French golf tour operator Mathieu.

"Would I be available to join him and his guests to play The New Course early the next day?"

With nothing arranged I texted back "Yes."

Mathieu replied great and was I a fan of F1, as one of his guests was an F1 driver ... Pierre Gasly. I had to admit that I didn't watch or follow F1, but I did the google 'Pierre Gasly' to find out more. He was a twenty-nine-year-old French racing driver for the Alpine Team, he had 5.6 million followers on Instagram and if the internet was to be believed he'd just signed a two-year contract with Alpine for 10 million dollars a year.!

Having just competed in the Miami Grand Prix the weekend before, he was in St Andrews this weekend before competing in the Emilia Romagna Grand Prix in Italy the following weekend. Quite literally life in the fast lane!

The next morning, I met Mathieu, Pierre and his family and played the New Course with them. Pierre radiated warmth and friendliness and seemed extremely down to earth. His family and friends were all the same, sharing that sense of friendliness and love for golf that joins us all.

Then on the late Saturday afternoon, we played the Old Course together in one of the last available dark times at 620pm. Sunset was at 910pm so we would only likely get to play fourteen holes before darkness fell. No 17th or 18th holes for Pierre and his brother Philippe! Still, it was better than nothing. They were getting to play the world-famous Old Course for the first time.

For a man who had travelled all over the world and whose workplace was in the cockpit of a 200mph racing car, the look of excitement and pleasure as Pierre stood there on the first tee on the most famous golf course in the world was amazing to see. He didn't look nervous, but he admitted after his tee shot that he was very nervous. The nerves were way different to waiting for the lights to change from red to green on the starting grid of a race. He was in control there, in automatic mode, ready for a moment he had trained all his life for, in front of millions of people. There on the first tee in front of just a few people, he'd been having real doubts over whether he would even connect with the golf ball!

He did connect, though, and fired it two hundred and twenty yards up the fairway, over Grannie Clark's Wynd towards the small gorse bush in the distance I'd pointed out as being a good line for him. Green for go. We were off.

We chatted round the course about Milan where he lived, about the French football club FC Versailles he had recently invested in, his hopes for PSG winning the Champions League for the first time. A keen golfer he had golfed with Tony Finau in Las Vegas at a 'Netflix Live' event and was trying to fit in a game with Rory McIlroy who was now an investor in the Alpine team.

He was a decent golfer and birdied the fifth hole, managed to avoid 'Bobby Jones' bunker on the eleventh and stopped to admire and photograph the extraordinary beauty of the sun setting over the Eden Estuary at the thirteenth tee.

As the shadows began to envelop the links, we started running to try and get all eighteen holes played. It looked like darkness was going to beat us but then two things happened. The full moon appeared from behind the clouds and gave us some light and to cut down on the time taken I stopped playing, to allow Pierre and Phillipe to try and finish as a two ball.

We were in our own race against darkness now and Pierre seemed to have found a DRS switch on his trolley and was running much quicker than me. He did have nearly thirty years on me, but I did manage to find an extra gear myself to keep up with him, shouting lines and finding balls for them as we made our way hastily round.

The tee shot over the hotel from the seventeenth tee is normally described as a 'blind shot' but this was truly a blind shot in the dark, as the moon had disappeared behind the clouds. Miraculously, we found their balls on the fairway. Voices drifted from The Jigger Inn across the fairway.

"There's still people playing out there" came the incredulous shouts through the blackness.

I gave Pierre the line for the second shot. It was towards the second lamppost I could see lighting up the road behind the green. Pierre swung blindly but smoothly. When we got up to the green The Golfing Gods had landed his ball eight feet short of the pin. Pierre had a putt for birdie in the dark on The Road Hole, one of the hardest par fours in golf.

I'd played this hole so many times before that I knew the line, even in the darkness. I gave Pierre the read and he putted, coming up agonisingly half an inch short of the hole It was a three and a half!

The rest of Pierre's family were waiting for us on the eighteenth tee. They'd already teed off. It was pitch black. We teed off to mobile phone torchlight shouting 'fore' into the darkness ahead. If only Pierre had put out a post to his 5.6 million Instagram followers with a request for help, maybe we could have had an 18th fairway lit up by thousands of his followers holding up their mobile phones lighting up the way to the green!

The walk down the 18th for their family group was punctuated by the customary group photo of then all on The Swilcan Bridge. A cigarette would have been handy to light up the photograph, but we made do with mobile phone torchlight again.

The lights from the historic buildings twinkling all around was magical, as was walking onto and putting on the 18th green, the scene of so many historic moments.

They had missed their restaurant booking as we had finished our round at 1015pm, but Pierre didn't mind. He said he would always trade food to have played The Old Course, even if the last few holes were in the dark and that he couldn't wait to return to play it again without the aid of torchlight!

I've ordered some fluorescent balls from Amazon, though, just in case!

THE DISAPPEARING GOLF TROLLEY

The twelfth hole, beside the Eden Estuary, also provided me with one of my funniest moments on The Old Course.

My podiatrist's father Andy was playing The Old Course with me for the first time. We'd just finished putting on the twelfth green when Andy looked up and around and, in a panic, shouted,

"Where's my trolley? Have you seen my trolley?"

It was an electric one, it wasn't where he'd left it and despite us searching the surrounding gorse bushes for three minutes, it was nowhere to be seen. I would have to contact The Links Trust to report the missing trolley and ask if they'd received any other similar reports of missing golf equipment in that area in case we were dealing with golf's version of The Bermuda Triangle.

When I was putting minutes before, I recalled seeing a trolley out of the corner of my eye, moving slowly on the third fairway of the adjacent Eden course. I'd thought it was a remote control one and that a player would be following behind. It couldn't have been Andy's trolley, could it?

I sprinted across the third fairway of the Eden course and then over the fourth fairway, but there was no trolley to be seen. Stopping at the edge of the estuary wall I peered over. There lying ten feet below was Andy's trolley with his golf bag still attached to it, but half buried in the sand. Thankfully, the tide was out, so the salvage operation was much easier and quicker, with me lifting Andy's equipment up and out to my fellow rescuer who grabbed it from above.

Trolley and bag were reunited with one very relieved owner on the thirteenth tee. I didn't know whether that moment was the appropriate time to joke with Andy that it should incur a two stoke penalty for his trolley and bag going out of bounds. His still-flustered face said I should keep that one to myself, for the moment at least!

TWO SPECIAL DAYS ON THE OLD COURSE

There are two special dates in the diary I look forward to every year …The Town Match and The Old Course In Reverse.

THE TOWN MATCH

The Town Match is when members of the R and A take on players from all the other clubs representing the town in foursomes matches. It's the largest golf match in the world and in 2024 consisted of eight hundred and eighty players. All the courses on the Links are used but the jewel in the crown is getting to play your match on The Old Course. Last year my partner Michael and I had the privilege of teeing off last at 350pm and coming down the eighteenth as players were gathering at the R and A steps to hear the winning result. Clearly our result had no bearing on it! Still, having to navigate the 'Valley of Sin' in front of two hundred suited and booted people was interesting and a little nerve racking.

Matches start across the Links from 7am and the first ones can be finished by 10am with players retiring for drinks and lunch and more drinks at respective clubhouses. The alternative is that players meet for lunch and drinks and then go out to play which makes for some interesting golf on the courses in the afternoon.

It's all played in great spirits and afterwards the town is awash later with local golfers trekking from local bar to local bar sharing stories of golf long into the night. Great fun is had by everyone.

THE OLD COURSE IN REVERSE

Once a year, like a mystical island appearing from the ocean, the Old Course is played in in Reverse. This was how it was originally played and until recently it was run for just one day in late November and only for the local clubs.

However, The Links Trust have now opened this up for anyone to ballot to play the Old Course in Reverse on a Friday and Monday in late March, with the Saturday being reserved exclusively for a Links Ticket Holder Tournament.

Playing The Old Course in Reverse is a must. I rank it as my second favourite course in the world ... after The Old Course!

It takes you a couple of times playing it in reverse, to get your head round just how to play it. Drive off the 1st tee, playing to the 17th green, drive off the 18th tee playing to the 16th green and so on-it's difficult knowing where the best lines off the tees are. Why some of the bunkers are placed where they are, suddenly becomes apparent though- they're there to catch balls when the course was played in reverse. Playing second shots into some greens across rough and gorse bushes is especially challenging, as is the carry from some tees to fairways, such as from the 8th tee down the seventh fairway to the sixth green!

You still get to finish off at the eighteenth green having teed off from the 2nd tee, so you do get your moment walking the eighteenth fairway-just across it though, not down it! If you've have played the Old Course before, then make sure you play the Old Course in Reverse too at least once in your lifetime. You'll not regret making that trip.

The Town Match and The Old Course in Reverse are the two times in the year that you are almost certainly guaranteed to see a double major winner playing The Old Course.

Both times the major winner uses his hickory clubs. I think it's to give the rest of us a chance, but he says it's because he loves playing with them.

It's quite a feeling to be stood on the eighth green which is shared with the tenth green, looking across and seeing golfing legend Sandy Lyle putting only yards away from you. Sandy is an honorary member of both the R and A and The St Andrews Club and never misses an opportunity to take part in both these occasions.

SANDY LYLE OWES ME AN ICE CREAM

The AIG Womens Open came to town in August 2024. It was to be Kerry's first experience of a major tournament in St Andrews, so rather than volunteer to be a marshal this time, I volunteered to play golf with her in the mornings and in the afternoons, we would enjoy walking The Old Course and watching the tournament unfold.

What a tournament it was with Lydia Ko prevailing over a stellar field on a cold, windy Sunday afternoon with Kerry and I watching the drama unfold on the 18th green from the steps of the R and A's Waldon House. We were joined there by a German couple, and the lady seemed to have been crying. Her husband explained that they'd just dropped off their son at St Leonard's School where he was going to be a boarder. I didn't think that it was the appropriate time to share with them that my Mum had been a boarder at the same school some seventy years before. Her feeling of homesickness there as a twelve-year-old had led her to draw up a map detailing her escape route from the school grounds across the Tay Rail Bridge and all the way back to Banff, some one hundred and twenty miles away! Luckily, her sense of direction wasn't very good, and she abandoned 'the great escape'.

An escape to Germany would be much easier now for their son with Ryanair flights departing daily! I decided to keep my mouth shut and headed back to The New Club with Kerry.

A couple of days earlier we'd dined upstairs in The New Club with my friend Kenny, who had recommended that I apply for my Links Ticket way back in 2012, and his partner Emma. Enjoying the delicious food served there, we were able to watch the world's best women golfers on the 1st and 18th fairways out of the windows behind us in the restaurant.

Kenny and Emma were leaving at 4pm to meet Sandy Lyle and his wife Jolande for drinks at the Champagne Tent, after Sandy had finished a Question-and-Answer event for the R and A. Kenny revealed they'd become friends after Jolande and Emma played golf together at the exclusive Skibo Castle where they were all members and had stayed in touch after that.

As luck would have it, for me at least, there was no Champagne Tent, so Kenny invited Sandy and Jolande into The New Cub to join us in the restaurant. As they arrived, we were still finishing our lunch and waiting for our desserts to be served. Pulling up two chairs for them, Sandy sat down beside me.

Quiet initially, but then with a little prompting from me, Sandy shared some wonderful anecdotes of Augusta and The Masters, Billy Casper at the Champions Dinner, Sam Snead, hickory clubs, Cypress Point and Seve Ballesteros.

Jolande shared stories of how they'd met and that she "had the most beautiful practice swing-it's perfect- but I just cannot hit the ball"

I shared my story of Sandy signing my Masters flag in 2014 and then asking to sign it again in 2018!

Drinks were ordered and desserts followed quickly with Sandy and Jolande deciding they'd order desserts too. This meal was on me as thank you to Kenny and Emma for having us to their house for dinner. Not being much of a cook, paying was more palatable for me and everyone else, than sampling my cooking.

I picked up the tab for Sandy and Jolande too. I didn't mind ... I was sitting next to a golfing legend, a double major winner. I'd watched The Masters in Ellon with my Mum and Dad in April 1988, all of us glued to the television. We sat mesmerised as Sandy played the best bunker shot I'd ever seen on the 18th at Augusta, firing a seven iron 145 yards over the lip of the fairway bunker, landing beyond the flag and rolling back to ten feet. We roared as Scotland's Sandy Lyle holed the putt to become a two-time major winner and the first British winner of The Masters, with the green jacket slipped over his shoulders by the previous year's winner Larry Mize.

Seve Ballesteros famously described Sandy as having "the greatest God-given talent in history," stating that if everyone played their best, Lyle would win, and he, Seve, would come second!

Whatever ... Sandy Lyle owes me an ice cream! Hopefully, I'll get it the next time The Open comes to town.

In the meantime, I ordered myself a golf ball marker with a photo on it from that afternoon ... with Kerry, Sandy and me sitting together enjoying ourselves.

Every time I putt I'm inspired by it.

WELCOME TO THE REAL THING

Whether you're a double major winner, an F1 driver or a first timer, I look forward to seeing you on The Old Course in the future.

Just be prepared and don't be disappointed when you don't eagle the first hole like you did on your 'X box'.

Nothing will ever prepare you for what it's like to play The Old Course for real.

CHAPTER 16: MY TAKE ON THE TOWN

THE BEST DRIVE IN GOLF

There are a couple of ways to come into St Andrews, but for me the most picturesque one is coming from Leuchars along the A91, with the Eden Estuary to the left-hand side of you. You turn a corner, and there in the distance, you catch sight of the imposing red building of The Hamilton Grand, standing majestically against the skyline.

You're nearly there. Turn another corner and you see the sign for St Andrews, which is twinned with another medieval town, the royal city of Loches, located in the Loire Valley of France.

You've finally arrived at The Home of Golf. At last!

Then you pass the vibrant and unmissable Balgove Larder and Steak Barn on the right-hand side and the road to the Golf Academy on the left, where you'll also find the Eden, Strathtyrum and Balgove courses.

Catch sight of The Old Course Hotel, knowing that just beyond that is The Old Course itself!

The modern North Haugh University Science buildings, which

are located to the right of the Petheram Bridge roundabout, give a hint of student life and the large free car park there is a great place to leave your transport for the day and explore the ancient town.

A TOWN OF NOUGHTS AND CROSSES

St Andrews is basically made up of four main streets all running parallel to each other, The Scores, North Street, South Street and Market Street…with a number of interconnecting streets cutting across these main arteries. Then there is The Old Course, New Course, Jubilee and Eden courses which all also run parallel to each other in a Town Planner's dream.

GIBSON PLACE

It would be remiss of me, though, not to mention that The New Golf Club is located here at Number Three - Five Gibson Place where you can stop and read the blue plaque on the front wall detailing the demise of Old Tom Morris. Look left and you can see the seventeenth green and the eighteenth tee of The Old Course from here. The easiest way to the most photographed golf bridge in the world, The Swilcan Bridge, is to turn left here and keep walking for less than a hundred yards to join the queue to have your photograph taken and look across to the first green and the infamous Swilcan Burn which snakes in front of it, ready to catch many an errant golfer's second, third or even fourth shot into the green.

THE LINKS

Turn right at 'Wow Corner' onto The Links to take in the stunning view of The Old Course looking back towards the first tee with the R and A Clubhouse behind it. Enjoy the walk down the edge of the eighteenth fairway, past Grannie Clark's Wynd, Rusacks Hotel, and The St Andrews and St Rule Golf Clubs, towards the eighteenth green to join the hordes of other golfing disciples standing there in awe. On the other side of the road is The Open Shop which used to be Old Tom Morris's shop. Further retail therapy can also be obtained next door at The Old Course Shop where you can buy all your official Old Course merchandise and, immediately behind the 18th Green, at the 'St Andrews Links By Travis Mathew' Shop.

GOLF PLACE

Turn right onto Golf Place, which is one of those interconnecting arteries between North Street and The Scores.

You can't miss the imposing red sandstone building known as **The Hamilton Grand**, which was built as The Grand Hotel in 1895. Over the years, it hosted royalty and film stars, before the University bought the building and turned it into student accommodation, calling it Hamilton Hall.

Herb Kohler, the owner of the Old Course Hotel had the foresight to buy the building in 2009, converting it into 27 luxury apartments. A penthouse there sold for £4.2 million in 2023. Others had looked at buying and converting the building, but a lack of parking was a problem for the planners until Kohler arrived and sorted the parking condition with valet parking for the owners at the nearby Old Course Hotel.

I played with a member of The New Club, who was one of the first to buy in the building in early 2015 and he told me that if you look closely at the images of Zach Johnson celebrating his victory on the eighteenth green, you can just see him and his family standing on the rooftop terrace celebrating too; they were some of the only occupants at that time.

The Dunvegan sits proudly on the corner of Golf Place and North Street. In its window are etched the following words: 'The coolest hangout in the world of golf.' The Golf Channel.

This is unashamedly a golf bar with photos on every inch of every wall, and every inch of every ceiling, of celebrities from golf, film and business standing with the owners or staff at some time in the past. The bar, which serves good, traditional bar food, is always busy with golfing visitors sitting or standing, exchanging tales of their round or rounds that day and they're joined by locals, caddies and members of the R and A in an eclectic mix of golfing afficionados from every corner of the world.

Auchterlonies, named after former Open champion Willie Auchterlonie's family, is a treasure trove of golfing shoes, clothes and every club manufacturer worth knowing. The staff there are knowledgeable and polite and any visit to St Andrews is not complete without a visit here.

Their newly refurbished fitting studio allows for best-in-class club and putter fitting for locals and visitors alike, with a visitor from the States recently getting fitted there for driver, irons, wedges and putter in a mammoth session and asking for seven sets of what he'd just been fitted for, so he could ship a set to each of the clubs where he was a member!!

A little-known fact is that they also rent out clubs to golfers and these can be booked ahead of your visit to the town directly with the staff [7].

Further along Golf Place past The Scores is the world-famous **R and A Clubhouse** which has stood behind the first tee since 1854. Behind that, the bronze statue of Old Tom Morris keeps a watchful eye over the Old Course, and to his right is the R and A World Golf Museum which is a must-visit attraction. Head upstairs afterwards to the newly refurbished Niblick Restaurant which offers good food and sweeping views of the links opposite.

Located to the side of the R and A Museum, you wouldn't

[7] sales@auchterlonies.com

imagine that a public car park would make the list of attractions, but **The Bruce Embankment Car Park**, which has 161 spaces including 4 disabled parking bays (Source: Fife Council), is located yards from the first tee and Starters Pavillion of The Old Course and is so reasonably priced that I had to list it. At the time of writing, it's free to park from 1st October to 31st March every year, with short stays (from 2 - 8 hours) from April until the end of September hardly breaking the bank. Newly refurbished public bathrooms, including disabled toilets, are located here too.

THE STARTERS PAVILLION
A friendly face will greet you here, be it from one of the starters on the day or someone on the other side of the food kiosk, where golfers can grab a coffee or a hot roll before venturing out to play.

THE WEST SANDS
This is where the iconic opening running scenes for *'Chariots of Fire'* were filmed. Nowadays the sands in the summertime will be full of families, dog walkers, beach volleyball players, windsurfers, jet skiers and swimmers. The Swilcan Burn finishes its journey into the sea here.

Further along, just beyond The Links Clubhouse, there is a beach bar called 'Dook', a windsurfing school called 'Blown Away', a pay-as-you-use sauna, and a hut for free beach wheelchair hire so everyone can enjoy this wonderful leisure space, regardless of their abilities.

THE CADDYSHACK
Closed to the public, and shrouded in secrecy, the Caddyshack is small in size but immense in importance. This is where the caddies hang out, waiting for their allocated time to share the golf course with a wide-eyed golfer eager to shoot the round of their life so

they can go home and share stories with friends and family alike. 'Double loopers', those who do two rounds in one day, will chill and eat between rounds here.

THE HIMALAYAS

To give it is full title, The St Andrews Ladies Putting Club, which was founded in 1867, is better known as 'The Himalayas' due to the hilly, undulating terrain you have to putt on. It's fun for all the family and, even if you haven't managed to get a game on any of the courses on the Links, then 18 holes of putting on here will at least give you some sense of playing golf in St Andrews. There is also a smaller, less undulating nine-hole course for younger children to enjoy too. It's open during weekends in March and then daily from April to October and it's best to book a time online at www.standrewsputtingclub.com so as not to be disappointed. Putters and balls are available to hire on top of the small green fee, which is £4 in 2025, but you are allowed to bring your own equipment. The official course record is 35 strokes and, as their website says, it's probably the best value entertainment in St Andrews.

I was recently beaten in a match against The Ladies Putting Club by Anne, a thirty-two-handicap demon putter. The ladies there know their lines for sure. Don't play them for money!

THE LINKS CLUBHOUSE

The beauty of St Andrews is that most of it is open to everyone. The Links Trust is a charity which owns and runs the golf courses, and the properties affiliated to the golf courses; The Links Clubhouse is one of those buildings. Located beside the Jubilee and the New Course, it offers a place for visitors to change into their golfing gear in the lockers and shower rooms downstairs and eat well before or after their round in the Tom Morris Bar & Grill upstairs.

With sweeping panoramic views on three sides across The Old Course, The Himalayas, the New and the Jubilee, this is a place for golfers or walkers to sit and relax and take in the astonishing surroundings from inside or from the outside on the rooftop terrace. There is also a small retail unit here to purchase some St Andrews Links branded merchandise, including clothes, whisky or wine glasses - or a Lego™ replica of the Swilcan Bridge! Parking for golfers with tee times is located within the car park outside The Links Clubhouse. Parking for walkers and visitors is located along from the Clubhouse near 'Blown Away' which is the wonderful beach-based outdoor experiences company.

THE SCORES

If you want to walk up a street with impressive houses and more impressive price tags, then this is the street. Walking past Old Tom's statue, the Victorian Bandstand and the Martyrs' Monument, you'll be able to enjoy sitting on one of the many wooden benches here, enjoying spectacular views of the West Sands and out to sea from here. Walk past The Aquarium and imposing houses tucked behind security gates into the clifftops. Further up the street are the ancient university buildings, The Wardlaw Museum and The Castle, the origins of which date back nearly 850 years to 1189. Complete with dungeon, its own cove and rockpools, this is a must-visit during your stay here.

Further along, walk past the high ancient walls of the Cathedral grounds and the two cannons on the clifftop which guarded the castle. Then head down the hill past the fishing baskets and brightly coloured houses overlooking the harbour wall towards the East Sands.

THE EAST SANDS

This is a highly rated family and dog friendly golden sandy beach with water sports, rockpools and free parking. Walk along to the end of the pier here and look back to get fantastic views of the Castle and the Cathedral. Beware the seagulls, though; the owners of the very popular Cheesy Toast Shack even offer optional 'seagull insurance' to replace your snack if a gull does swoop in and steal it!

ST LEONARDS AND THE CATHEDRAL GROUNDS

You can walk back into town uphill and past the ancient walls of St Leonards School within the grounds of which is situated Mary Queen's House, where Mary Queen of Scots stayed whenever she visited St Andrews.

From here you can access North Street, South Street and Market Street but before that take in the breathtaking ruins of The Cathedral and The Cemetery where eight Open Champions are buried. Climb the 156 steps of St Rule's Tower to enjoy the magnificent views from the top.

NORTH STREET

North Street will take you back past the ancient University buildings and past Younger Hall where Bobby Jones was made a Freeman of The City in 1958 and Jack Nicklaus made the equivalent, an Honorary Citizen, in 2022.

St Andrews would not be the place it is without the ancient University, Scotland's first, dating back to 1413. The ten thousand or so students who grace the town from September until the end of May come from all corners of the world to be educated in ancient and modern buildings throughout the town. They bring with them different accents, perspectives and cultures which offer a unique window to the outside world, with residents and students mixing well to create a special vibrant atmosphere in and around the streets of St Andrews.

MARKET STREET

Once you have got used to the genius of the ancient and quirky town planning, you'll be able to find most venues. Cut through Union Street onto Market Street where the medieval marketplace has been replaced by a modern marketplace of shops, restaurants and bars. At the end of Market Street on St Marys Place is the University Union, and the impressive St Marks Church stands opposite St Andrews Bus Station on City Road.

SOUTH STREET

As you return from The East Sands you may come across a large queue on the street. Children and adults are waiting for a serving of their favourite flavours of ice creams, sorbets and desserts at Jannetta's Gelateria, choosing either to sit in or continue their walk around the town, tubs in hand. Further along just past The 51 Club, owned by my barber McGiff, is The Criterion where one of the 'Cri pies' needs to be tried, although maybe before the ice cream from Jannetta's.

The Holy Trinity Church dates to 1412 and sits close to the ruins of Blackfriars Chapel. At the end of the street lies The West Port, the medieval town gate built in 1587 and providing a symbolic entrance to the old part of the town.

So that's my take on the town. It's easy to navigate by car and even easier to walk as a couple, a family, with friends or just by yourself as you ponder how good it is to be in this magical place.

EAT, DRINK AND BE MERRY

Places change, so check out the website at www.kevindavidsonauthor.com for my up-to-date recommendations on where to eat, drink and be merry.

CHAPTER 17: OTHER PEOPLE'S STORIES

Since I've been in St Andrews, I've heard some great stories from other people. Here are just a selection of them. They are all reproduced by kind permission of the main actors in each story.

THE KEYS TO CYPRESS POINT

A man walks into a bar with his dog … it sounds like the start of a joke, but for Malcolm, a pal of mine from The New Golf Club, it was the start of an amazing golfing adventure.

Malcolm and his wife had taken their little dog Jasper, a cute red working cocker spaniel, into the Keys Bar on Market Street for their usual Thursday early evening drink. The super friendly 'locals' bar in the centre of St Andrews is frequented by regulars including caddies and with groups of visiting golfers.

When a young American girl bent down to stroke the sociable Jasper, Malcolm, always a great conversationalist, started chatting to her and was invited over to her table where her family were sitting. The girl introduced her mother, father and brother and as the conversation flowed Malcolm mentioned that he was heading over to the States the following week.

His table hosts asked him where he was playing.

"Bethpage Black, Pinehurst and Pine Valley," said Malcolm.

"Wow, Pine Valley is uber-exclusive. Non-members can only play if invited and accompanied by a member. How are you managing to get in there?" they asked Malcolm.

Malcolm didn't want to name drop as his Pine Valley host was a well-known personality.

His integrity struck a chord with the family, who insisted he contact them next time he was coming to America, with the father offering to host him at his own club, none other than the Alister MacKenzie designed course, Cypress Point in California.

Recently voted number one golf course in the world[8], pushing Pine Valley into second place, this famously secretive and exclusive private course, will have showcased itself to the world again as host of the 2025 Walker Cup, after decades of being shrouded from public view.

That was some invitation, and one Malcolm has excitedly taken up on a couple of occasions, having struck up a lasting friendship with his hosts.

Dog treats for life for little Jasper too I'd imagine, for engineering that particular piece of magic!

FROM LEMA TO LEMA

Jack Nicklaus in his heyday was almost a certainty to win three Open Championships at St Andrews, but in 1964 he was beaten

[8] Source: https://www.top100golfcourses.com

by ex-marine, 'Champagne' Tony Lema by five strokes. This was the culmination for Lema of a momentous four wins in thirty-three days and a fifth tournament win in 1964, so he was undoubtedly the player bang in form.

Lema had done a deal with Arnold Palmer when they were rooming together during the Ryder Cup in 1963 in Atlanta, Georgia. Palmer was unable to make the trip across to St Andrews to play in the 1964 Open because of a scheduling conflict and instead of giving Tony his putter as requested, Palmer said he would go one better and give him his Open caddy Tip Anderson, who caddied on The Old Course. Tip was a descendant of previous Open winer at The Old Course Jamie Anderson who had won it back in 1879 and he knew the links like the back of his hand.

For the likeable Lema though, there would be no everlasting 'Magic In St Andrews' after he and his wife Betty, tragically died in a plane crash on 24th July 1966, just two years and two weeks after his victory at St Andrews.

After listening to a podcast with Tony's son David from 2017 at the Jack Nicklaus Memorial tournament, at which Tony, amongst others, was remembered, I changed my mind on this.

David was just five years old when his father died and didn't remember too much of his dad, but he tells the story of a trip to St Andrews in 2010 to get close to the place where immortality came his father's way. His father's caddie Tip was still caddying on the Links and joined David for his round, clubbing for him round the Old Course and reliving his father's win with David.

When David walked into a pub in St Andrews after the round, magic was in the air when by chance he bumped into a caddy there who told him that his own father had caught Tony Lema's ball when he threw it into the crowd after making his two-foot putt to win on the 18th. He even took David Lema back to his house to show him the Slazenger ball. Holding it, David felt closer to his father than he'd perhaps ever felt before in his life.

Only forty-six years separated the passing of the golf ball from father to son.

FROM LEFT TO RIGHT

I found myself sitting next to New Golf Club Member Robert at the annual prizegiving night one year. I'd always found Robert a larger-than-life character but had never had the chance to really get to know him before then. That evening I found out just why he had that zest for life.

When he was fifty and living in Saudi Arabia, Robert went to get a scan on what he thought was sciatica. The scan showed up two cancerous tumours on his spine which he had to have removed in a series of agonising operations.

The dapper gentleman sitting in front of me in his dinner suit at the prize giving, had previously shrunk to seven stone with the effects of the treatment nine years before.

A small child at a Christmas event where Robert had volunteered to be Father Christmas caught Robert out when he shouted, You can't be Santa, you're too thin to be Santa"

What's this got to do with golf? Well, Robert was a one handicap golfer when they found the tumours and had been that low for years. He'd never quite managed to hit the dizzy heights of scratch, but he had been Club Champion on four occasions at his Club in the west of Scotland and he played left-handed.

When he returned from his tortuous treatment, he could no longer turn his left side. The first time he ventured onto a golf course again and discovered he could no longer play the game he loved the way he used to, he got back into his car and sat there disconsolate.

If he hadn't gone through everything he had done already, and come out the other side of it, he said he would have burst into tears. A lot of people would have given up and found themselves another hobby, but not Robert. He loved the game, the tests of the course and the banter with his buddies

So Robert taught himself to play right-handed, returned to a respectable twelve handicap and laughed when he recalled not having lost a club match for The New Club in over two years, wishing he'd the audacity to tell some of his beaten opponents that he used to play left-handed and was now playing right-handed!

His burning ambition is to get near scratch again and I for one will be following his remarkable journey closely over the coming years.

Robert staunchly attributes St Andrews and The New Golf Club with its friendly, encouraging membership to his remarkable recovery.

PLAYING WITH POSITIVITY

Willie G took up golf in 2019, just before the pandemic, and his WHS handicap was 21.6 when we played together in a Stableford competition on the Eden Course in early November 2024.

His first tee shot pulled one hundred yards left off the tee. His second shot wasn't much better and his golf ball decided enough was enough and made its own great escape from the round, burying itself in the gorse further up the fairway, hoping it wouldn't be found. It wasn't. Shots four and five took Willie just short of the green and three putts landed him with an eight and zero Stableford points. Not a great start!

Willie G ended the round up with forty-five Stableford points and score of 82 (adjusted for WHS purposes to 81), which was his best ever gross score, even with that eight from the first hole on his card. He won the competition that day and earned an overnight cut to a career low WHS of 18.6.

His twenty scores up before that were nothing startling and had consisted of the following:

95, 103, 87, 107, 90, 100, 89, 113, 104, 111, 107, 101, 88, 95, 96, 95, 95, 97, 87 & 93

and there was nothing to suggest that his next round was going to be the round of his life.

So what was the difference that day, from the second hole onwards? I'll let Willie describe what was different in his own words.

Willie G's words …
"As a high handicap golfer, I've always struggled to relax and play my best golf when playing in competitions. Not only do I have first tee nerves when setting up for the first drive, but I'm also often playing with complete strangers, and have no control over how they behave or their attitude on the course.

"Normally I have all sorts going through my head, a lot of which can be caused by fellow golfers losing the plot and swearing if they duff a shot. It's not only bad for their round, but it also makes me nervous, and I put pressure on myself to play a good shot, so as not to annoy them further. Rather than praising me if I hit a good shot or have a good hole, I'm often called a 'bandit', with comments coming my way like "There's no way you're a 21 handicapper!"

"I was lucky enough to play with two calm, good natured golfers in Kevin and Brian in a recent competition. They were fun, positive and never once got angry during the round. Almost every shot was good for my standard (except the first hole!) and I won the competition with forty- five points and was net nine under par.

"When we got back to the clubhouse, Kevin was looking at my previous competition scores on the Scottish golf app and asked what the difference was today. I replied instantly that Brian and he had been the difference. Not once did I hear a negative word from either of them. All I heard was praise, encouragement, jokes, fun and laughter. My nerves were non-existent- it was like playing a Sunday round on my own with my dog or my best pal.

I cannot thank Kevin and Brian enough … maybe some golfers need to reflect on how their own behaviour on the course affects other golfers"

****

Well said, Willie G … I'm sure we've all spent time with 'Angry Golfers' where their attitude and behaviour, including swearing, tantrums, club throwing and club thumping, contributes negatively, not just to the demise of their own game and mental state, but also to that of their playing partners and to any caddies in the group as well. A thoroughly unpleasant experience for everyone!

DR JIM'S WATERY END

My friend Dr Jim was playing The Old Course in Reverse in 2024 and was drawn with a father and son combination. Dr Jim doesn't watch much golf on tv so had no idea who one of the players was. He was still none the wiser when the father asked his son "if he was going to go for it from the first tee?'

Playing the Old Course in Reverse means that you tee off at the first and play to the seventeenth green and the father was asking his son if he was going to carry the Swilcan Burn with his drive! Alarmed by this and desperate to impart his local knowledge, fifteen handicapper Jim said to the son, "I wouldn't try that son, it's quite a carry."

Jim was disappointed to note that the son didn't seem to be heeding his unsolicited advice and stood up with his driver and lined up straight at the Swilcan Bridge. With a one hundred and seventy mile an hour swoosh, the driver flashed in the air and the ball ricocheted off the club face towards the Bridge, took one bounce in front, leaping the six feet of water, drawing nicely as it hit the ground and left a wedge into the green.

As the son popped his driver back into his bag and walked off, Dr Jim saw that there was a name on his oversized golf bag. Connor Syme, the DP World Tour Professional was playing with his dad Stuart, the teaching professional at the nearby Drumoig Golf Centre, and Jim was making up the threesome.

Jim maintains that Connor should dedicate his first victory on the DP World Tour to him, because what Jim did next would have left a lasting impression on Connor.

As Jim was playing his second shot, he heard some people shouting and waving and pointing over towards Jim's group- Jim thought they had recognised Connor and were waving at him. They weren't though. Jim had forgotten to engage the trolley's brake and they were trying to let Jim, who was facing the other way, know that his trolley, assisted by a very strong wind, was making its way of its own accord, towards the Swilcan Burn which was swollen by recent heavy rainfall.

Jim turned round just in time to see his trolley falling into the Burn, leaving Jim red faced and his clubs and bag soaked through. With Connor and Stuart's help, Dr Jim spent five minutes fishing bag and trolley out of the Burn. (It took Jim a further full week to dry out his bag and empty all the sand from it.) The Symes just about managed to contain their laughter as Dr Jim tried to compose himself for the rest of his round.

I was reminded of Jim's story again, as I sat looking over the Old Course from The Peter Thomson Suite in The New Club on the first Friday in April 2025, a year on from Dr Jim's watery end.

Connor and Stuart were walking up the 18th again having come out in The Old Course in Reverse Ballot. There was no Dr Jim this time and it was Connor who was fishing his ball out of the burn after his ball didn't benefit from last year's kindly bounce.

I swear I saw Connor turn to his dad and say, Remember that guy we played with last year whose trolley ended up in the Swilcan Burn?!"

I made sure to text Jim with my version of events.

SWORN TO SECRECY!

Andy was a starter for the Links Trust for several years and tells the story of arriving for his shift at The Old Course Starters Hut as normal, only to be told to expect a VIP guest in thirty minutes time.

As is usual in these circumstances, the name on the ballot didn't match the person who turned up to play. Andy immediately texted one of his American pals Skip and someone else texted one of their friends and so on.

By the time former President Barrack Obama turned up twenty minutes later to hit one or two putts on the practice putting green, he was met with a crowd of several hundred people and spent the last few minutes before his tee time, shaking hands and speaking to locals and tourists.

An accomplished left-handed golfer with a handicap of seven and despite being more used to speaking to crowds rather than playing golf in front of them, Obama managed to launch his drive up the first hole to a round of applause from the assembled masses. Obligingly he doffed his cap and walked up the fairway smiling and waving as he went.

The armed marksmen on top of the Hamilton Grand building continued to scan the crowds for any irregular movements.

By the time, Obama strode down the 18th fairway four hours later the crowds along Links Place and surrounding the 18th green had swelled to several thousand people. The marksmen on the Hamilton Grand had been joined by more sharpshooters on top of the Old Course Hotel.

I've not been able to confirm reports that instead of having the normal conversation about which letter to hit over the sheds at the 17th tee, the president and his caddy debated about which marksman to hit over!

Other notables who have turned up under pseudonyms are Tom Cruise, Rory McIlroy (ahead of the 2024 Olympics) and Harry Styles who probably had more spectators around the 18th green than Barrack Obama, although admittedly the age and gender demographic was markedly different for Harry, with one marshall remarking that he thought he was in the front row of a Harry Styles concert, such was the level of shrieking and screaming coming from all around him.

AN 80TH HOLE IN ONE

A long-standing stalwart of the New Club and Old Course Walking Tour Guide, David Millar, turned eighty and scored his first hole in one on The Old Course at the par three eleventh hole three days later.

I was playing my second shot into the seventh hole which crosses over with the eleventh and shared David's moment of joy as he walked onto the eleventh green and beyond the small hump which had hidden the final resting place of his ball from view from the tee.

I toasted David in the club afterwards too, partaking with a dram from one of the two bottles of whisky he'd put behind the bar. The one which he had placed there just days before to celebrate his eightieth birthday, was quickly joined by another one for his hole in one.

With David being one of the club's most well-liked and respected members, it couldn't have happened to a nicer person. Well done, David.

SEVE THE GREAT

I went to The Open in 1984 with my Dad to see the great Severiano Ballesteros and Seve ended up winning the tournament in dramatic 'Seve' fashion.

Two to three times a week at the Golf Academy on the wall behind Reception, I see the iconic image of Seve fist pumping on the 18th Green after he holed his putt, and I loved hearing this next story about the great man.

I was caddying for a man called Arturo, at a Sponsors Day for the machinery company Toro™ at The Castle Course in early June 2025. As we were nearing the end of the round, I mentioned that I was writing this book and Arturo told me a story about his father and Seve Ballesteros and gave me permission to include it here.

Club Car™ who make quality golf carts, were presenting Seve with his own bespoke golf cart and had commissioned Arturo's father to transport the car one thousand kilometres, all the way from Sotogrande in the southern tip of Spain to Seve's home in Pedreña in the northern most part of Spain.

After the ten-hour journey north, he arrived at Seve's house, unloaded the vehicle and proceeded to show Seve how it worked. Having done this, he was packing up his van getting ready to leave, when Seve asked him where he was off to now. Arturo's father replied that he was going to drive back home.

"But you left at six this morning and you have already driven for ten hours. No, no, no" Seve said firmly "You can stay in my guesthouse, and I'll phone the restaurant nearby and they will look after you. Then at least you will be refreshed in the morning for your long drive back"

And that's what happened. Arturo's father ate and slept that night as a guest of the great Severiano Ballesteros.

I now look at the image of Seve on the wall behind the reception desk at The Academy as Seve The Gentleman as well as Seve The Golfing Great.

TO BE CONTINUED ...

St Andrews abounds with stories like these. Spend time here and you'll hear many, many more.

Memories are constantly being made, stories are always being told.

You may even have your own stories, and I'd love to hear them. Just email them to me at kevin@thepositivegolfer.com with the subject matter 'Other People's Stories'. They may even feature in the next book.

I look forward to hearing from you.

CHAPTER 18: WHERE THE MAGIC NEVER ENDS

MY GLORIOUS SUMMER PLAYGROUND

As the battle with my former employers unfolded, thankfully I'd been accepted to caddy on the Links while I waited for a judgment to be issued by the Employment Tribunal. My workplace and playground for the summer was going to be The Castle Course.

The world comes to St Andrews, and I was fortunate to caddy for players from seventeen different states in America and from eight different countries across the globe, getting paid to read putts, give lines, find balls, carry bags and hand clubs to:-

An ex-Chicago cop who had gone deep undercover in the drug dens of the south of the city. He had seen some sights and had some tales to tell. He told me if I passed them on, he'd have to come back and find me.. so my lips are sealed!

An armoured car maker who used to make vehicles for The President of The United States. (He shared that the glass windows of 'The Beast' were eight inches thick and designs kept having to be updated as more sophisticated, powerful weapons and bullets were produced.)

A venture capitalist who had flown his seven buddies over in his private plane for a week's golf together with his own private wine collection, so they could enjoy their own wine wherever they ate out in the evenings.!

The Director of Golf at Sandy Lane Hotel in Barbados who had worked his way up through the ranks from waiter to head of golf there. Incredibly we worked out that he would have been working as a waiter in the restaurant when I got married there in 2007. It's a small world.

The owner of a vineyard in California.

A Volunteer from New York who had just come from a conference for 11,000 Jehovah's Witnesses at The Hydro in Glasgow. I had four and a half interesting hours engaging with them about matters I'd never discussed before.

A supplier of tyres to F1 cars (They loved my story of playing The Old Course in the dark with Pierre Gasly)

A honeymooning couple who had chosen to play golf in Scotland as their preferred way to spend their first married fortnight together. 'Gimmes' between the two were few and far between and my fellow caddy Paul and I laughed and speculated on whether this was a sign of things to come?

Manhattan lawyers, Manhattan dentists, Manhattan real estate agents.

Manhattan must have been closed for the summer!

I got paid to chat, I was interested in these golfers, and I got my 15,000 steps in a day as well! Health, Wealth and a Worldly Education all in one round of golf. I managed to lose a stone in weight, and an even bigger weight was lifted from my shoulders, as I pounded the healing fairways.

I caddied for a guy who shared he was going to propose to his girlfriend the following month. He told me before he told her. I hope she said yes!

I caddied for a thirteen-year-old Austrian boy, with a handicap of thirty-two. Poor boy … I didn't know what he'd done to deserve being made to play the 'monster course', as it was described to me by some Italian guests staying at The House of Golf, but his mother took me aside on the first tee and asked me to persevere with her son as he was a shy boy.

By the fifth hole we'd developed a 'bond' because his wooden tees kept breaking. I said to him with a smile that he needed to write his letter to Father Christmas asking for more tees …

"Dear Father Christmas. Last Year you gave me some tees for Christmas. I would like to ask you for plastic ones this year as I've broken all of last year's wooden ones." I joked

Without drawing breath he fired back, "And I promise to be good this year so please don't lock me in the basement again!!"

I didn't know whether he was joking or was it a cry for help! Hopefully, the shy boy just had a wicked sense of humour!

Caddying with other caddies in a group was always fun and as close to dressing room banter as it gets. We looked out for each other, looked out for other balls and kept each other going in poor weather.

Not that there was too much of that, with 2025 being the sunniest spring on record in Scotland, and the summer being not far behind. What a time to be between jobs on this glorious playground!

JUDGMENT DAY.

Nine long months after I'd last been paid, I finally received the extract judgement from the Employment Tribunal. It was in my favour against my former employers. With the help of my pal Holiday Ronnie's wife Linda, a retired former HR professional, I had won my case for wrongful dismissal and breach of contract, and I was to be fully paid and compensated for my losses, said the Judgement. Many thanks Linda.

My mounting credit cards debts could be paid off and sadly there would be no more 'caddy dances'[9] for me, at least for the time being. I would miss the chat with players, caddies, starters and staff alike and would gladly have remained walking the fairways of the stunning Castle Course on a permanent basis.

However, now that the 'monkey' of the Tribunal was finally off my back, I had a legal career to resume. I was looking forward to helping new and former clients with matters of life and death again. That wouldn't stop me yearning for The Castle Course, though.

FIVE YEARS A BELIEVER

On 25th July 2025, it was five years since I moved to the St Andrews area. Incredibly, my five-year anniversary in the town was marked by another Medal win exactly five years to the day after the first one. However, my 2025 round contained ten single putts for the first time ever, which contributed to a total of twenty six putts and and a gross score of two under par 70 (nett 65) round the Jubilee course!

Maybe it was a gift to me from The Golfing Gods for my 'wooden' anniversary! I must remember to get this inscribed on the

---

[9] A caddy dance is where a caddy hangs about at the end of the round, hopping from one foot to the other, waiting patiently for their player to pay them, silently hoping that their 'great' caddying will reap a rewarding payday.

back of the medal when I get it engraved:

'Happy Wooden Anniversary, Kevin - From The Golfing Gods."

Having experienced the Magic In St Andrews as The Positive Golfer in between these two rounds five years apart, my stats spreadsheet showed that I'd played 890 rounds of golf, won the Thistle Club Championship, the R & A Quaich, the Tom Watson Trophy, the Neil Westwood Cup, helped The New Golf Club win the Winter League Handicap Cup twice, the Bobby Jones Cup and the Bute Trophy once each, won five monthly medals, qualified for the 2023, 2025 and 2026 Monthly Medals Final Day on The Old Course and I'd had a hole in one on The New Course at the par 3 13th hole in Jan 2023.

My lowest gross rounds on each course were:-

The Strathtyrum Course: .... 3 under par 66
The New Course: .... 3 under par 68
The Jubilee Course: .... 3 under par 69
The Eden Course : .... 1 under par 69
The Castle Course: ....2 over par 73
The Old Course: .... 5 under par 67

I'd been fortunate enough to play The Old Course one hundred and seventy-six times during that period, having birdied every hole on the course including two birdies on the Road Hole! My favourite course remains The Old Course, with The Old Course in Reverse coming in a close second.

My handicap reduced from ten to scratch and I came within a four putt of playing off a plus handicap.

All in all not too shabby for someone who only played golf occasionally before moving to St Andrews.

HAPPY BIRTHDAY, DAD.

The Golfing Gods delivered a further touching gift just a day after that 'wooden' anniversary medal win, on what would have been my Dad's 85th birthday. The luck of the draw had me caddying for a wonderful father and son combination which reminded me of my own early times on the golf course with my Dad. I caddied for Drew the father and Drew caddied for his son. When I jokingly asked Drew what he was getting paid for caddying, he replied that his fee had already been agreed, and it was 'hugs from his son'. That was lovely ...but I was quick to point out that although I'd be happy to accept hugs from Drew as payment, that would have to be in addition to cold hard cash!! He laughed and wished my Dad a Happy Heavenly Birthday.

I HAVE A DREAM

I've caddied and played with family groups and witnessed the joy they get from playing together and sharing memorable moments on the 18th of The Old Course.

I won't ever get that opportunity with my Dad, but he'll be there in spirit as my brother Rory, and my nephew Calvin walk down the 18th fairway on one side of me, with Kerry on the other side. My Mum will be watching, with her other grandson Josh, waving at us from the large windows of The Peter Thomson Suite upstairs in the New Golf Club.

I hope The Magic in St Andrews delivers my dream.

THANK YOU, ST ANDREWS

I've found love on the links, made my home here and made some great golfing buddies along the way (you know who you are). My business ambitions were quelled but my golfing ambitions were ignited ... and I've written this book!

I'm excited for the 2027 Open returning here and I look forward to welcoming many more guests to The House of Golf, playing golf with Kerry and seeing just how good a player she can become.

I also look forward to having many more fantastic experiences on the course and around the town. I love this place. This is home now and where I learned that almost anything is possible if you have a positive mindset.

Thank you, St Andrews.

Kevin
The Positive Golfer

ACKNOWLEDGEMENTS

Thanks must go firstly to Kerry and my Mum for their invaluable feedback when reviewing each chapter. Your suggestions and support have been greatly appreciated.

To my beta readers Chloe, Franck, Ally, Stephen, Cliff, Ian, Adam and my brother Rory for giving me the confidence to continue writing after the first six chapters.

To everyone who is mentioned in the book - thank you for agreeing to have your stories shared. It has been a pleasure sharing the original experiences with you and reliving them with you during the writing and reviewing process.

To all the wonderful staff at The New Golf Club for making it the place that it is and for keeping me fed, watered and motivated during my writing process.

To Zack for providing the first-rate illustrations.

To Brian The Putt Reader for giving up his time trying to sort out my chipping ... and for reading my putts for me at Royal Aberdeen!!

To Hector The Tinkerer for constantly tinkering and passing on your tips!

To Whispering Dave for providing me with plenty of material for the book.

To the Caddies on the Links for your knowledge and support.

To the Members of the Fellowship for your friendship.

To my friend Willie Miller, a hero of mine who became a friend.

To Byron Casper and his dad Billy, without whom a lot of these stories would not have been written.

To you for sharing my journey in these pages ... I look forward to seeing you on the Links sometime.

And finally thanks to my Dad for introducing me to the wonderful game of golf.

APPENDIX: MY FAVOURITE GOLF COURSES ... SO FAR!

The Old Course (History)
The Old Course In Reverse (Scarce, History)
Pebble Beach (Views, History)
The Olympic Club-Lakes (Tough, History)
Muirfield (Tough, Great Layout, Exclusive, Lunch)
Adare Manor (Manicured, Ryder Cup Course)
Trump Turnberry (Tough, Views, History)
Carnoustie (Tough, History)
Royal Dornoch (Tough, Views)
Trump International-Old (Tough)
Kingsbarns (Views)
Royal Troon (History)
Royal Liverpool (History)
The K Club North (Tough, Ryder Cup Course)
Dumbarnie (Tough)
Skibo Castle (Tough, Views, Exclusive)
PGA Gleneagles (Tough Ryder Cup Course)
Royal Aberdeen (Tough)
The Belfry-Brabazon (Condition, Tough, Ryder Cup Course)
Seaton Carew (Tough, History)
Cruden Bay (Tough, Views)
The Castle Course (Tough, Views)
Murcar, Aberdeen (Tough)
North Berwick (Views)
Gullane 1 (Challenging)
Balcomie, Crail (Views)
Spyglass Hill (Challenging, Views)
Meadow Club (Views, Lush Alister MacKenzie course)
Castle Stuart, Inverness (Views)
Duff House Royal (Lush Alister MacKenzie Course)

Always:
McDonald Golf Club, Ellon (My First Course-what a closing last two holes!)

PHOTOGRAPHS ACCOMPANYING THE BOOK:

Check out some of the photographs from the stories in the book at www.kevindavidsonauthor.com

SOCIAL MEDIA:

Keep in touch with what's going on with me at my socials..

Instagram:
@the-positive-golfer
@themagicinstandrews

Facebook:
The Positive Golfer
The Magic in St Andrews

TikTok:
The Positive Golfer
The Magic in St Andrews

Youtube Channels:
The Positive Golfer
The Magic in St Andrews

X:
The Positive Golfer

www.ingramcontent.com/pod-product-compliance
Lightning Source LLC
LaVergne TN
LVHW040042080526
838202LV00045B/3446

The Magic In St Andrews is a rich tapestry of vivid memories and uplifting tales, detailing a heartfelt and inspiring memoir of enduring connections with the ancient town of St Andrews. The author is repeatedly drawn back over the years by a calling he cannot fully explain, with the town having a profound and transformative impact on his golfing and personal life. It will resonate with every golfer who has felt the game stir something deeper, something beyond scorecards and swings...something closer to the soul.

∴

'This book feels like visiting St Andrews. Good memories come flooding back'

Monique Kalkman
PARALYMPIC GOLD MEDALLIST & INTERNATIONAL TENNIS HALL OF FAMER

'This is a great story. Thank you for honouring my Dad. God bless you and this amazing game we call life...& golf!'

Byron Casper
IPGA GOLF PROFESSIONAL & SON OF THREE-TIME MAJOR WINNER BILLY CASPER

'Kevin has a natural gift for storytelling'

Ally Ross
TV CRITIC, THE SUN

'Wonderfully written. Beautiful sparse language reminds me of Hemingway'

Dr Doug Given
US GOLFER & SILICON VALLEY VENTURE CAPITALIST

'I was so excited for the Pebble Beach story, and it didn't disappoint, keeping the humility, but very entertaining!'

Chloe Thackeray
PROFESSIONAL GOLFER AND COACH

www.KevinDavidsonAuthor.com

Design: Spiffing Publishing